A Trip Through

METRO·GOLDWYN·MAYER

LAND

SANTA
MONICA
PRESS

Published by:
Santa Monica Press LLC
P.O. Box 850
Solana Beach, CA 92075
1-800-784-9553
www.santamonicapress.com
books@santamonicapress.com

Printed in China

Santa Monica Press books are available at special quantity discounts when purchased in bulk by corporations, organizations, or groups. Please call our Special Sales department at 1-800-784-9553.

ISBN-13 978-1-59580-055-8

Library of Congress Cataloging-in-Publication Data

Bingen, Steven.
  MGM : Hollywood's greatest backlot / by Steven Bingen, Stephen X. Sylvester, Michael Troyan.
      p. cm.
Includes bibliographical references.
ISBN 978-1-59580-055-8
1. Metro-Goldwyn-Mayer. I. Sylvester, Stephen X. II. Troyan, Michael, 1968- III. Title.
PN1999.M4B56 2010
384'.80979494—dc22

2010002730

Cover and interior design and production by Future Studio

Above: A forlorn façade on the distant outskirts of New York Street in the 1930s.
Previous Page: The title page from a 1929 studio promotional book.

This book is dedicated to the memory of Robert W. Nudelman,
who fought a gallant, doomed battle to save MGM's backlot from the wrecking ball.

—The Authors

CONTENTS

PART TWO: POTEMKIN'S VILLAGES

PART THREE:
MYTHIC LANDSCAPES

PART FOUR:
BACKLOT BABYLON

Opposite: MGM's mysterious Lot One backlot as it looked in 1925.

Someday, a guidebook will be written to America's most pictorial ruin—the ruins of Hollywood.
—*New York Herald Tribune*, July 19, 1936

So much of Hollywood is a façade.
—DAVID O. SELZNICK

FOREWORD

The first time I found myself at the gates of Metro-Goldwyn-Mayer Studios it was 1950. I was a normally innocent teenager from Burbank and I didn't really have any knowledge that MGM was the greatest studio in the world. What I really wanted to do was go to college and become a gym teacher. Working at a movie studio just seemed like something to do while I waited for my real life to start. I guess you could say that I'm still waiting.

Maybe I should explain that I didn't grow up in a movie-going family. I didn't sit in the audience watching pictures and thinking how wonderful it would be to work in such a glamorous business. So I didn't have any romantic notions about show biz like other people my age probably did. When casting director Solly Baiano drove me to the lot that day, and I first saw the gigantic "Metro-Goldwyn-Mayer" sign atop Stage 6, well, it was certainly impressive, but I hardly thought the moment life-changing.

And yet, I did feel at home at MGM from the very first. I used to spend days walking around the big, busy lot while they tried to figure out what to do with me. I'd hang out in the Makeup Department or the Music and Property Departments, or the Scoring Stages, or Rehearsal Halls, or out on the backlots. I never dreamt or cared that the composers and writers and performers I was mingling with, and not taking particularly seriously, were the finest and most famous in the world.

And yet somehow MGM, and show biz too, eventually got to me in a way I never could have predicted when I was that indifferent kid. I grew to love the studio, not only because of the thousands of memorable movies made there, but because MGM became my hometown, my prep school, my university. I grew up there. I learned about friendship and responsibility there. I laughed and cried there. Certainly I learned everything I know about acting there. Later my children grew up there as well, playing on those same backlots while their mother earned a living on them. And later, when those same beautiful, magical backlots were being sold off and destroyed, I first tried to save the place itself, and then its legacy.

Well, it's all gone now. That big Metro-Goldwyn-Mayer sign atop Stage 6, which I first saw all those years ago, has been replaced. Those unbelievable backlots are now suburbs with different children playing in the streets. Children who would never believe that castles and pirate ships and Mississippi riverboats once stood exactly where their homes are now.

The good news is that, although the studio is gone, it lives on vividly in the pages of this remarkable and beautiful book. Just like I first did all those years ago, this work approaches the studio not through the perspective of its films, but rather as a very real community with its own politics and personalities and legends. Come inside and look around like I once did. Like me, you may never want to leave.

DEBBIE REYNOLDS
Hollywood, California

INTRODUCTION AND ACKNOWLEDGMENTS

I went to the lands of the moviemakers and saw them at work. As I go back over the weeks I spent within the innermost walls of these great studios and watched the master minds and master hands at their appointed tasks, I am filled with the wonder of it all. I thrill at the miracles performed before my eyes, at the sight of a thousand threads in a tangled skein wrought into a fabric of exquisite design.
—JOHN J. FLOHERTY, *Moviemakers*

In *The Wizard of Oz* (1939), one of Metro-Goldwyn-Mayer's most enduring films, Dorothy Gale explores a wondrous land woven entirely of her own imagination. Significantly, movie studios in Hollywood's Golden Age were labeled "dream factories" for their imaginative entertainments that have inspired, encouraged, and enchanted generations of filmgoers. Today, MGM—the most prodigious of those dream factories—now seems like a dream itself. Time has not been kind to the former empire of Louis B. Mayer and Irving Thalberg and their lands of make-believe. Living memories of the place are quickly dissipating with the erosion of time.

Time and again, many of the people with whom we have discussed the studio and this project with have fondly mentioned a book from 1975 called *The MGM Story*. In that long-out-of-print book, near the title page as wallpaper for the graphics, author John Douglas Eames included a partial studio map under a superimposed section of text. More than one person we spoke to about this book has admitted to wistfully taking a virtual tour of the studio lot and exploring the various sets found there using their imagination and this truncated map as their jumping-off point.

Remarkably, we discovered that these misguided romantics weren't touring the places these sets were created to mimic. No one was imagining visiting Algiers or the Bastille or the 1904 World's Fair. Instead, they were exploring Hollywood, which, to some of us anyway, must have been even better.

Our purpose in producing this book is not to discuss the films that MGM produced. That particular road has been well traveled else-where. Our interest here is not in the product at all, but rather the factory *responsible* for that product. Our goal is to preserve, in print and in memory, if not in brick and mortar, the actual physical place that was once Metro-Goldwyn-Mayer for the first time.

No attempt has been made to ratchet the focus of this story outward and discuss the backlots of the other six studios of Hollywood's Golden Era, except in cases where these other properties affected or reflected upon MGM's. In looking at Hollywood as a physical place, it soon becomes apparent that exploring the approximately 175 acres of real estate occupied by MGM for more than half a century is actually a poignant and apt microcosm for the entire studio system and for Hollywood itself.

We would like to thank the following for generously sharing their priceless memories and memorabilia, including those whose names appear below who actually *did* visit, play, work at, or climb the fences at the studio—namely, MGM vice president of administration Roger Mayer and his wife Pauline; MGM vice president of rental facilities Ben Cowitt; directors Ralph Senesky and Roger Corman; producers Daniel Selznick, Walter Seltzer, and George M. Lehr; actors Richard Anderson, Clint Eastwood, Betty Garret, Marsha Hunt, Debbie Reynolds, Warren Stevens, Rod Taylor, Robert Vaughn, George Wallace, Fredd Wayne, and the late Delmar Watson; writer George W. Schenck; *Twilight Zone* authors George Clayton Johnson and Earl Hamner Jr.; art director Robert Kinoshita; actor/editor Pierre Jalbert; assistant cameraman Brainard Miller; production accountant John Valasek; costume designer Deborah Nadoolman; reading department staffer Nancy

Richards; production office employee Jan Murree; photographer Dave Freeman; and Special Effects Department technicians Don Jarel and Marcel Vercoutere. The late MGM makeup genius William Tuttle was kind enough to grant us his last interview. Special thanks to Keath and Cynthia Graham, and to the family of special effects ace A. Arnold "Buddy" Gillespie for providing access to his unpublished memoirs.

Thanks are due also to Richard Adkins, Keith Anderson, Fred Basten, Marty Black, Billy Blackburn, Scott Brogan, June Caldwell, James C. Christensen, John Divola, John Ellicott, Glenn Erickson, Todd Fisher, Stuart Galbraith IV, Martin Grams Jr., Dave Heilman, Jon Heitland, Kit Hudson, Michael J. Kouri, Randy Knox, John Landis, Robert Lane, Bruce Lao, Eleanor Lyon, Paul D. Marks, Paul Mavis, Ray Morton, Scott Mokal, Bill Nelson, the late Robert Nudelman, Beth Orsoff, Steven Richard Osborn, Kristina Rivera, Richard Rownak, Natasha Rubin, Giovanni Secchi, Steven C. Smith, David L. Snyder, Chris Soldo, Brian Stowell, Stan Taffel, Craig Tanner, John Thomas, Lou Valentino, Reece Vogel, Tom Walsh, Paul Welsh, Mike Wetherell, and to John Bertrum, who spent many a lonely hour transcribing dates and titles from paper that was literally crumbling to dust as he worked.

This product, and perhaps any Hollywood product, would have been impossible without assistance from the following film historians extraordinaire: Marc Wanamaker (and his invaluable, infinite Bison Archives), Kevin Brownlow, Leonard Maltin, Richard Schickel, and Rudy Behlmer. Thanks are also due to Rudy's wife, Stacey, and to the entire staff of the Academy of Motion Picture Arts and Sciences, Margaret Herrick Library. Ditto to Ned Comstock at the USC Cinematic Arts Library.

On the corporate front, Walt Disney Company archivists David R. Smith and Rob Klein furnished invaluable assistance and wisdom and Marianne Laurenson and Gary Martin at Sony Pictures, MGM's old homestead, helped us illuminate both what was and what is in Culver City, as did city historian Julie Lugo Cerra.

The project would have truly been impossible without the cooperation of Warner Bros., which controls much of the MGM library and legacy. Special thanks to Warner Bros. corporate archivist Leith Adams and his staff. Also at Warners, much gratitude is due to Lisa Janney, Ray Olivera, Jeremy Williams, Elaine Piechowski, Steve Fogelson, Linda Cummings-Whelan, Kim Steelsmith Paine, Elaine Patton, Mark Greenhalgh, Dougie Cringean, Pat Kowalski, Lynn Borzumato, Nina Smith, Art Nunez, Maria Garcia, Geoff Murillo, Mike Arnold, Ana M. de Castro, and George Feltenstein. Cynthia Martinez, Genevieve McGillicuddy, and Eric Webber at Turner also deserve a mention.

We'd also like to acknowledge, decades after the fact, the work of one George P. Erengis, who—until this volume's publication—was responsible for the only comprehensive historical work ever attempted on the Hollywood backlots; this in the early 1960s, when the studio's fabled kingdoms were still intact. Our hats are off to you, George, wherever you are.

STEVEN BINGEN, STEPHEN X. SYLVESTER, MICHAEL TROYAN

PROLOGUE

What castles built for a few hours, what phantom towns, what still-new ruins! In Hollywood they used to take tours through these plywood and plaster cities, these imitation streets where the fake patina of paint was covered by the patina of time. A romantic poet could have dreamed among these decrepit buildings that once imitated the past and later caricatured it, and today have disappeared. Fiction or reality? Méliès or Lumière? In our own memories, the real world where we thought we lived blends with the world of illusion.

—René Clair

It has been estimated that historically a *fifth* of all movies made in the United States were partially shot somewhere at MGM studios. Without belaboring the point, this means that if an individual has seen 25 movies in his life, then perhaps five of them would have been shot on these grounds. The math escalates and compounds as we add upward: A hundred films viewed means 20 shot here; a thousand films equals 200 locations shot here.

Like a visit to any hometown from which we have been long absent, touring the world of MGM's vast backlots can be disarming and disorienting. The path is confusing and thorny. The size of the place and the number and variety of sets can be overwhelming. *Twilight Zone* writer George Clayton Johnson remembered being completely overwhelmed by the "sheer vastness of it all," and this impression is by no means unique. At MGM, perspective and memory can warp, and appearances can indeed be deceiving. Spend some time here with us and it soon becomes infuriatingly tempting, near impossible in fact, not to look upon these familiar façades and tie them to movies and to memories that they were never meant to evoke. A courthouse set may *look* like a building from a thousand remembered movies, or like a thousand real courthouses. Make no mistake, the set may well have those thousand or more actual credits on its resume, but it's difficult not to try to tie the same building to even more titles and even more memories due to its overwhelming familiarity. Our filmography, chronological and reasonably comprehensive for each of the various sets, although by no means complete, will be helpful in avoiding such misappropriate nostalgia.

Included in this book is the most complete and accurate map of each of the major MGM lots ever created. Each major set is assigned a number that corresponds with the same designation on our map. Photographs of the various sets, both as they would have looked during our visit and dressed for their various film appearances, are also included.

We encourage our readers and fellow backlot historians to read these lists, enjoy the text and photos, and join us in contributing to our backlot tour—the first of its kind ever undertaken. Although the studio is gone, the list of titles that utilized these sets will paradoxically continue to grow as long as the films, if not the physical place, survive to be enjoyed and explored and revisited.

Welcome aboard, the studio gates are swinging open.

Opposite: An aerial view of Lots One and Two in the 1940s. This photo was used in studio publicity for decades.

PART ONE:

LANDS OF MAKE-BELIEVE

The place is somewhere near the trail that led from the Rancho El Rodeo de Las Aguas to Rancho del Sausal Redondo. The haciendas were rich. The walled gardens were afire with poinsettia by day and scented with tuberose at twilight. There were great ladies, pale, dark-eyed señoritas, and gay blades, and great dignity of family. It was the land of such as the Picos, the De La Guerras, the Verdugos, and the Carillos. It was a realm of romance. And there was melodrama, too, and such flitting flames of violence as that charming bandit, Don Tiburcio Vasquez.

Now it has a crisp Yankee name—Culver City—and across those acres spread the studios of M-G-M. So again the land is drenched with romance and drama and splendors, a world of make-believe, the like of which the most spend-thrifty of the old grandees could not have dreamed, nodding over his oporto in the patio shade of palm and vine.

—Motion Picture Herald,
June 24, 1944

MISTER CULVER AND THE MOVIES

*Say it's only a Paper Moon, sailing over a cardboard sea . . . but it
wouldn't be make-believe if you believed in me.*
—"Paper Moon,"
music by Harold Arlen,
lyrics by E. Y. Harburg and Billy Rose

The land where our story takes place was first occupied by a loose confederacy of Native American peoples, the Gabrieliños, approximately 10,000 years ago. Very little is known of these mysterious people, whose lives and culture have vanished into the Santa Ana winds. Even their very name is lost to us, "Gabrieliños" being an appellation given to the locals by the Spanish because of their proximity to the nearby Mission San Gabriel.

The acreage that concerns us became part of two, vast early Spanish homesteads: Rancho La Ballona, controlled by the Machado family, and its southerly neighbor, Rancho Rincon de los Bueyes, operated by the Higuera clan. The resourceful Machados in particular managed to retain control of their 14,000-acre hacienda through the rise and fall of both the Spanish and Mexican regimes, and even after California was admitted into the Union in 1850.

The man to whom the city surrounding the future MGM studios owes its name was born in Nebraska in 1880. Harry C. Culver was an entrepreneur who followed his instincts west in 1910. Within five years, he had laid out the community of Culver City, California, and formed an investment company to attract local merchants. His diligence was rewarded in 1914 when the citizenry in his little community rejected annexation into greater Los Angeles and supported Culver City's official incorporation in 1917.

Culver fretted over his shiny new township like the diligent father that he was. He sponsored picnics and fairs and baby contests. He placed ads in local papers extolling the virtues of his little community.

Most importantly, he encouraged local industries—including motion picture companies—to come to Culver City.

The majority of these rather disreputable little operations were already based up the road in neighboring Hollywood. Unlike the original, conservative, temperate citizens of that community—settled by a strict prohibitionist from Kansas—Culver tolerated, even encouraged the "movies," as early filmmakers were then called. He befriended producer Thomas Ince, and fast-talked the fast-talking "movie" into building a new studio in Culver City on 16 vacant acres in August of 1915.

Ince had partnered with fellow moviemakers D. W. Griffith and Mack Sennett to secure financing for a dream studio that, unlike other film lots of the era, was to be both functional and, at least from the outside, aesthetically pleasing. The three-story administration building, with its Corinthian-columned entrance, rose just as the dirt road in front was pretentiously christened "Washington Boulevard."

The sign proclaiming the place "Triangle Studios" seemed both a nod to the three partners, as well as to the physical shape of the studio, which formed a triangular arrow pointing northeast in a direct line towards Hollywood. Oddly enough, the current studio property, after nearly 90 years of growth and contractions, now forms a similar triangle.

By the spring of 1916, the little studio had taken shape with an administration building, commissary, producers and writers buildings, wardrobe, dressing rooms fronting Washington Boulevard, and six glass stages for silent film production. In March, the Ince/Triangle studios

Above: An aerial view of the property in the early 1920s.

ners Samuel Goldfish and Edgar Selwyn. "If we had jumbled them the other way around it would have been called 'Selfish Pictures,'" Goldfish used to quip. To the surprise of no one, he subsequently adopted the name Samuel Goldwyn as his own.

Goldwyn shared Ince's vision of the industry as both an art and a science. He took an interest in his studio's physical operation, and construction continued on crafts buildings and in technical departments. For $50,000, he added 23 additional acres to the studio, expanded the administration building to a total of 15,324 square feet, and extended the studio's impressive exterior wall almost a half mile along Washington Boulevard. Inside, a lawn was planted near the front of the lot, bringing these new buildings and the six glass soundstages together into a cohesive campus for the first time. Exterior sets were constructed as needed on the western end of the lot, which faced Overland Avenue. A *Los Angeles Times* article on July 25, 1923, used the phrase "back lot" (the quotation marks and word spacing are the paper's) for one of the first times in print to describe this corner of the property. The phrase originally was intended to describe the rear or back of a studio property where permanent outdoor sets were stored. Recently, it has been used more broadly to refer to any production-related property on a studio lot. Paramount, for example, now refers to its entire production-related process as "Backlot Operations."

J. J. (Joseph J.) Cohn, brought aboard to manage the new lot as executive head of production, wryly declared, "Rome wasn't built in a day. It took us a week." It was his job to organize the various studio departments into a filmmaking process that would turn out a picture a week at a set cost. He happily held the job on the property for the next four decades.

But all was not well in the refurbished Triangle administration building. Movies had grown up—and grown more expensive to finance. The developing star system and the elaborate epics of Griffith, Cecil B. DeMille, and Ince had pushed films, filmmakers, and film audiences

were officially inaugurated with such stars as actor-director William S. Hart, actress Bessie Barriscale, and Charles Ray in attendance.

For three years, Triangle was a dominant force in the film industry, producing a string of prestige pictures and gaining exclusive bookings to thousands of motion picture theatres at higher-than-usual ticket prices. But the union was as doomed as the Gabrieliños. A combination of internal management disagreements, and the painful financial losses incurred by Griffith's *Intolerance* (1916) caused the group to break up in 1918.

The next tenant was Goldwyn Pictures, which purchased the studio facilities for $325,000 in October of 1918. This time, the studio's name was actually an anagram created by combining the names of part-

Above: An early photo of Ince/Triangle Studios in Culver City, California.

into a new era of sophistication and higher expectations. With an inability to control production expenditures, poor box office returns, and a lack of stars, the Goldwyn Pictures Corporation needed a convenient scapegoat. Studio investor Frank Joseph Godsol pointed the finger at Goldwyn himself. The board agreed, and in 1922, the company's president was out of a job.

In an effort to save the studio, the now Goldwyn-less executives became even more extravagant by inviting prestigious directors like Rex Ingram and Erich von Stroheim to the lot. They wanted von Stroheim to film their most ambitious undertaking yet: an epic interpretation of General Lew Wallace's best-selling novel *Ben-Hur: A Tale of the Christ*. But von Stroheim preferred another project—an experiment, actually. He wanted to dispose of screenwriting—and most of the other ready-and-waiting studio departments, including the backlot—and to film Frank Norris's infamous novel *McTeague* page-by-page on the actual locations described in the novel (including sweltering Death Valley) as *Greed* (1924).

At the same time, Ingram set to work on *Mare Nostrum* (1926)

with his wife, noted actress Alice Terry, and promptly went over budget as well. Thus, even as *Ben-Hur* floundered on location in Italy (with third-choice director Fred Niblo shouting into the megaphone), Ingram and von Stroheim set the new studio on a disastrous path towards bankruptcy.

Enter Marcus Loew, a diminutive wheeler-dealer from the east respected for his extraordinary business acumen. Loew had started his empire by cobbling together a syndicate of penny arcades that featured, among the vaudeville acts and games of chance, motion pictures. With rapid-fire speed, these nickelodeons, as they were eventually known, became full-scale vaudeville houses and then movie theatres that could accommodate thousands of patrons per day. By 1919, Loew's chain of theatres stretched from Atlanta to Ontario.

Loew's problem was keeping his huge, eager audiences constantly supplied with a new product befitting the quality theatres the films were shown in. In order to insure this, in 1919, Loew negotiated the purchase of Metro Pictures (established in 1915 by Richard A. Rowland) for $3.1 million. With this purchase, Loew became a

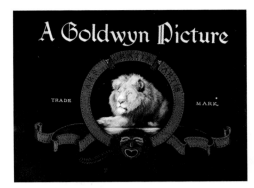

Above: The lion was chosen for the Goldwyn logo to represent the "King of all beasts" at a time when other studios were using lesser animals for their logos.
Center: A gathering of early Goldwyn studio personnel that includes Samuel Goldwyn (center), actress Mabel Normand, director Rupert Hughes, actress/opera singer Geraldine Farrar, and writer Rex Beach (1919).

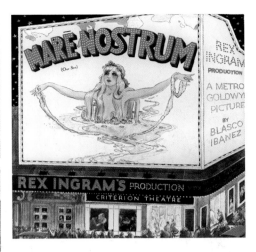

Above: An early promotional poster for the 1926 film *Mare Nostrum.*

producer with his own studio located at the corner of Cahuenga Boulevard and Romaine Street in Hollywood.

But Metro actually turned out to be teetering on the brink of bankruptcy. In 1924, Loew purchased the outwardly more prosperous Goldwyn Pictures. However, the would-be empire builder failed to realize that with von Stroheim, Ingram, and Niblo each madly flushing countless dollars into their own epics and no one in charge to stop them, the Goldwyn company was nearly as debt-ridden as Metro had been.

Nicholas Schenck, Loew's New York hatchet-man assistant, realized that in order to make the unwieldy merger work, someone with experience and a strong hand would be needed to run the plant in Culver City that had fallen into Loew's lap as part of the merger. Their choice would affect them all—for better and worse—for the rest of their lives.

Louis B. Mayer was a child of penniless Jewish-Russian peasants who immigrated to the United States in 1904. By the early 1920s, he had formed Louis B. Mayer Film Company and was a small, but busy independent producer of a 32-acre studio on Mission Road, near Downtown Los Angeles. Something about Mayer impressed Loew enough to buy Mayer's company (for a meager $75,000) under the condition that Mayer would be retained as vice president of operations at the new and newly renamed company: Metro-Goldwyn-Mayer. (The hyphens between these three words were and are officially part of the name but were never used onscreen in the logo, so we have taken the admittedly arbitrary liberty of eliminating them henceforth, except when quoted as such.) His job: to handle studio business arrangements, oversee the hiring and firing of all employees, formulate studio policy, and be the last word in deciding how to spend the studio's money.

On April 18, 1924, formal papers were signed for the Metro, Goldwyn, and Mayer merger. Mayer signed the contract with the understanding that he would "supervise, manage, and generally control the manufacture of all its pictures." The agreement required that 15 completed feature-length motion pictures be delivered to Loew's theatres within two years. In order to meet this ambitious goal on time,

Above: **The Metro Goldwyn Mayer merger celebration in 1924.**

Mayer streamlined the then-existent scattershot filmmaking process by, in a stroke of entrepreneurial genius that influences the motion picture industry to this day, borrowing Henry Ford's phenomenally successful assembly line method for the Model T. In order to instigate this radical new process, Mayer turned to his supervisor of production: 25-year-old Irving Thalberg.

"Mayer often claimed that the Lord singled him out for special benedictions," recalled MGM story editor Samuel Marx. "The day he met Thalberg was one of them."

Thalberg would earn his stripes at the new company almost immediately. Salvaging the three white elephants inherited from the Goldwyn Company—*Greed, Ben-Hur,* and *Mare Nostrum*—Thalberg would also produce the early silent films that put MGM on the Hol-

lywood map: *The Big Parade* (1925) and *The Merry Widow* (1925). By 1925, he was already well respected in Hollywood as the "Boy Wonder," an appellation coined by the *Saturday Evening Post* during his remarkable career as production head at Universal.

Unlike Mayer, who demanded recognition, Thalberg believed that "credit you give yourself isn't worth having." None of the MGM films he produced carried his name. After his death, the studio would dedicate two to him: *The Good Earth* (1937) and *Goodbye, Mr. Chips* (1939). Despite their differences, the two executives did share some key beliefs. Both had a cost-conscious nature that would affect the studio's creations—both its films and its factory. This shared vision would permeate the studio for more than 30 years, raising it to unparalleled heights but, eventually with changing times, also helping to bring about

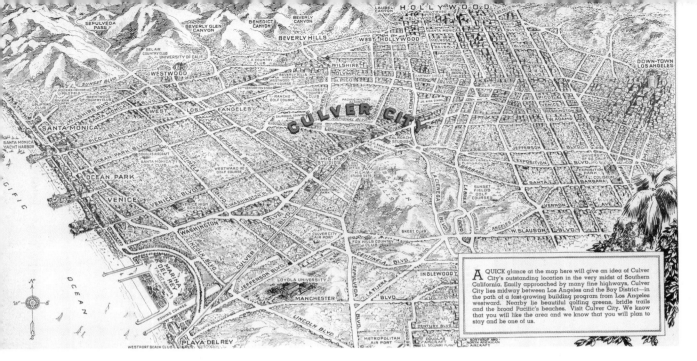

Above: The Landmark Cultural Resource plaque installed on the wall of the studio colonnade entrance by the City of Culver City in 1990.
Left: A 1940s promotional map of Culver City produced by the city to promote its many amenities, while nearby "Hollywood" is downplayed.

A QUICK glance at the map here will give an idea of Culver City's outstanding location in the very midst of Southern California. Easily approached by many fine highways, Culver City lies midway between Los Angeles and the Bay District—in the path of a fast-growing building program from Los Angeles westward. Nearby lie beautiful golfing greens, bridle trails and the broad Pacific's beaches. Visit Culver City. We know that you will like the area and we know that you will plan to stay and be one of us.

its destruction.

Former Goldwyn production manager J. J. Cohn was impressed with his new bosses, and remembers it as "not a difficult transition. . . . It was a marvelous thing for [Mayer's people] to be able to walk into a studio with standing sets, which they didn't have on Mission Road. . . . They were a much firmer and stronger company with Thalberg and Mayer."

Mayer hoped to bring his studio logo of an eagle to MGM films. But the studio's New York-based head of publicity, Howard Dietz, convinced everyone that the Goldwyn company's motto, *Ars gratia artis*—which he somehow interpreted as "Art for art's sake"—and its lion logo be retained. Dietz is also responsible (long before it became a fact) for the studio's famous publicity offering of "more stars than there are in heaven!"

Harry Culver, meanwhile, was proud of MGM's burgeoning success. But he must also have looked toward the Santa Monica Mountains into Hollywood with more than a little irritation. Hadn't he, after all, been the only prominent citizen in Los Angeles to embrace the "movies" and their eccentric ways? Hadn't he actually welcomed Ince into his community, while Hollywood residents had initially done ev-

erything in their power to uproot this unsavory little business? In fact, those original, God-fearing, Hollywood citizens had hung signs in boarding house windows proclaiming "no dogs or movies," and yet the town of Hollywood had nevertheless almost immediately become associated with the industry itself. How could this be?

Through the years, as motion pictures became the great, defining industry of Los Angeles, Hollywood's perceived dominance continued to gnaw at Harry Culver. In 1934, MGM and the Culver City Chamber of Commerce—*his* chamber of commerce—actually tried to change the name of the city, Culver's namesake, to "Hollywood." In 1936, Culver City adapted the nickname "The Heart of Screenland" as part of the city's seal. In 1937, Culver participated in a ceremony at Grauman's Chinese Theatre—in Hollywood—pleading, to no avail, for recognition of Culver City's contributions to Hollywood. Similar deaf ears would certainly have prevailed at MGM had Culver lived long enough to complain to studio executives about the fallacy of releasing hundreds of films made in Culver City under the designation "Made in Hollywood, USA."

Harry lost. The man himself ceased to matter; Culver City had ceased to matter. There was and always would be—will be—only Hollywood.

In 1946, Culver died of a stroke at a hospital in Hollywood.

It will interest you as a phenomenon. You see, the film studio of today is really the palace of the 16th century. There, one sees what Shakespeare saw. The absolute power of the tyrant, the courtiers, the flatterers, the jesters, the cunningly ambitious intriguers. There are fantastically beautiful women. There are incompetent favorites. There are great men who are suddenly disgraced. There is the most insane extravagance. And unexpected parsimony over a few pence. There is enormous splendor, which is a sham; and also horrible squalor hidden behind the scenery. There are vast schemes abandoned because of some caprice. There are secrets that everybody knows and no one speaks of. There are even two or three honest advisors. These are court fools, who speak the deepest wisdom in puns, least they be taken seriously, they grimace, and tear their hair out privately, and weep.

—CHRISTOPHER ISHERWOOD, *Prater Violet*

The New York corporate office of MGM-Loew's Incorporated celebrated a profit of $4,708,631 in its first year of operation. Mayer and Thalberg had done their job in Culver City, efficiently delivering their contracted 15 pictures *eighteen months* ahead of deadline. Clearly, Mayer's Detroit-inspired business model was paying off. By 1926, the company was leading the industry with profits of $6,388,200.

This production process was deceivingly simple. Once a script—or a purchased property (like a Broadway play)—was approved, production manager J. J. Cohn would initiate "pre-production" by routing 25 copies to the various studio departments to cast, design and build sets, and promote the new production. Within a month, the studio was ready for actual filming. The film was shot on the stages and the resulting celluloid was sent to post-production, where a team of 32 editors would cut and shape the footage, which was then sent to the titling department. From each edited film negative, 150 prints (usually) were made by the studio's lab for shipment.

The studio earned the title of "The Friendly Company" from exhibitors by including a cutting synopsis with each film. If any portion of a print was damaged during shipment, replacement scenes could be ordered from the Culver City lab using this synopsis, which had each scene numbered in order and broken down into footage measurements. "Do it right . . . do it big . . . give it class!" became the studio slogan.

Now that a successful mechanism was in place, profits would double and quadruple variably over the next 20 years. With these profits and need for production expansion, Lot One would grow to 44 acres. Goldwyn's six glass stages would eventually be replaced by 30 concrete ones (with the coming of "talking" pictures), and the 42 original buildings of Goldwyn's day would grow to 177 administrative and support buildings. All of which once caused later executive Roger Mayer to joke that "you could get anything done on the lot except be born or buried—and there was a mortuary down the block."

A walk across these 44 acres could include any of the following stops or departments as identified here on the MGM Lot One map. . . .

Opposite: An aerial view of Lot One in 1932.

LOT ONE

BUILDINGS AND DEPARTMENTS

1 Lion Building
2 Purchasing Department
3 General Wardrobe Building
4 Accounting, Payroll, and Insurance Departments
5 East Gate
6 Thalberg Building
7 Writers Building
8 Film Editing Rooms, Film Storage, and Ladies Wardrobe
9 Music Department (A)
10 New Film Lab Building
11 Property Department
12 Camera Department
13 Music Department (B)
14 Portrait Studio
15 Old Film Lab Building
16 MGM Special Trolley
17 Fire Department
18 Research Department
19 Commissary
20 Barbershop and Newsstand
21 Art Department
22 Scoring Stage (Stage One)

23 Screening Room (Stage Two)
24 Production Department
25 Sound Department
26 Makeup Department
27 Dressing Rooms
28 Marion Davies Bungalow
29 Little Red Schoolhouse
30 First-Aid Department
31 Short Subject Department
32 Rehearsal Halls A, B, and C
33 Water Tower
34 Power Plant
35 Special Effects Department
36 Scene Docks (A, B, C, D, and E)
37 Scenic Arts Department
38 Saucer Tank
39 Mill Complex
40 Transportation Department
41 Film Vaults

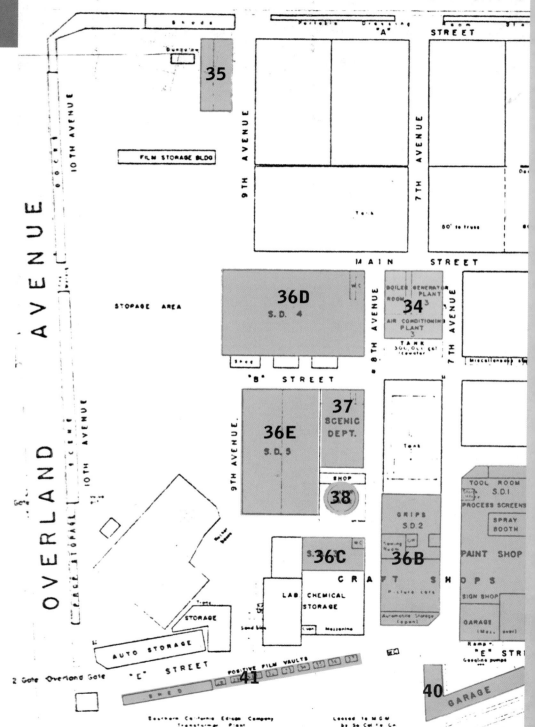

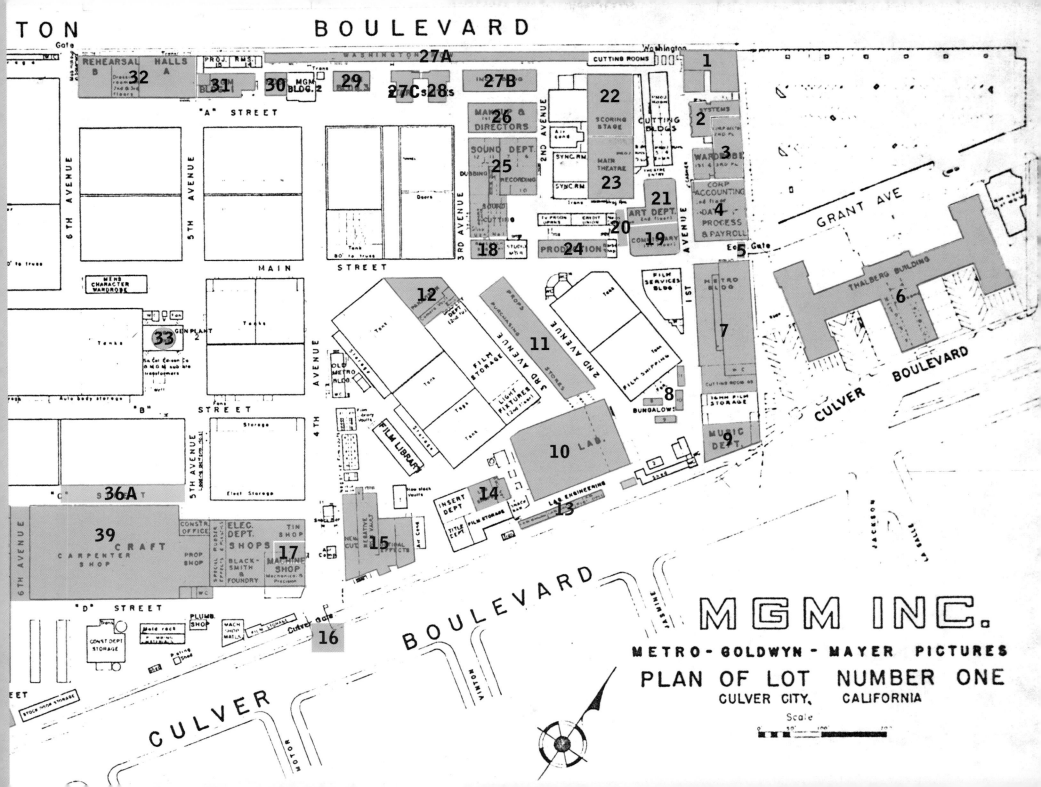

MGM INC.

METRO-GOLDWYN-MAYER PICTURES

PLAN OF LOT NUMBER ONE

CULVER CITY, CALIFORNIA

Left: An intimidating Louis B. Mayer at his infamous desk in his all–white office.
Right: The "Boy Wonder," Irving Thalberg, surrounded by piles of scripts and books.
Opposite: The original MGM colonnade entrance off Washington Boulevard in 1924, where stars would enter the studio in their custom cars and limos.

By 1934, the studio would house 4,000 employees, incorporating 61 stars and featured players, 17 directors, and 51 writers. To lead this army of filmmakers, MGM's central command center was the very same suite of offices once used by Thomas Ince, and redesigned by Sam Goldwyn and his architect Stephen Merritt. It was located in the northeastern corner of the lot, in the aptly named Lion Building, amongst the columns and adjoining the main studio gates fronting Washington Boulevard.

Here can be traced the highs and lows of the Mayer-Thalberg regime. In these offices, the dreams were spun that led to the creation of the studio's phenomenal output between 1924 and 1937. These were the halcyon years when director Frank Capra remembered that "MGM's lion . . . brought 'anticipatory applause'" and, put simply by MGM publicist Eddie Lawrence, "MGM was the Tiffany's of the business."

On the first floor was the casting office, as well as Mayer's of-

1 LION BUILDING

fice. The mogul was flocked protectively by three secretaries. "It was very difficult to see [Mayer]," recalled Lillian Gish, who made four films for the studio in the 1920s. "And he had a secretary who was one of the most formidable women I've ever seen in my life. She virtually ran Hollywood."

That "secretary" was Mayer's executive assistant Ida Koverman, a much-feared legend on the lot. This fearsome power, once an assistant to President Herbert Hoover and a major force in the California Republican Party, could help make a star or destroy one. "We called her Mount Ida," said Van Johnson's wife, Evie. "How to explain her? She was Margaret Thatcher, but much worse. She was dictatorial, unbending, and unyielding. She was not a nice old grandmother."

Irving Thalberg's office was on the second floor, in a corner with his secretary, Vivian Newcom. "When you were shown into his office, he was invariably standing behind the desk, looking at a letter or fid-

Top Left: The star of the circus themed film *Billy Rose's Jumbo* (1962) has his pass checked by an attentive studio guard.
Top Right: Bert Lahr shows a lack of "courage" as he hands the MGM guard his studio pass.
Bottom Right: Buster Keaton sneaks past a stern studio guard in the 1930 film *Free and Easy*.

Above: A line-up of MGM's stable of directors as photographed in June 1925: (from left to right) Victor Seastrom, Mauritz Stiller, J. Ernest Williamson, Monta Bell, Rupert Hughes, Joseph Von Sternberg, Erich von Stroheim (rear with face blocked), Jack Conway, Tod Browning (rear with hat), Hobart Henley, King Vidor, William A. Wellman, Reginald Barker, Marcel De Santo, Al Raback, William Christy Cabanne, and Benjamin Christiansen.

dling with various objects with an abstracted air, as if he were quite unconscious of your presence," recalled screenwriter Lenore Coffee. "After a good moment, he would look up as if startled to find you there."

Due to his busy schedule, it was very difficult to meet with Thalberg. At least until the Marx Brothers invaded the studio in 1935. As Groucho Marx recalls:

> After *Duck Soup*, we [Groucho, Chico, and Harpo] signed with Thalberg. We started to talk about *A Night at the Opera* and then at 11:30 or 12:00, he said he needed to go and talk to [screenwriter] Bob Sherwood and that he'd be back. He didn't come back until 2:00 or 3:00—and he did this more than once. So the fourth time he did this, we lit a fire in his huge fireplace and we sent to the commissary and got eight baked potatoes.

And we lit a fire and we took off all our clothes. When he came back, we were sitting in front of the fireplace, toasting these baked potatoes. After that, he loved us because no one ever cracked a joke around him. They were too afraid of him—even Mayer was afraid of him.

It was in his own office that he proposed to the studio's reigning "Queen of the Lot," actress Norma Shearer, by displaying trays of engagement rings and asking her to pick one. Their marriage was a successful private and professional relationship that would last until his death. "She was breathtakingly beautiful," recalled her protégé, contract star Janet Leigh. "Classic patrician features, porcelain skin, and a smile that could melt stone."

Also melting at this time was Thalberg's relationship with Mayer, which had started out cordial, but disintegrated even as the company's success skyrocketed. "Mayer left the production, the artistic end, to Thalberg," recalled director King Vidor. "Irving said that since MGM was making enough pictures and enough money, we could afford an experimental film every once in awhile. It would do something for the studio and something for the whole industry. That was a pretty good attitude for a top production executive."

But that attitude clashed with Mayer's anti-prestige-picture management style. Thalberg felt oppressed by Mayer's domination of the studio, and felt his salary did not equal his contributions. Just as Ince and his partners, and then Goldwyn and Godsol, turned to bitter rivals in the same offices, Mayer and Thalberg reached a stage where they barely spoke to each other. Thalberg had planned to leave the property, like Goldwyn, to form his own independent company when his studio contract ended in 1939.

Typical of their dissension was Mayer's refusal to green light three Thalberg films: *It Can't Happen Here*, based on Sinclair Lewis' novel of dictatorship in America ("Too controversial!"); Mildred Cram's extramarital love story *Forever* ("It will offend the Catholic Church!"); and Franz Werfel's *The Forty Days of Musa Dagh* ("Its subject matter—Armenian genocide—will offend the Turkish government!").

"What can the Turks do if we make *Musa Dagh*?" Thalberg argued. "Okay, let them keep us out of their 30 movie theatres! We've lost our guts, and when that happens to a studio, you can kiss it goodbye!" Thalberg's increasingly expensive prestige pictures became a financial headache for Mayer, who preferred an assembly line of inexpensive family pictures like the *Andy Hardy* series. But the young producer did have a point. The eventual blandness and factory-like feel of Metro Goldwyn Mayer's films in the decades to come would indeed help spell the studio's doom.

An iron bridge was built from the second floor of the executive offices to a private projection room across the studio street, where Thalberg could preview all film shot each day. The room, complete

Left: Some of the MGM star power under contract included Clark Cable, seen here with Louis B. Mayer.
Right: The colonnade entrance in 1938, and Thalberg's "Bridge of Sighs" above.

with three pianos in the Silent Era, was dubbed the "Bridge of Sighs" by nervous filmmakers who would watch Thalberg cross it to judge their work.

That projection room was also the scene of numerous gatherings of the studio's stars, writers, directors, and department heads. During one historic meeting, in the midst of the Great Depression, Mayer wept as he told the gathering that the studio demanded a 50 percent pay cut of everyone. Struck by his emotion, everyone agreed to the cut.

"The group dispersed and I was a few steps ahead of Mayer . . . as we crossed the iron bridge to the front-office building," recalled Samuel Marx. "Oblivious to the fact that I could surely hear him, he asked a talent expert, 'How did I do?'"

With tricks like this one, Mayer and Thalberg would see to it that MGM survived the Great Depression better off than any other studio. Paramount (once the industry leader), Warner Bros., RKO, and Fox all toppled into bankruptcy by 1932—but not MGM, which roared out an $8 million profit thanks to its unrivaled production team and star power.

The studio's unrivaled dominance over the entire industry continued until 1936, when Irving Thalberg, always in frail health, suc-

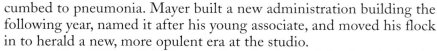

Top Left: Artists in the Publicity Department fine-tune film posters in 1938.
Top Right: New contract star Jane Powell boards the "The Showbuilder," a MGM publicity billboard bus, in 1944.
Bottom Left: The staff of the Publicity Department, including Howard Strickling (center right) and Howard Dietz (center left).
Bottom Right: An elaborate roadside advertisement for the upcoming *Queen Christina* booked to screen at Hollywood's Grauman's Chinese Theatre in 1933.

cumbed to pneumonia. Mayer built a new administration building the following year, named it after his young associate, and moved his flock in to herald a new, more opulent era at the studio.

The old Lion Building continued to be used for decades by the Talent, Fire, Security, Casting, Labor Relations, Travel and, perhaps most importantly, the Publicity departments.

Although Pete Smith (later famous for his comic short subjects) and Lawrence Weingarten (later a prolific producer) made at-

tempts at heading the Publicity Department, Howard Strickling eventually made the department his own. His office featured a desk dominated by a carved ivory lion; his favorite tattered leather chair; and photo stills everywhere, including a favorite of Joan Crawford

thumbing her nose at him.

Studio publicists were aware that scandal could sometimes improve a contract star's reputation. "After reading about the twentieth new romance I'm supposed to be having this month," Lana Turner once confided to June Allyson, "all I can say is I only wish I had the time."

For decades, studio employees would pass on the tale of a new girl who was brought to the lot in the mid-1920s. She was a lonely, underused Swedish actress who spent her time wandering listlessly along studio paths. This "brooding, reflective figure" came upon a tree that grew beside the old Lion Building and, to the surprise of bystanders, grabbed some fruit and ate it. Her name was Greta Garbo. Reflecting with surprise on the studio's expert ability to create illusions, story editor Samuel Marx wryly added, "There was a widespread belief that fruit that grew inside a movie studio must be inedible." Actually, Budd Schulberg, then a child who often played on the lot with executive Harry Rapf's son, Maurice, found another use for the figs. The two boys would pick the fruit and throw it at passing luminaries, once hitting the ethereal Garbo right in the kisser.

The Lion Building would be renamed for the studio's longest-running contract star, Robert Taylor, in 1987. Taylor, born Spangler Arlington Brugh, was once asked to explain his longevity at the studio.

"My metabolism doesn't lend itself to the Davis-Cagney brand of high-pressure careering. I stayed with one studio for 20 years, took what they gave me to do, did my work. While I wasn't happy with everything, I scored pretty well."

This building was subsequently renamed for the studio's famed director George Cukor in 1989 after the current tenants of the building circulated a petition requesting that the name be changed because the mild-mannered Taylor had once been a friendly witness before the House Un-American Activities Committee and an alleged supporter of the Hollywood blacklist. Taylor and Cukor died in 1969 and 1983, respectively.

In the 1990s, this building was torn down and replaced. This accounts for a strange sight awaiting those working inside the current studio on West Washington Boulevard. The windows and exterior wall of the old executive building facing the street have been preserved by city ordinance as a historic landmark. But inside the front gate, it is apparent that the imposing wall looking out into the real world is only a façade. The new building replacing the old was built a few feet inside the gate, creating an inadvertent and erroneous echo of the long-gone MGM backlot.

Above: The interior of the Purchasing Department, where a focused staff types up a never-ending series of purchasing forms.

2 PURCHASING DEPARTMENT

Proceeding south, away from the old front gate, one passed MGM's Purchasing Department, "where everything from a package of needles to a brace of *Kismet* camels may be found on the auditing books," reported the *Motion Picture Herald* in 1944.

The main office for the studio's police force, discussed in the East Gate section, was also once housed here.

Above: The men's costumes are housed in the "Heidelberg Building," one of Lot One's oldest structures (1960s).

I n 1924, Mayer and Thalberg found the three-story, 25,004-square-foot General Wardrobe Building—a relic from the Triangle days—still storing costumes from Griffith and Ince epics. The moth-besieged costumes inside the building were indicative of the generally poor condition of most of the former Goldwyn studio. Although improvements would be made, the physical look of the plant was unimportant to Thalberg, who instead set to work updating and streamlining the departments into his overall plan for assembly-line efficiency.

"The look of the studio inside those walls was never really that important," recalled assistant cameraman Brainard Miller. "It was always very clean and well-kept, but the money was poured into the films. That's an additional reason why MGM films looked so lavish."

"MGM fooled everybody," agreed actor Richard Anderson. "Despite the studio's reputation for excess, it was actually the best below-the-line studio in Hollywood."

Anderson also recalls the immaculate nature of the studio as well. "If you have ever worked on a film, you know that moviemaking is messy. It's the nature of the business. That's why I was all the more

3   GENERAL WARDROBE BUILDING

amazed at how clean the studio was kept at all times. It was a matter of pride."

Thalberg directed immediate changes in the Wardrobe Department, but was frustrated in his attempts to find a primary wardrobe designer. Mayer thought he had found the answer by hiring, with great pomp and circumstance, Romain de Tirtoff (or "Erté," for short) as supervising Art and Costume Department director in 1925. Erté did indeed impress by developing lavish costumes for *Ben-Hur* and the concurrent "flapper" films, but with a disapproving tone as subtle as many of his designs, he would later recall Hollywood studios—and MGM in particular—as "a world of fantasy in themselves. There were royal façades without palaces: stupendous interiors without walls, kings and queens in full regalia eating sandwiches in the cafeteria with beggars in rags."

But Erté's sly and romantic Deco style clashed with the fast-paced, assembly-line methods imposed by Thalberg. In November of 1925, *Variety* reported that the "fiery French designer" had left after clashing with Lillian Gish over her *La Boheme* (1926) wardrobe and with studio officials over his work not being "performed in the speedy

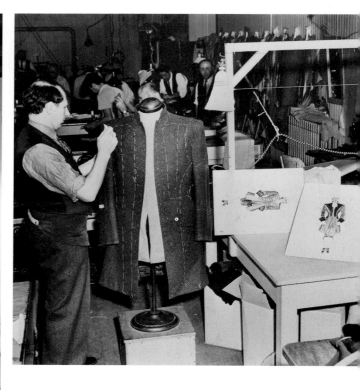

Left: Rivets are punched through a leather strap attached to a Roman breastplate in the Wardrobe Department.
Center: Employees of the Wardrobe Department ready a rack of costumes for an upcoming production.
Right: Chalk markings are made on a period costume to be sewn in the Wardrobe Department for the 1951 production of *Scaramouche* (1952).

Opposite: Four heavy-duty sewing machines are used to create draperies that will be used to dress the sets of future productions.

way required."

Mayer tried again in 1928 by grabbing the designer Cecil B. DeMille brought to the lot for his three-picture deal: renowned designer Adrian (born Adrian Greenberg). This time the mogul was much luckier. For the first time, the studio found a designer who could create MGM costumes that complemented MGM sets. Mayer and Thalberg began a concerted campaign to keep their new costumer at the studio by publicly billing him as the most important designer in Hollywood. The appeal to Adrian's vanity worked and the designer actually lived up to the studio-created ballyhoo by displaying a unique ability to design costumes that reflected the individuality of the char-

acters in each film again and again for decades. "Designers in real life seldom worry about dramatic values," Adrian observed in 1936, "for they know little about the events in the life of the individual wearing their creations. . . . On the other hand, a designer for the screen knows, before he starts his sketch, every experience the wearer of the gown will have. It is his business to dress his character in a manner that will intensify, to an audience, the mood of the scene."

By the time Adrian left the studio in 1941, with a fat scrapbook of studio clippings under his arm, studio publicists would brag that 178 people worked in the costume building; that the racks held over 250,000 costumes of almost every historical period in world history

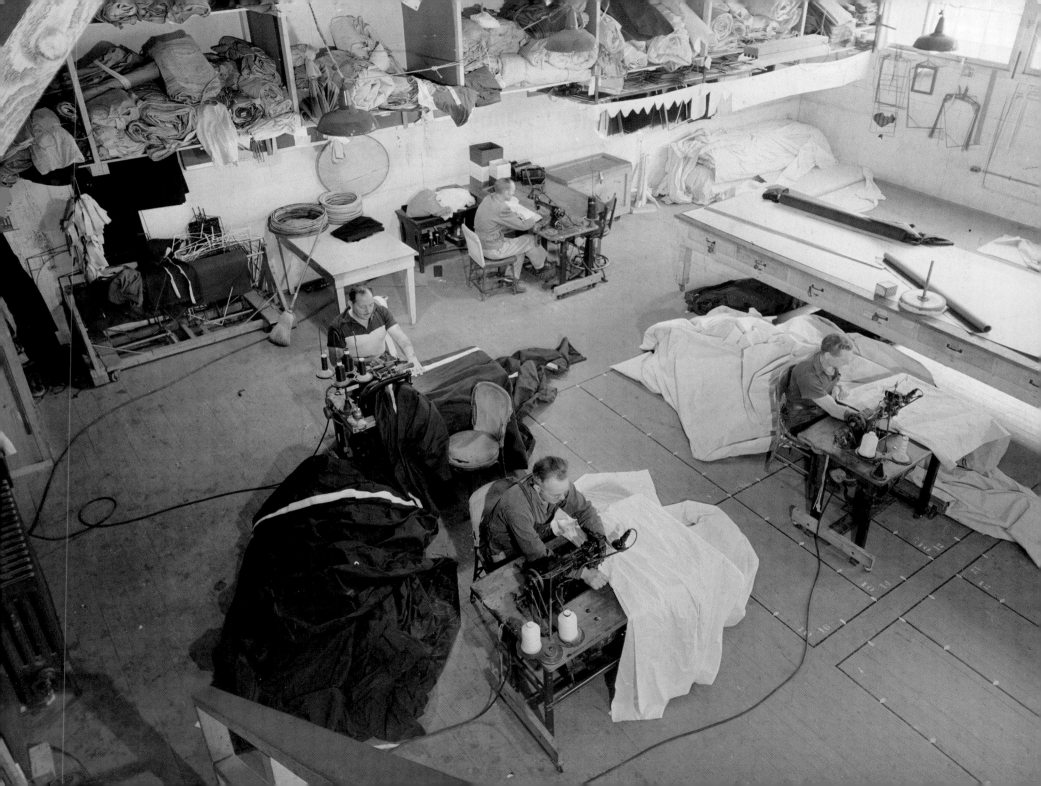

Left: Ann-Margret models the latest fashion as she passes the Wardrobe annex in 1964.
Right: Shoes are set out for pick-up by actresses and extras in the Wardrobe Department.

inventoried at a value of $1,500,000; and that 100,000 yards of material were annually cut in the department, which now included 15 separate warehouses.

In the decades to come, many gifted designers would work at MGM. They included Irene (*Gaslight* [1944], *National Velvet* [1944], *Green Dolphin Street* [1947], *Neptune's Daughter* [1949], among others); Walter Plunkett (*Gone with the Wind* [1939], *The Sea of Grass* [1947], *Show Boat* [1951], *Singin' in the Rain* [1952], *Kiss Me Kate* [1953], *Forbidden Planet* [1956], *Raintree County* [1957], among others); Helen Rose (*A Date With Judy* [1948], *High Society* [1956], *Cat on a Hot Tin Roof* [1958], *The Courtship of Eddie's Father* [1963], among others);

Mary Ann Nyberg (*Lili* [1953] and *The Band Wagon* [1953]); and Irene Sharaff (*Ziegfeld Follies* [1946], *An American in Paris* [1951], *Brigadoon* [1954], among others). But none would ever equal Adrian's output or influence, as evidenced by the fact that the star fitting rooms continued to bear his name until 1959.

Costumes were stored across the lot. The so-called "Heidelberg Building" (kitty-corner to the water tower), constructed in 1916 as a military barracks, was known for many years as "Men's Wardrobe," instead. Today, inexplicably, the surviving structure is referred to by employees by that odd, World War I-era moniker.

Above: The staff in the Tabulation Department creates employees' eagerly awaited paychecks.
Inset: A 1937 check made out to Greta Garbo.

4 | ACCOUNTING, PAYROLL, AND INSURANCE DEPARTMENTS

Further south, past a row of editing rooms (discussed later) were the Accounting, Payroll, and Insurance departments. These departments are mentioned here only as a not-so-subtle reminder of the second word in the term "show business."

Left: The alternative Culver Boulevard entrance to Lot One in 1935.
Right: The East Gate in 1939, the most used entrance and exit on Lot One.
Opposite: In 1944, the East Gate entrance reflected a world at war with a banner above the gates signifying the number of studio personnel currently serving in the Armed Forces, marked with a blue star (1,062), and the number who lost their lives while serving, marked with a gold star (4). An enemy attack on the United States had a major impact on those living on the West Coast, and the sign above the guard shack pointing to the Air Raid Shelter reflects that concern.
Inset: An employee's pass from 1944.

Beyond was the famed East Gate, adjacent to the Thalberg Building and accessed by Grant Avenue (Thalberg's middle name). From the late 1930s, when the old gate at the colonnade became too small for modern truck traffic until Sony Pictures purchased the studio in 1989, this was the primary entrance to the studio. The only other option for studio employees to avoid the hordes of fans, tourists, and lineup of visitors was to duck into Lot One by a small gate on Culver Boulevard.

The gate and the nearby Thalberg Building became Hollywood icons, appearing in dozens of promotional films and movies. Both were used, for example, as "Meglopolitian Studios" in *The Loved One* (1965).

5 EAST GATE

In *Anchors Aweigh* (1945), Frank Sinatra made his MGM debut attempting to crash the East Gate as a lovesick sailor. His last film at the studio was a hosting job standing near the East Gate for *That's Entertainment!* in 1974. The crooner's MGM career had come full circle.

Security at the studio gates was a serious business. At its peak, the studio employed 50 policemen under the direction of Police Chief Whitey Hendry, who once quipped that MGM "is the only insane asylum I've ever known that people try to break *into*." Gate guards were expected to recognize and salute the studio's stars. Policeman Harry Keating, who was hired in 1928, recalled failing to recognize a star only

EMPLOYEES PASS

[PAYROLL No. 1]

LOEW'S INCORPORATED
Metro-Goldwyn-Mayer Pictures
CULVER-CITY CALIFORNIA

EXPIRES
APRIL 1ST, 1944

4054

45464   Jack Jancich
102
187-40   AS 4-3311

BY   W. R. Craig
      G. Lewis

J. G. Mayer.
STUDIO MANAGER

NOT VALID UNLESS SIGNED BY EMPLOYEE ON REVERSE SIDE

INTERNATIONAL DEPT.

AIR RAID SHELTER

Top Left: A screen capture from *Anchors Aweigh* (1945) shows a "dressed" streamlined-Moderne guard shack set, much fancier than the actual structure. An example of the glamour MGM was so good at promoting is reinforced by the pretty blonde leaving the studio in a flashy convertible.

Top Right: Glenn Ford exits through the East Gate behind the wheel of the 1955 Lincoln Futura. This $250,000 Ford concept car was purchased by MGM for *It Started with a Kiss* (1959), co-starring Debbie Reynolds. The vehicle would later be transferred to Hollywood car customizer George Barris and reinvented as TV's Batmobile.

Bottom: Officers from the Security Department line up for inspection on Lot Two's Cohn Park that fronted the Girl's School set (1938).

Left: The East Gate entrance with a more "modern" logo and lettering in the 1970s.
Right: The East Gate entrance to Sony/Columbia Studios in 2009, after an expensive studio overhaul. The new façade-based architecture is meant to conjure up a resemblance to a studio backlot. Well meaning, but it is a cramped, impractical location and a poor substitute for the real thing. Note that the arch above the gate has now been entirely removed.

once: He greeted Carole Lombard at the gate as "Miss Stanwyck."

The lot's most famous security guard was named Kenneth Hollywood ("It's an old Irish name"), who worked for MGM for more than 30 years. Like many of the most trusted security men at the studio, Hollywood held special responsibilities over the years. When Clark Gable had a heart attack, Ken was positioned at the star's door at Hollywood Presbyterian Hospital. When producer Mike Todd died, Hollywood acted as personal bodyguard to his bereaved wife, Elizabeth Taylor. Many famous personages became friends. Among the fringe benefits of sporting badge #1 was a cameo in Elvis Presley's *Jailhouse Rock* (1957).

"On my 25th wedding anniversary, Elvis stopped in the middle of his act and told the audience it was my anniversary," said Hollywood. "He told the people he'd known me for a hundred years. Which was very nice—to stop your act and do that. People just don't do that."

Surprisingly, Hollywood's security style rarely required the use

of the word "no" or calling for police backup. "You can talk almost anyone down. You just got to remember never to put your hands on them. I don't tell them no. I have them park their cars and let them use my phone to try and get their authorization. By letting them call, you've accommodated them, right? You haven't refused them. Now if the producer or whoever turns them down, they can't be mad at you. They may be mad as hell at the producer, but. . . ."

Still, there were those who tried that famous Hollywood placidity.

"Shirley Peeps—he was this guy who would always try to drive through on a girl's bicycle," recalled Hollywood. "For years he did this. And if a new cop was on the gate on my day off, he would tell them he was Hollywood's cousin. . . . That guy, he could drive you nuts."

The iconic arched gate, where a thousand stars once entered and exited the studio, was removed in 2009.

Opposite: An aerial view of the Thalberg Building in 1945. Behind the building are the railroad tracks, which trains used to transport supplies to Lot One.

Left: The Thalberg Building, recently landscaped, after being completed in 1938.

Just outside the East Gate was the iconic Thalberg Building, the studio's executive administration building designed by Claud Beelman and built between 1937–1938.

The Thalberg Building was Mayer's magnificent public tribute to the "Boy Wonder" and his considerable achievements at MGM. It is not known if it was genuine affection, humility, or even guilt that motivated Mayer in erecting such an impressive altar to the memory of the man who Mayer had come to resent. Known as the "Iron Lung" (or "White Lung"), both for its shape and primitive, early air conditioning, the Thalberg Building heralded a new era for MGM—with Mayer in charge.

Among the Iron Lung's original 235 offices, totaling 115,000 cubic feet, each producer was awarded a richly appointed corner suite. But they were in fact gilded cages, for the producer's power (to select scripts, stars, sets, and costumes) did not project much further than this building. It was the writers and directors—whose offices lined the walls in-between the producer suites—who created the magic with their typewriters and soundstages.

"I was one of 27 or 28 producers," recalls Frank Davis, "and we only made somewhere around 40 pictures a year. We were always

6 THALBERG BUILDING

supposed to make 52, but we never did. That meant that the producers could barely make one picture a year. Yes, there were jealousies."

Ultimately, the Mayer regime (1936–1951) would yield an incredible bounty of film classics and the array of musicals for which the studio remains famous today—lacking perhaps only the depth of variety and sophistication that Thalberg could deliver. These include: *Libeled Lady* (1936), *Boys Town* (1938), *Ninotchka* (1939), *The Women* (1939). *The Philadelphia Story* (1940), *Woman of the Year* (1942), *National Velvet* (1944), *Gaslight* (1944), *Easter Parade* (1948), *Adam's Rib* (1949), *Father of the Bride* (1950), *Annie Get Your Gun* (1950), and *An American in Paris* (1951). Mayer's personal favorites were the *Andy Hardy* series (1937–1958), *The Human Comedy* (1943), and *Madame Curie* (1943).

The third floor of the Thalberg Building was the seat of power with Mayer's office in the center, surrounded in the wings by his favorite producers and administrators, including Ida Koverman. "You entered this enormous room, all in white, for what some people called the 'quarter-mile walk' to a desk the size of a small helicopter pad, all highly polished and shining," recalls Debbie Reynolds. "Because Mr. Mayer was not very tall (about five-and-a-half feet), and rather roundish and portly, he had his desk built on a platform, lest some big temperamental

Above: MGM's mascot, Leo the Lion, lounges in front of the Thalberg Building on the occasion of the studio's 25th Anniversary in 1949.

Left: The Thalberg Building ablaze with light.
Right: Former MGM contract star Frank Sinatra stands in front of the Thalberg Building in *That's Entertainment!* (1974).

star or director come in and forget who was boss."

The fourth floor contained a private gymnasium, chiropractor's office, and Mayer's executive dining room, which played host to the studio's dazzling array of stars and America's most famous and infamous. "It was that private dining room to which Mayer invited Ethel Waters, Lena Horne, and the rest of the black cast of *Cabin in the Sky* when the studio manager—his brother, Jerry—refused to allow them to sit at tables in the commissary," noted *Wizard of Oz* film historian Aljean Harmetz. "And the next day, the commissary was open to them. Black or white, L. B. Mayer's stars were *his* stars."

The mogul had a seemingly bottomless bag of tricks to keep his stars in line. "He could foam at the mouth if he was upset with us," recalls Esther Williams. "I always wondered how he did it."

"You can say what you like about the Louis B. Mayers and the heads of the studios in my day," said contract star Allan Jones. "They were not educated, they were pretty crude, but they wanted to improve themselves and they wanted to improve the public."

"Mayer used [MGM] as a pulpit to establish values for the whole nation," said Mickey Rooney.

"He did this by telling stories, not about the way the world was, but about the way he loved running the studio—it was like an empire," adds former MGM publicist Jim Mahoney. "You just can't do that anymore. There isn't anyone in this business that can make a star—not anymore. Louis B. Mayer could."

In 1941, it was at the side entrance to the Thalberg Building, inside the East Gate, that two stars met and become one of the best studio (and real-life) pairings: Spencer Tracy and Katharine Hepburn. "That's the spot where I met Spencer Tracy," Hepburn recalled. "He was coming along from the commissary with Joe Mankiewicz. Joe had produced *The Philadelphia Story* and, God willing, was going to produce *Woman of the Year*. I had on very high heels—I was about five-seven-and-a-half then. Spencer was about 5'10". I said, 'I'm sorry, I've got these high heels on.' Joe looked at me and said, 'Don't worry, Kate, he'll cut you down to his size.'" The couple would make nine films together over the next 25 years.

"I think he was the best American actor we ever had in motion pictures," future MGM production chief Dore Schary would say of Tracy.

The Thalberg Building was only occasionally used as a set to portray anything other than a motion picture studio administration building; *The Subterraneans* (1960), the *Dr. Kildare* (1961–1966) TV series, and *Marlowe* (1969) were rare examples, all of which ironically cast the Iron Lung as a hospital. Cliff Robertson won an a Oscar as the title character in *Charly* (1968), visiting Claire Bloom's apartment played by this building's rear entrance.

Left: Inside the Writer's Building multiple copies of scripts are being processed and sorted.
Right: The old Writer's Building has recently been covered with façades in order to evoke not an actual city street, but a studio backlot (2009).

7 WRITERS BUILDING

Writers in Hollywood were never terribly high on the Hollywood totem pole. Mayer was once reported to have said that profits from actress Joan Crawford's pictures had paid for the Writers Building. The truth is that he probably could have housed his writers in a tent in the parking lot and gotten away with it.

The Writers Building stood on the site of the original studio mill complex. Originally, the long, narrow structure was referred to as the Scenario Building and, later still, as the Metro Building and the TV Building. Like most studio departments, the "scenario writers" moved about the lot over the years. Originally, the unappreciated writers were housed in an ancient Thomas Ince building, built circa 1916, which lined the northern side of the studio's Main Street. It's not known if they were grateful or resentful of Crawford or the substantial profits from her pictures for moving them closer to Mayer's ever-watchful eye.

In the 1930s, the intelligentsia in the media often found, or pretended to find, the inhabitants of the Writers Building more interesting than the studio's stars. Such was the case in 1932, when a *Fortune* magazine reporter observed that "more members of the literati work under [department head] Samuel Marx at MGM than it took to produce the King James version of the Bible!" Indeed, no less than the very greatest writers of the 20th century worked in this unassuming building at various times over the years. F. Scott Fitzgerald, George S. Kaufman, Lillian Hellman, Moss Hart, Ben Hecht, P. G. Wodehouse, Anita Loos, Joseph L. Mankiewicz, James Hilton, Philip Wylie, Robert Sherwood, Robert Benchley, Dashiell Hammett, S. J. Perelman, Sidney Howard, and Dorothy Parker were among the many notable men (and women) of letters who toiled away behind Underwood typewriters in little offices here.

But it was the brilliant (but unhappy-to-be-in-Hollywood) William Faulkner who got the last word for all his underappreciated brethren when, upon meeting Clark Gable in the 1930s, was subjected to Gable's inquiry, "So I hear you're a writer, Mr. Faulkner."

Faulkner answered, "That's right, Mr. Gable. What do you do?"

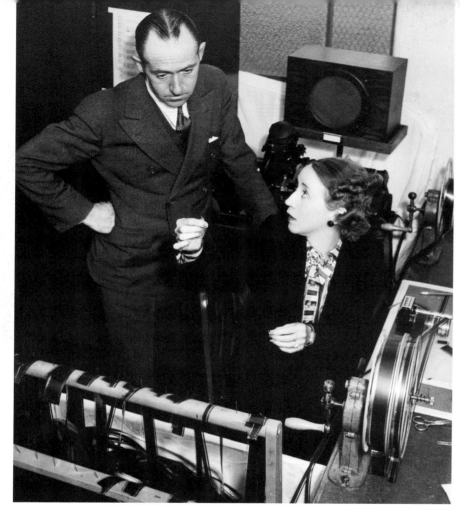

Left: Danny Gray, manager of the Film Editing Department, and editor Margaret Booth (1936).
Right: A reel of processed film is examined before edits are made.

<table>
<tr><td>8</td><td>FILM EDITING ROOMS,
FILM STORAGE, AND
LADIES WARDROBE</td></tr>
</table>

Some buildings on the lot never had a clear identity of their own. Further south, toward the southeastern corner of the lot on Culver Boulevard, are hives of adjoining buildings that variously served as film editing rooms, film storage, and a ladies' wardrobe annex.

Left: Members of the Music Department work to complete a musical score for an upcoming production.
Right: A rare surviving cache of original music scores from the MGM archives.

The Music Department's sheet music library, housed in this unassuming gray building, eventually swelled to over 4,000,000 selections, ranking with the Library of Congress and the New York Public Library as one of the three largest in the world.

"Just to the left when you came in the gate was the music department," recalls Debbie Reynolds. "Andre Previn, Conrad Salinger, Johnny Green, Roger Edens, Lena Horne's husband Lennie Hayton, and Bobby Tucker were there. You might hear Andre Previn on the piano, or Connie Salinger. Everyone had the windows of their offices

opened because there was still no air conditioning at that time."

This was actually the second building with this name. The first one consisted of a row of bungalows described later.

It has been reported that most of the contents of both of these buildings were unceremoniously tossed into the nearest dumpster in the 1970s. Fortunately, this is not true. Although the orchestrations for individual instruments were destroyed, the complete conductors' scores survive intact at Warner Bros. Studios.

Left: The massive interior of the state of the art New Film Lab Building as it looked in the 1940s.
Right: The Capra Office building stands on the site of the original lab at the now Sony/Columbia lot (2009).

Across from these buildings to the west lies the Metrocolor Building. This film processing plant rose from the site of one of the original glass stages in 1930, and was long-publicized as the largest laboratory erected inside a motion picture studio.

It was in this lab that the studio (like others in the cost-conscious 1950s) began to process its own color film stock, known appropriately as Metrocolor (a trade name for Eastmancolor). The process was cheaper than using Technicolor, then (as now) the industry standard, but as the years would prove, less durable. As internal production slowed in the 1960s, the laboratory began processing with great success for outside clients and other studios, as well.

The building, an upper floor of which housed the studio gymnasium, was completely rebuilt as the Metrocolor Building in 1979. At

10 NEW FILM LAB BUILDING

that time, it could boast of four 25-seat screening rooms and storage facilities for 25 million feet of raw stock. These additions cost the company $1.5 million at a time it could ill-afford it. The expansion included the removing of Stages 16 and 17 to build Metrocolor offices and processing equipment. Yet the lab would be closed only 10 years later by Lorimar (which had purchased the lot), as part of an agreement with rival Technicolor.

MGM publicist Dore Freeman's favorite story was the time he escorted Princess Grace and her two young children on a tour of the studio. The children were most fascinated by the barrels of 70 mm and 35 mm film found outside the Metrocolor Lab. The princess and the children enjoyed rummaging through the barrels and took souvenirs of the snippets of film home with them.

Left: The back of the Property Department building in 1936.
Right: The furniture used in *Marie Antoinette* (1938) is a small sample of the treasures found in the Property Department building.

11 PROPERTY DEPARTMENT

Further west along the studio's Main Street was the four-story Property Warehouse. Built in 1925, and remodeled and enlarged in 1937, this was the primary storehouse for MGM props. The top three floors contained furniture for dressing sets from ancient to futuristic times. The lower floor contained thousands of "hand" props such as phony money, clocks, lamps, dishes, gold- and silverware, typewriters, radios, and much more.

Teenager Maurice Rapf, when not throwing fruit at Greta Garbo, remembered the place in the '30s as being "a square brick building three or four stories tall that looked like a warehouse, but on each of its floors were exotic accoutrements from scores of movies." Rapf and his friend Budd Schulberg (later the author of that poison-pen letter to Hollywood *What Makes Sammy Run?*) used to rampage through the building—indeed the entire lot—as boys.

"Schulberg's father was head of Paramount and my father was one of the heads of MGM. We chased down autographs on both lots, but preferred MGM as a playground because it had more space than Paramount and more glamorous sets to act out our stories," he recalled

Left: Dominating this set for *Rasputin and the Empress* (1933) is a prop moose head mounted on the wall.
Top Center: The same moose made a cameo in *Peg 'o My Heart* (1933).
Bottom Center: On the set of *The Garden Murder Case* (1936), the stuffed moose can be seen yet again hanging on the wall.
Props were often used over and over for several decades.
Right: The Property Department building as seen in 2009. The current owners of the studio have "dressed" the exterior façade for the purpose of filming.
Opposite Top Left: This section of the Prop Department, with its clocks and silver plate, resembles an exquisite boutique of antiquities.
Opposite Top Right: Every style and type of lamp imaginable could be found in the Prop Department.
Opposite Bottom Left: Displaying some Hollywood magic, employees of the Property Department "age" these freshly minted plaster statues.
Opposite Bottom Right: Surrounded by enough weapons to outfit a large army, actor Stewart Granger (left) admires a bolt-action rifle in the Gun Room.

in his memoirs.

"The prop department at MGM was like a museum, a glorious collection of real and unreal, of every period, every style you could imagine, and some you could never imagine," marveled actress Jane Powell. "If they couldn't find it, they made it—and made it accurate in every detail."

The Property Department eventually outgrew the Property Building. Adjuncts and annexes sprang up across Lot One and eventually Prop Department pieces would be stored inside warehouses and sets on Lots Two and Three, as well.

The building, now an office complex, is today known as the David Lean Building.

Above: Audrey Totter kisses a camera for *Lady in the Lake* (1947). In a daring act of originality, the movie was told from the camera's point of view.

12   CAMERA DEPARTMENT

Across the street from the Property Department was the Camera Department. MGM, like other studios, owned their own cameras, camera accessories, and lenses. In 1969, however, the department would be closed and the Janitorial Department would move into the building. When Sony Pictures first moved onto the lot, the building became the new Property Department. Today, the structure is primarily an office complex, and is known as the Robert Young Building.

Top Left: Camera Department employees inspect a camera and lens before filming.
Bottom Left: What couldn't Lassie do? Here she sets up a shot for *Son of Lassie* (1945).
Right: MGM had a way of making everything look glamorous, even the Camera Department.

Lot One: Buildings and Departments | **53**

Left: The Music Departments's (A and B) staff in 1938: (left to right) George Bassman, Dave Snell, Lew Finston, Edward Cordner, Al Columbo, Herbert Stothart, I. Friedman, Daniele Amfitheatrof, Bronislau Kaper, I. Halperin, George Stoll, Johnny Green, Arthur Bergh, Max Terr, Rudy Kopp, Minneletha White, and Nat Finston.
Right: The Music Departments's staff of songwriters in 1944: (back row left to right) Music Department Director Nat Finston, Johnny Green, Johnny Mercer, Harry Warren, Ralph Freed, Ralph Blane, and I. Friedman (Finston's assistant); (on floor) Sammy Cahn, Jule Styne, and Hugh Martin.

13 MUSIC DEPARTMENT (B)

A modest row of five bungalows once bordered the now-vanished track rails on Culver Boulevard. They were the humble beginnings of the studio's soon-to-be-unrivaled Music Department, where MGM virtually had its own Tin Pan Alley of composers and songwriters once upon a time.

The most ambitious and talented of these songwriters were Arthur Freed and Nacio Herb Brown, who had collaborated on songs (Brown wrote the music, Freed was lyricist) since 1921. The pair convinced Thalberg to let them compose the score for the studio's first "All-Talking, All-Singing, All-Dancing" motion picture, *The Broadway Melody* (1929), for which the pair contributed the standards "You Were Meant for Me," and "The Broadway Melody." That picture single-handedly ushered in the genre of the movie musical, earning a then-fabulous $4,366,000 and the Oscar for best picture. Freed convinced Thalberg to use them again for *The Hollywood Revue of 1929* (1929), for which they wrote the studio's subsequent theme song, "Singin' in the Rain."

Freed and Brown continued to write songs that the studio continued to recycle. Take "Pagan Love Song" as an example. Written for the 1928 (partial) talkie *White Shadows of the South Seas*, it was replayed constantly through the years as background music in films that required a South Seas atmosphere, including *The Pagan* (1929), *Never the Twain Shall Meet* (1931), *Three Kings and a Queen* (1939), and *Night Club Girl* (1945). The song, now a film title as well, was used again in 1950 for the eponymous South Seas musical starring Howard Keel and Esther Williams.

Many of the Freed-Brown evergreens were permanently and most entertainingly memorialized in *Singin' in the Rain* (1951).

Not satisfied as a lyricist, Freed worked his way up the corporate ladder to producer. His knack for discovering and nurturing talent matched Mayer's. He developed the "Freed unit," which produced the studio's most famous and award-winning musicals through the years such as *Meet Me in St. Louis* (1944), *An American in Paris* (1951), *The Band Wagon* (1953), and *Gigi* (1958).

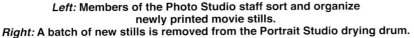
Left: Members of the Photo Studio staff sort and organize
newly printed movie stills.
Right: A batch of new stills is removed from the Portrait Studio drying drum.

Squeezed between the old and new (circa 1931) film labs, and another dance rehearsal hall, was the single-story Portrait Studio. Built in 1918, MGM fashion editor Ann Straus once referred to each of its 8,660 square feet as "a very ugly, uninspiring place," and indeed it was ironic that the most beautiful photographs of the world's most beautiful people were made amidst the machine and construction shops.

Straus worked extra hard to make the experience pleasant by decorating the room with flowers and always providing refreshments. Some stars, like Joan Crawford and Norma Shearer, loved this process.

14   PORTRAIT STUDIO

Others, like Greta Garbo and Greer Garson, hated it.

Janet Leigh considered these photo sittings "the most difficult aspect of being an actress. . . . The minute the photographer says, 'Hold it!' I freeze. I felt stilted, unnatural. And when I started, color flashbulbs had to be replaced after every shot and each exposure took two-to-three seconds—forever, it seemed. It was almost impossible to catch a spontaneous expression. Gradually, I learned to ignore the bulbs and time, and just concentrated on a thought—any thought. That helped some."

Left: An employee prepares the chemical tanks inside the Old Film Lab Building.
Right: The original film lab as it looked in 1926.

Above: When the new lab was built the old building was used for optical effects. A cameraman films a title card for a promotion for *The Wizard of Oz* (1939).

15   OLD FILM LAB BUILDING

Nearby was the original film lab. In this low stucco building, erected in 1918, 200-foot film rolls would be developed after being stretched on wooden racks, which were immersed in deep, narrow tanks of chemical solutions.

With the opening of the new lab in the early 1930s, the building continued to be used for processing, titles, prints, stills, and special effects.

16   MGM SPECIAL TROLLEY

One of Metro's most unique luxuries in early Hollywood was its personal connection to Culver City's Pacific Electric Railway System. In 1934, a spur was laid directly into the rear of Lot One so that the "MGM Special," a chartered private trolley as large as a Pullman, could arrive on film preview evenings at 6:00 PM. With the advent of talking pictures, Thalberg introduced sneak previews to the industry. Instead of counting on the opinions of studio "yes-men" in his private projection room, the young executive could judge for himself what the public thought about MGM films by traveling from this "depot" to Santa Ana, Pomona, Glendale, Riverside, or San Bernardino, where "real people" could be recruited for their opinions on upcoming features.

"We were ridiculed in the industry as 'Retake Alley,'" recalls chief film editor Margaret Booth. "We came back from the previews and fixed the pictures. The other studios didn't do it as well as we could."

A separate, trackless trolley was utilized to transport staffers and crew across the studio grounds and onto the backlots.

Above: Members of the MGM Fire Department test their equipment on the Lot Three Lake set in 1951.

17 FIRE DEPARTMENT

A staff was maintained at the on-lot fire department 24 hours a day, 7 days a week, for over 50 years. The department itself was housed here in the early years before the Mill Complex, specifically the sheet metal shop, forced the Fire Department to relocate to the first of several buildings it occupied until the 1970s.

Left: Research Department head Nathalie Bucknall at work with employees in a publicity photo used in 1938.
Right: The exterior of the Research Department building used as a filming location in 1960.

Above studio manager Eddie Mannix's office, in a building that could trace its history to 1916, was the Research Department. The staff of researchers employed here could, at its peak, handle up to 500 queries a day to provide accuracy, inspiration, and authenticity to films in production. The material was an invaluable tool for art directors, production designers, set decorators, prop men, costume designers, writers, and producers. Every outdoor set on the studio's backlots was born here among the books and picture files depicting every period in world history.

This was the largest of all movie studio research libraries, with over 20,000 books and 250,000 clippings cross-referenced on 80,000 index cards and stored here and in three other buildings across the lot. The department was managed by the formidable Nathalie Bucknall

18 RESEARCH DEPARTMENT

until the 1950s, Elliott Morgan through the 1960s, then by James J. Earie and, lastly, by Bonnie Rothbart until 1988, when Warner Bros. acquired the collection.

Unlike any other library in the world, here you could find historic Sears catalogs cohabitating with old menus, 19th century travel guides, a volume on industrial art published in 1885, and a copy of *The Voyages of Captain Cook*, dated 1785. There was also a special section of 19th century Russian books used for the Greta Garbo film *Anna Karenina* (1935), a dozen carefully maintained scrapbooks on fashions of the French Revolution, and individual files on New York manhole covers, World War II Quonset huts, and French Foreign Legion kepi caps.

In later years, the studio's Security Department would occupy this building, which would be remodeled in 1981.

Left: The studio Commissary Ice Cream Parlor was a favorite spot for: (left to right) Peggy Ann Garner, Elizabeth Taylor, Marshall Thompson, Jane Powell, and Roddy McDowell (1948).
Right: The streamlined-Moderne architecture of the Commissary in 1938.
Opposite: A MGM luncheon in 1933. Among those visible are Irving Thalberg, David O. Selznick, director Jack Conway, Norma Shearer, Hunt Stromberg, and Louis B. Mayer.

19 COMMISSARY

In his or her recollections of Metro Goldwyn Mayer, every employee recalls the legendary commissary with great affection. Built by Ince in 1916, art director Cedric Gibbons remodeled it in chrome and green in 1935. "The MGM commissary was a remarkable experience," recalls Esther Williams. "It was not only the local watering hole, but a respite from whatever was going on in those soundstages. It was on a little side street just past the East Gate, across from the barbershop. Although the tabletops in the commissary were Formica, the clientele was pure platinum!"

"I remember eating there with Ray Bradbury," *Waltons* creator Earl Hamner Jr. remembered, "and at the next table would be Gary Cooper!" Even *other stars* tended to be impressed by the commissary's dazzling clientele. "Although I wasn't star struck, I was amazed at the famous faces I saw at the Metro commissary," recalled Lana Turner. "What a sight," remembered Janet Leigh. "I could never eat, I was too busy gawking. In that huge room—God, I was always so self-conscious walking to a table—I'd see Clark Gable in one corner, Elizabeth Taylor and her mother in another, Gene Kelly tucked against the wall, and on and on and on."

Believing that excellent, well-prepared food would keep his

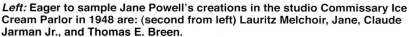

Left: Eager to sample Jane Powell's creations in the studio Commissary Ice Cream Parlor in 1948 are: (second from left) Lauritz Melchoir, Jane, Claude Jarman Jr., and Thomas E. Breen.
Right: The art deco styled interior of the Commissary in 1939.

employees on the lot and avoid long lunch breaks, L. B. Mayer originally put his wife in charge here. Margaret Mayer trained the chef herself, supplying him with the recipe for her husband's favorite chicken soup ("Take nine fat, two-year-old kosher hens for every three gallons of liquid, stewing them overnight, then separating the broth from the chicken. Add chunks of chicken and delicate matzoh balls") for 35 cents a bowl.

"It was the best chicken soup I've ever had," recalled contract child star (and later producer of TV's *M*A*S*H*) Gene Reynolds. "It had big chunks of chicken and noodles. It was delicious, almost a lunch

in itself. It became *the* traditional offering on the menu."

The commissary's other legendary dish was a chocolate malt that was so large that the overflow was served in a smaller side-car glass that was known as the "associate malt." Thanks to the fine food, the 8,730-square-foot commissary (seating 225) was the most famous and star-filled in Hollywood. It even included its own bakery in the basement, which sent tantalizing smells through studio alleyways.

Today, the commissary is known as the Rita Hayworth Dining Room. Mrs. Mayer's chicken soup is still on the menu.

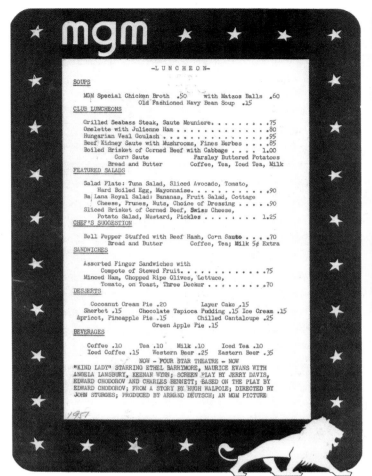

Top Left: A menu from the Commissary in 1957 featured the "MGM Special Chicken Broth with Matzos Balls."
Top Right: (left to right) Marlon Brando, Paul Ford, Glenn Ford, and Machiko Kyo in makeup for *The Teahouse of the August Moon* break for lunch in the Commissary (1956).
Bottom Right: The MGM Commissary has been remodeled and renamed the Rita Hayworth Commissary (2009).

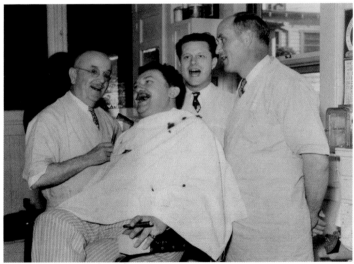

Top Left: Howard Keel reads the latest issue of *Look* magazine in the Barbershop and Newsstand during the 1950s.
Bottom Left: A classic barbershop quartet, featuring Jean Hersholt (seated) and the MGM barbers, singing a tune after finishing a hair trim (1930s).
Right: Ann Sothern checks out the magazine selection at the Barbershop and Newsstand in the 1940s.

20 BARBERSHOP AND NEWSSTAND

Across from the commissary was the studio's busy barbershop and newsstand. "Spencer Tracy, Walter Pidgeon, or Brian Donlevy is apt to be next in line for a haircut," noted a reporter for the *Motion Picture Herald* in 1944. "Fritz, the veteran barber, is said to have trimmed more wealthy and famous persons than anybody else in Hollywood."

Louis B. Mayer usually showed up here in the late afternoons for a haircut. A chiropractor was also available to employees here, as was the studio's venerable shoeshine man. A bookie—who several employees remembered as being named Rudi—was also to be found in the area daily, taking bets for all the major racetracks for any employee.

Democracy only went so far. Every day at five o'clock, the barbershop was locked and for the next hour only executives could use it.

Above: Using drawings and scale models, members of the Art Department create sets for up-coming productions in 1940.

21 **ART DEPARTMENT**

Above the commissary was the Art Department, run most famously by Cedric Gibbons. Circa 1944, Gibbons operated from this command center with a staff of 17 art directors, 4 assistant art directors, 43 draftsmen, and 10 sketch artists.

"Mr. Gibbons was a handsome man and an impeccable dresser," recalled George Gibson, head of the Scenic Arts Department. "That impeccable taste extended to everything he touched. I think Gibbons was the MGM look—in person and his initial was on every drawing. He built the finest art department in the business, so everything that came out of that department was first-rate."

Staff member Jack Martin Smith once said that "when you went home at night and left a working drawing on your desk, you had to be very sure it was complete. Because when you came back in the morning, the thing you had designed was sitting there waiting for you."

Above: Herbert Stohart conducts an orchestra in the Scoring Stage in 1939.
The picture being scored is a sequence from *The Wizard of Oz*, which was cut from the film and lost.

Over the years, the legendary 9,987-square-foot scoring stage—inexplicably referred to as "Stage One"—although unique on the lot and, in fact, the largest such structure in the world, has echoed the voices and the music of just about every famous entertainer and composer of the 20th century and beyond.

This vast, but squat and physically unimpressive room was entered through padded doors that looked more appropriate to a butcher shop meat locker than to a place where artists gathered. Inside, the room itself consisted of a 93 × 66-foot open area with brown-paneled walls buttressed by three closed-off booths in the rear and a theatre-sized

22 SCORING STAGE (STAGE ONE)

screen in the front. Despite its less-than-inspiring appearance, this room is where hundreds of famous and forgotten vocalists and composers, single musicians and vast orchestras of up to 110 pieces, have created the soundtrack for the lives of millions.

The material recorded inside for movies, television, and records ultimately ran the entire gamut of musical taste, style, and fashion. From the Tin Pan Alley stylings of Irving Berlin to the jazz melodies of Ethel Waters and Louis Armstrong; from operettas performed by Luciano Pavarotti, Jeanette MacDonald, and Nelson Eddy to the big band riffs of Tommy and Jimmy Dorsey, Harry James, and Xavier Cugat; from popular melodies performed by Frank Sinatra, Bing Crosby,

Above: Lena Horne returns to the Scoring Stage in *That's Entertainment! III* (1994), and watches a clip of herself singing "Where or When" from *Words and Music* (1948).

Lena Horne, and Judy Garland to iconic recordings by Kathryn Grayson, Sophie Tucker, Howard Keel, Jane Powell, Doris Day, Nat King Cole, Mario Lanza, Debbie Reynolds, Grace Moore, and Betty Hutton; from country and Western riffs by Hank Williams Jr. to Elvis Presley's genre-defining rock and roll.

Occasional movies photographed the stage as an onscreen set. *Words and Music* (1948), *Anchors Aweigh* (1945), and *Love Me or Leave Me* (1955) are good examples. But the primary purpose of the stage was, and fortunately still is, to record orchestral scores and vocals for motion pictures filmed elsewhere.

Composers like John Williams, Danny Elfman, and John Barry continue to create musical magic for the world on the same spot, in the same room—now updated for the digital age—in which their musical predecessors did their best work.

In 2004, the stage was rededicated and renamed the "Barbra Streisand Scoring Stage." Over the course of her career, Streisand has recorded selections from 10 albums and three movies in this most magical sounding of rooms.

(Sony Pictures, the current owner of the building, likes to mention in publicity material that Max Steiner recorded the score for *Gone with the Wind* [1939] on this stage. Actually, this is incorrect. *Gone with the Wind*'s score was recorded at the Goldwyn stage in West Hollywood.)

Left: **A Screening Room was used as a set in *Two Weeks in Another Town* (1962). Edward G. Robinson (right) talks to Kirk Douglas (seated), while Claire Trevor looks on.**

23 SCREENING ROOM (STAGE TWO)

A second "soundstage"—Stage Two—is connected to Stage One. Like Stage One, it isn't really a soundstage at all, but rather the studio's largest re-recording stage and theatre (with a capacity of 332), used for press and outside screenings.

In 1981, the screening room (actually one of 21 on the lot) was renamed the "Cary Grant Theatre."

"Spectacular pyrotechnics, hundreds of brilliant klieg lights, a soundstage transformed magically into a lavish ballroom, and many of the movie capital's most famous celebrities greeted Cary Grant on the October 3 dedication of the Cary Grant Theatre here on the MGM/UA lot," trumpeted the studio newsletter at the time. "Before a star-studded audience in the newly refurbished and technologically renovated theatre, Grant was presented with the company's first Leo Award—a 10-inch, full-bodied gold lion with diamonds for eyes, designed for MGM/UA by Cartier and inspired by the studio's famous feline trademark."

It is not known what the long-retired, yet still debonair Grant (actually an occasional member of the MGM board of directors) did with his Leo, or if the company ever bothered to give away a second one.

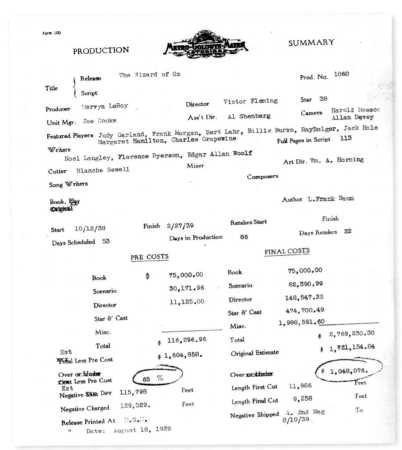

Left: The original, final budget for *The Wizard of Oz* as tabulated by the Production Department (1939).
Right: The entrance to the Production Department is barely visible here (ground floor, left), but the Department's importance was wide ranging indeed.

24 PRODUCTION DEPARTMENT

The Art Department also had offices in the building across from the Commissary: the Production Department. This was appropriate, for as production head J. J. Cohn noted, "[Gibbons] approved every set that was built. And I approved every set that was built. . . . It was a fusion of work and we had very good art directors under Cedric Gibbons. Very good men."

Cohn's Production Department contained a blackboard chart noting where each film in production was located at any given time. The entire spectrum of the physical execution of every picture the studio created was plotted and organized out of this office. "The background noise of the department was caused by the incessant chatter of estima-tors, figuring the costs of films planned, in work or completed," recalled Story Department head Samuel Marx.

There was, however, no incessant chatter being generated by booking and billing out the usage of backlot sets. During the entire studio era, using the backlot was not a billable expense for internal pictures. So in the 1960s, when the studio was looking for ways to trim the fat, the backlots were an easy target because the Production Department's legers reflected very little income generated by the vast real estate holdings these sets stood on.

No one realized it at the time, but the seeds of destruction for the backlots were inadvertently sewn in these offices.

Left: **The Recording Building in 1928.**
Right: **The soundtrack for *Show Boat* is fine-tuned on an ADR stage in 1951.**

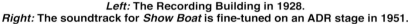

Built in 1925, the Recording Building was run by head soundman Douglas Shearer (Norma Shearer's brother). And it was here where much of every picture's elaborate post-production process was centered. The term "recording" actually was indicative of the entire post-production process, which was scattered across all of Lot One. Entire technical books have been written about this process.

Once a script had been prepared in the Writer's Building, cast in the Thalberg Building, designed in the Art Department, and produced on the soundstages and backlot, the resultant film ended up in the hands of the post-production unit. At its command over the years were the film labs where the raw stock was processed and work prints—disposable copies of the camera negative—were struck. The negative itself was the most valuable result of the entire production process and was never touched or cut until the very end.

Next, the film went on to one or more of the 200 cutting or editing rooms where a version was assembled. Once an acceptable print (to the producer) was ready, the film would travel to one or more of the five dubbing stages, mostly located here, where the sound mixing was accomplished. Technicians in ADR (Automated Dialogue Re-

25 SOUND DEPARTMENT

placement) rooms dubbed lines of dialogue, or entire scenes. When an acceptable recording had not been created on set, Foley stages (named after sound mixer Jack Foley) recreated sound effects, such as footsteps or falling rain, which had not been miked or recorded successfully during production.

Music was added next. The film was usually scored (in Stage One) at this point, and often went back to the editing rooms for re-cutting and fine tuning, before traveling back here for final mixing, where all the audio elements would be combined.

During the entire post-production process, and during principle production, the footage would be viewed in one or more of the 21 screening rooms (small theatres with viewing capacity from 10 to 332 seats) available on lot. A studio press agent once claimed that these screening rooms projected enough film every day to maintain a circuit of 40 actual movie theatres.

Once the film was deemed finished, the much-spliced work-print used in all of the above steps was matched against the camera negative, which was finally and carefully cut and used to make release prints (the actual film screened in theatres) back in the lab.

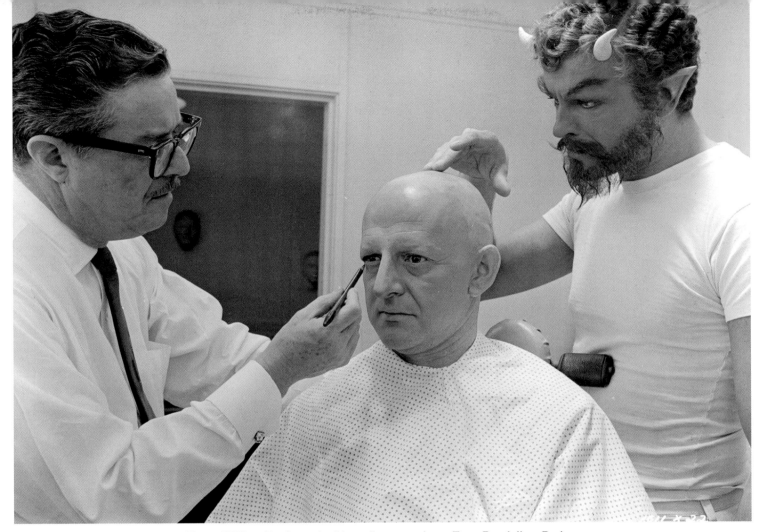

Above: William Tuttle works his makeup magic on Tony Randall as Dr. Lao, and is watched by John Ericson as Pan from *The 7 Faces of Dr. Lao* (1964).

26 MAKEUP DEPARTMENT

The Makeup Department was run by Jack Dawn and then William Tuttle, who also supervised the hairstylists, of whom Sydney Guilaroff was the most famous. By the 1950s, studio publicists boasted that the department could change the appearance of 1,200 actors an hour and handle as many as 12,000 faces in a single day. Among its achievements was transforming brunettes into famous blondes (Lana Turner) and redheads (Lucille Ball and Shirley MacLaine). Once in a while, the department heads had some fun in films and television programs themselves—Tuttle appeared in an episode of *The Girl from U.N.C.L.E.* in 1966.

"Bill Tuttle and Sydney Guilaroff supervised all the makeup men and hairdressers," recalled actress Betty Garrett. "Every MGM

Left: William Tuttle, head of the Makeup Department, shown here in 1974, surrounded by the life masks he created during his long career. The masks enabled him to experiment with various makeup techniques and effects without requiring the actor to be seated for countless hours.
Right: The original Makeup Department building is now called the "Clark Gable Building" (2010).

contract player had a mimeographed photo with lines drawn on it to instruct the makeup men how to improve our faces with makeup, such as how to shade the nose and cheekbones. My photo was literally a roadmap of lines!"

"With those 5:30 AM makeup calls . . . the women envied the men because they didn't have hairdos and makeup sessions to contend with," recalls Jane Powell.

The makeup men and hairstylists have their own memories—

and favorite actors. One of Judy Garland's favorites, Keester Sweeney, was himself a favorite of visiting actress Doris Day, who made four films for the studio. She asked him to leave with her, but Sweeney held back, loyal to the studio even in its decline.

Like his department, Tuttle also rode out wave after wave of regime changes and corporate cutbacks. He lasted 35 years at the studio.

In the 1970s, this building, built in 1937, would be renamed the "Clark Gable Building."

Above: The General Dressing Room Building in 1926.

For decades, any actor important enough to warrant a room to change clothes in or relax off set would be assigned a room somewhere in this complex. Within this quarter-mile of honeycombs could be found, at different, but overlapping times, the General Dressing Rooms, the Featured Players Dressing Rooms, and the Star Suites.

Until 1935, when the Star Suites were erected, most of the big names resided in the original, General Dressing Rooms—a two-

story barracks-style building backed up against Washington Boulevard, and adjacent to where producer-director Cecil B. DeMille had his offices from 1928 to 1932.

Myrna Loy recalled this original structure as having "open verandahs running along the front, which we traversed in our dressing gowns to and from the bathrooms. For obvious reasons, we called the building 'the bordello,'" she added wryly.

Left: A wall directory illustrating the location of the women's Star Suites. When this picture was taken in 1937, the name of recently deceased actress Jean Harlow had just been removed, and in fact is still poignantly visible on line A.
Right: Lana Turner leaving the Star Suites in 1939.

These dressing rooms are on display themselves in many early MGM films, including the studio's 1931 Christmas short subject, in which Jackie Cooper visits Norma Shearer's dressing room to enlist her help in getting a soundstage for his party. Also look for them in Jean Harlow's near-autobiographical *Bombshell* in 1933.

The old General Dressing Rooms continued to be used by the up-and-coming newer talent even after the Star Suites and Featured Players Dressing Rooms were constructed. Esther Williams, before becoming a major star with a major dressing room, remembered looking from the old building to the newer, more glamorous structures to the east. "The MGM star dressing rooms would have impressed anyone," she said once. "I was awed by the names on the doors. 'Lana Turner' was

Left: MGM star Robert Taylor takes a call in his private dressing room.
Right: The 1937 directory signage for the men's star suites.

on A, 'Greer Garson' on B, 'Judy Garland' on C, 'Joan Crawford' on D, and 'Katharine Hepburn' on E."

The Star Suites included kitchens, fireplaces, living rooms and, yes, bathrooms inside the units.

Unlike the more ornate Star Suites and Featured Players Dressing Rooms, which have been largely redeveloped, the General Dressing Rooms building itself is surprisingly still there, although rebuilt and smaller. Today, the rooms are used for production and post-production office space, rather than as dressing rooms. (No one refers to the structure as "the bordello" any more, either.)

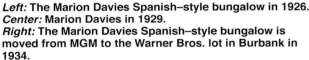

Left: The Marion Davies Spanish–style bungalow in 1926.
Center: Marion Davies in 1929.
Right: The Marion Davies Spanish–style bungalow is moved from MGM to the Warner Bros. lot in Burbank in 1934.

28 MARION DAVIES BUNGALOW

In the studio's history, or in *any* studio's history, no star ever had as lavish a dressing room as did perpetual starlet Marion Davies. Her palatial 14-room white stucco bungalow stood amidst (and yet dramatically apart) from all the other stars' smaller, lesser dressing rooms due to its size, opulence, and most unique history.

The bungalow was constructed in 1924 by tycoon William Randolph Hearst for Davies, who was his mistress. Mayer had been thrilled to sign a production deal between MGM and Hearst's Cosmopolitan Pictures, whose product had previously been distributed through Paramount, and whose primary reason for existence was to produce Marion Davies films.

But this ideal arrangement, offering the studio unending free publicity from Hearst's legendary newspaper empire, was not long lasting. Hearst wanted complete control over the creation of Davies' films. And the wealthy publisher's taste tended to run towards expensive, unprofitable costume pictures in which his mistress's genuine comedic talents were usually buried amongst all the resplendent costumes and soaring emotions. Many of the resultant films, except for an oc-

casional comedy—like the delightful Hollywood-set *Show People* (1928)—lost money and, not surprisingly, the relationship with MGM eventually soured.

Hearst was often asked if there was money in the movies. "There sure is," he would snort. "Mine!"

In 1934, Davies and her mentor (and even the massive bungalow) moved to Warner Bros. The dressing room allegedly had to be chopped into four pieces in order to be transported to its new home. But the same pattern of interference and unsuccessful pictures followed the starlet, the tycoon, and the bungalow up to Burbank, and less than four years later, Davies and her bungalow again relocated, this time to the Fox lot.

Upon her retirement from acting, most of Marion's amazing and well-traveled bungalow was moved to somewhere in Beverly Hills, where it survives, in truncated form, even today. An annex structure, in the same architectural style, and itself as large as many homes, is still on the Warner lot as office space for über-producer Joel Silver.

Left: The original MGM School House (1937). Among the pupils attending that day are Freddie Bartholomew and Mickey Rooney.
Right: The new Spanish Revival Little Red Schoolhouse in 1941.

29 LITTLE RED SCHOOLHOUSE

In the midst of these glamorous star dwellings stood a low, one-story white stucco bungalow with a red-tiled roof built in 1927, and was later expanded. Like most buildings on Lot One, it can be seen in movies like *Anchors Aweigh* (1945). Today, it is known as the Crawford Building, after a star whose dressing room it once was, but in Metro's heyday it was the "Little Red Schoolhouse."

No school in the world turned out graduates like this: Jackie Cooper, Mickey Rooney, Judy Garland, Freddie Bartholomew, Darryl Hickman, Roddy McDowall, Debbie Reynolds, Dean Stockwell, Claude Jarman Jr., Margaret O'Brien, Jane Powell, and Elizabeth Taylor were among its students.

Under the regulations of the State Board of Education and the Producers Association, Metro's young stars worked an eight-hour day at the studio: four hours each for schooling and performing. Schooling was done primarily in the Little Red Schoolhouse. For many years, Mary McDonald was the head instructor. "I think everybody was scared to death of her," recalled Margaret O'Brien. "She was very strict and none of the children liked her, and the studio didn't like her either because she obeyed the law and yanked us out of a scene when the time came, even if it they only wanted to get that one last shot."

"Miss McDonald didn't do much teaching," recalled Jane Powell. "She was more of an organizer, the principal, but she was always there to greet us. Coldly. We didn't always have the same teacher. The teachers were generally good. They all came from the Los Angeles public school system. Every year, we had to go down to L.A. for exams and all those normal high school rituals. I'd say our education was merely adequate."

"We'd usually go to the red schoolhouse for three hours every morning, from nine to noon, then spend the other two with our tutors on our respective sets," recalled Mickey Rooney, who was much more animated in recalling that the young ladies in these classes "were, after all, budding movie stars. . . . As soon as [Lana Turner] arrived, I assumed full gazing rights."

For young actresses like Turner and (later) Elizabeth Taylor, who were already in their late teens, playing adults on camera and being groomed as sex symbols by their studio, the ritual of being forced to attend an "artificial" school mostly made up of children younger than they were—like Mickey Rooney—must have seemed a bit ridiculous.

In the 1960s, the school was moved to a smaller building behind Stage 18. The original Little Red Schoolhouse building became production offices, which it remains today.

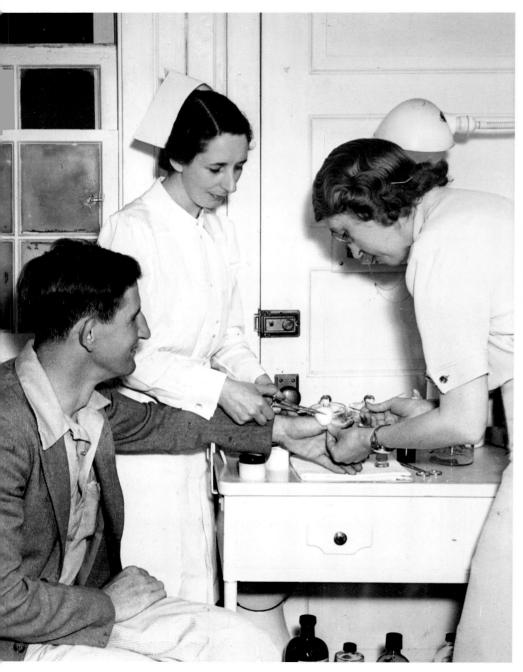

Left: Studio nurses offer aid to an injured MGM employee.
Right: The First Aid Building as it looks today (2009).

30 | FIRST-AID DEPARTMENT

Marked by a red cross was the First-Aid Department, where—unlike at most other studios—actual doctors, nurses, and even a dentist kept office hours. "I've got fond memories of those days when MGM was like a city and we had two doctors and a dentist," Robert Relyea, who was an executive at the company until 2001, remembered.

Like every other building on the lot, this little office is haunted by memories. June Allyson recalled the studio dentist trying to convince her to have her teeth straightened here. Gail Storm, who was shooting the TV series *My Little Margie* (1952–1955) at the nearby Roach Studios, once had to come here to seek a doctor for treatment because her own studio only had a nurse on staff—a statement about either the quality of care at MGM as opposed to a *real* hospital, or about the general clannishness of Hollywood people.

Top Left: John Gilbert's Spanish Colonial Bungalow would later house the Short Subject Department (1928).
Bottom Left: A scene from *The Big Dog House* (1930), one of several Dogville Comedies produced by the Short Subject Department.
Right: A publicity photo for *A Night at the Movies* (1937 Short Subject), starring Robert Benchley (left) and directed by Roy Rowland (right).

31 SHORT SUBJECT DEPARTMENT

Fred Quimby, a veteran of the old Pathé studio, was chosen to form the Short Subject Department in 1926. The Short Subject building was originally constructed as a bungalow for stars like John Gilbert before it was remodeled in the mid-1930s.

The department released an astonishing array of quality material. "We made about 70 shorts a year in different series," remembered Richard Goldstone, who eventually became head of the department. "Mayer was very good at delegating, once he was satisfied. If a unit was cooking successfully, he was pretty much hands-off. He was delighted with the product as a whole. As long as the machinery was working, and there were Oscars every year—that was important to him—then you were left alone."

Like many studios, MGM also had its own newsreel, "News of the Day," which had its roots from the Hearst-Selig weekly of the General Film Corporation days of 1912. It was administered by former newspapermen E. B. Hatrick and M. D. Clofine.

With the rise of television in the 1950s, the Short Subject Department became something of an expensive redundancy. News and short subjects could now be found at home and were accessible in the time it took a viewer to warm up a television's vacuum tube. The department would close its doors in 1956, after which this building would house, ironically enough, television production offices.

Today, this is known as the Garland Building.

Left: The dance Rehearsal Halls in 1937.
Right: The Rehearsal Halls as they look today (2009).
Opposite: June Allyson and Peter Lawford rehearse one of their dance numbers for *Good News* (1947).

32 REHEARSAL HALLS A, B, AND C

In neighboring Rehearsal Halls A, B, and C, the *Motion Picture Herald* reported that "one is likely to find the Dorseys, Harry James, or Xavier Cugat doing their stuff, along with 36 or 48 handpicked Hollywood beauties putting together a *Ziegfeld Follies*, a *Bathing Beauty*, or another top-flight musical extravaganza."

Debbie Reynolds remembers these halls as the place "where Gene Kelly and Fred Astaire, Roland Petit and, eventually, Elvis Presley worked." Reynolds has a special memory of this place, where dancers and choreographers worked weeks to perfect a few minutes of musical movie magic. It was here, at 19, that she worked eight hours a day to perfect her dance numbers with Gene Kelly and Donald O'Connor for *Singin' in the Rain* (1952). "I felt inept and exhausted all the time," she admitted. An annex to the Makeup Department could be found in the basement of this building.

Today, the Sony Pictures Wardrobe Department, which once ranged across three lots and included miles of racked clothing, is housed in the former Rehearsal Hall C.

Left: The iconic MGM water tower, now Sony/Columbia Studios (2008).
Right: The "Significant Cultural Resource" plaque on the historic MGM water tower, now owned by Sony/Columbia Studios (2008). The name "Esther Williams" was most likely placed there by a fan, perhaps because of the gallons of water used to fill the Stage 30 water tanks for Williams' numerous films, both *Take Me Out to the Ballgame* and *Neptune's Daughter* were released in 1949, which was a banner year for Williams professionally.

33 WATER TOWER

The studio's famed water tower, which rose in 1932 and was originally one of two on the lot, holds some 100,000 gallons of water. The tower is still there today, but is kept empty. Sony Pictures, the current owners of the lot, like many studios, have continued to maintain their historic, non-functioning water tower as a visual link to their storied past.

Above: A massive Westinghouse generator helped supply the power needs for the Lot One Power Plant.
Bottom Left: The CAL Edison substation in the southwestern corner of Lot One (1948).

34 POWER PLANT

In the southwestern corner of the lot existed the main, 2,600-square-foot power plant (there were four!) that ran the studio. Leased from the Southern California Edison company, this transformer plant was ballyhooed by MGM publicists in 1959 as having the power to light a city of 50,000 people. It certainly had the ability to illuminate these lands of make-believe.

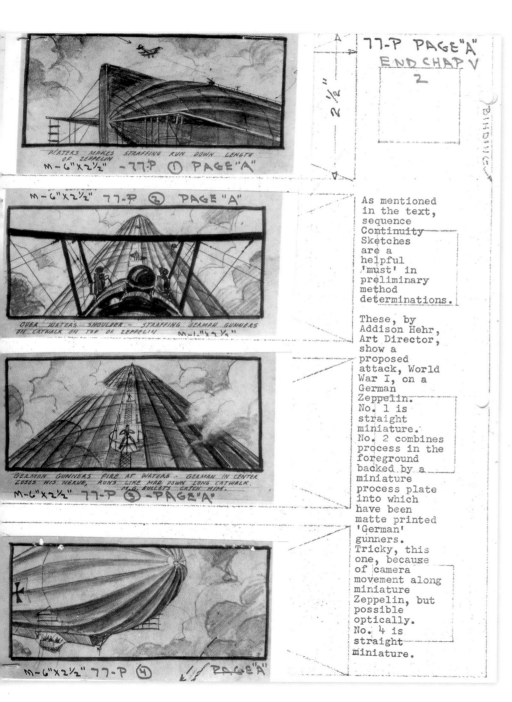

WATERS MAKES STRAFFING RUN DOWN LENGTH OF ZEPPELIN
M-6"×2½" -77-P ① PAGE "A"

M-6"×2½" 77-P ② PAGE "A"

OVER WATER'S SHOULDER - STRAFFING GERMAN GUNNERS ON CATWALK ON TOP OF ZEPPELIN   M-6"×2½"

GERMAN GUNNERS FIRE AT WATERS - GERMAN IN CENTER LOSES HIS NERVE, RUNS LIKE MAD DOWN LONG CATWALK. M.G. BULLETS CATCH HIM.
M-6"×2½" 77-P ③ -PAGE "A"

M-6"×2½" 77-P ④   PAGE "A"

77-P PAGE "A"
END CHAP V
2

As mentioned in the text, sequence Continuity Sketches are a helpful 'must' in preliminary method determinations.

These, by Addison Hehr, Art Director, show a proposed attack, World War I, on a German Zeppelin. No. 1 is straight miniature. No. 2 combines process in the foreground backed by a miniature process plate into which have been matte printed 'German' gunners. Tricky, this one, because of camera movement along miniature Zeppelin, but possible optically. No. 4 is straight miniature.

35 SPECIAL EFFECTS DEPARTMENT

As long as MGM occupied the lot, company maps would most often identify this building with the words "matte painting." Yet, every employee knew that the building was, in fact, one of several bases of operations for the studio's special visual effects master, A. Arnold Gillespie.

"Although 'A. Arnold Gillespie' is his formal moniker, few (if any) have ever addressed him thusly," remarked Spencer Tracy in his introduction to Gillespie's unpublished memoirs (from which illustrations are reproduced here), "It has been 'Buddy' Gillespie for all of his 42 years of uninterrupted residence at MGM. He is a magician. There's nothing he can't do. There's nothing too odd, too strange. Nothing sur-

88-PTOP ~~BOTTOM~~ - 6½"X 4½" - A

Esther Williams in
"Jupiter's Darling"
making that prodigious
leap.

Not the 'Real' Esther,
but the one we used.
A 3" scale miniature,
31 INCHES FROM
NOSTRILS TO REAR
HOOVES.

88·P

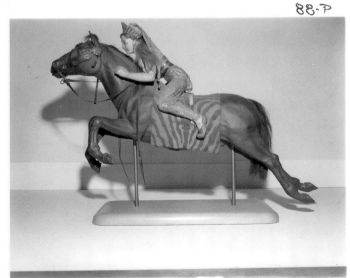

A-6½"X 4½" ~~TOP~~ BOTTOM

Q - 2¼" X 2¼" ⑤

The "Wizard" wicked
witch, pre backfiring
smoke 'bomb'.

Left: A process shot using rear projection and the 31-inch-long model of Esther Williams on horseback used for the film *Jupiter's Darling* (1955).
Right: Preparing the special effects for the disappearing "Wicked Witch" from the film *The Wizard of Oz* (1939). The scene required a soundstage trap door and some pyrotechnics to create a dramatic "smoke and flames" exit. Unfortunately, actress Margaret Hamilton was badly burned during the second take of filming.

prises him . . . he can do "that." Burn down Rome. Destroy San Francisco by earthquake. Provide a swarm of locusts, a hurricane, a typhoon, an air battle. He is a wonder worker."

Gillespie learned his extraordinary trade working for eight months in Cecil B. DeMille's Art Department before entering this studio's gates in February 1923 to work for Sam Goldwyn. His job as draftsman in Gibbons's Art Department led to a self-paid trip to Italy late in 1923 to join the *Ben-Hur* (1925) troupe and figure out how to get the mighty ship battle onto the screen. Returning as a unit art director in the spring of 1925, he was later offered (and accepted) the position of head of special effects, which, with assistance from optical effects maestro Warren Newcombe, he held until his retirement from MGM in March of 1965.

Left: The Lumber and Scene Docks of Lot One. The railroad spur in the lower left corner brought a wide array of supplies to the studio (1946).
Right: Remnants of the original Lot One Scene Docks (2009).

36   SCENE DOCKS (A, B, C, D, AND E)

F ive large and several more annexed, or smaller, scene docks existed on Lot One alone, the first of which was constructed along the wall of Stage 11, but quickly proved too small for the job. All were used to store "flats," or scenic elements, constructed for past pictures that the Production Department apparently had hopes to use again. However, a walk through these vast, shadowy areas was, in its way, actually a tour of the world's architecture and a pictorial history of American cinema as well; what with the walls, floors, staircases, pirate galleons, fighter planes, and spaceships stored here from half-remembered movies.

Top Left: Lot One photographed in 1925. The Scenic Arts Department building can be seen in the upper center portion of the photo.
Inset: That's' Entertainment! III (1994) star Cyd Charisse poses in front of the same backdrop used in *Brigadoon* (1954), which she co-starred in.
Top Right: Staff artists paint a realistic backdrop for an upcoming production in the Scenic Arts Department building.
Bottom Right: Director Ernst Lubitsch's *The Merry Widow* (1934) provided a good example of the Scenic Arts Department at work. A miniature city in front of the painted backdrop completes the illusion.

37   SCENIC ARTS DEPARTMENT

The Scenic Arts Department, long managed by George Gibson, housed five paint frames ranging from 40 × 40 feet to 100 × 40 feet. Most of these frames stood on either end of a raised floor, from which an artist could work on the elaborate cityscapes or photographically realistic backdrops created here without the aid of ladders or scaffolding. Eventually, more than 2,500 separate painted backdrops would be painted and stored here.

The department still exists and is operated today by J. C. Backings, an independent scenic arts company.

Left: The iron Saucer Tank hosted many an underwater adventure, seen here in *That's Entertainment! III* (1994).
Right: An episode of the TV show *Perfect Strangers* ("Father Knows Best" 1989) films in the Saucer Tank.
Bottom Left: Seated next to the Saucer Tank, Esther Williams takes a break while filming a segment for *That's Entertainment! III* (1994).
Opposite: The Saucer Tank in 1936.

38   SAUCER TANK

Incredibly, one relic from the early studio era survived until the 21st century and was still in use until its removal in 2003: the famous "saucer tank"—a 5,250-square-foot watertight iron bowl constructed above ground with portholes bored into the sides from which a camera could take "underwater shots" without going through the expense and trouble of being submerged. Famously, Johnny Weissmuller's *Tarzan the Ape Man* (1932) introduced many a rubber jungle crocodile to his knife blade from inside the murky waters of that 20-foot-deep tank. Buddy Gillespie recalled that a sack of nigrosine dye was planted in the monster's throat to portray the blood that squirted out when Weissmuller stabbed it with his knife.

But the performer who suffered the most from puckered fingers and swimmer's ear inside its bowels was Esther Williams in more than a dozen bright, watery musicals between 1942 and 1955. It was in *Andy Hardy's Double Life* (1942) that Williams first appeared onscreen swimming in this tank. Neither she, nor the world, ever forgot that moment.

But all things must eventually pass. The tank outlasted Esther Williams's film career, and it survived MGM's long tenancy at the studio. By the 1970s, it was such an anomaly in Hollywood that other studios (having probably forgotten that they had ever owned just such a contraption themselves) rented it, amazed at how well this ancient movie relic worked—most notably Universal, briefly in 1975 for *Jaws*, as well as its first sequel. Sony used it intermittently, as well, for underwater inserts in pictures like *The Prince of Tides* (1991). It finally starred as itself in 1994 for *That's Entertainment! III*, in which Esther Williams introduced her old screenmate. Just before Sony Pictures dismantled it to put up a Coke machine, they bled a few last dollars out of it, renting its rusty, trusty hull in 2001 to Fox for the *Planet of the Apes* remake, and to Warners for *The Majestic* (2001), starring Jim Carrey.

And then they bulldozed it all away to salvage the scrap metal.

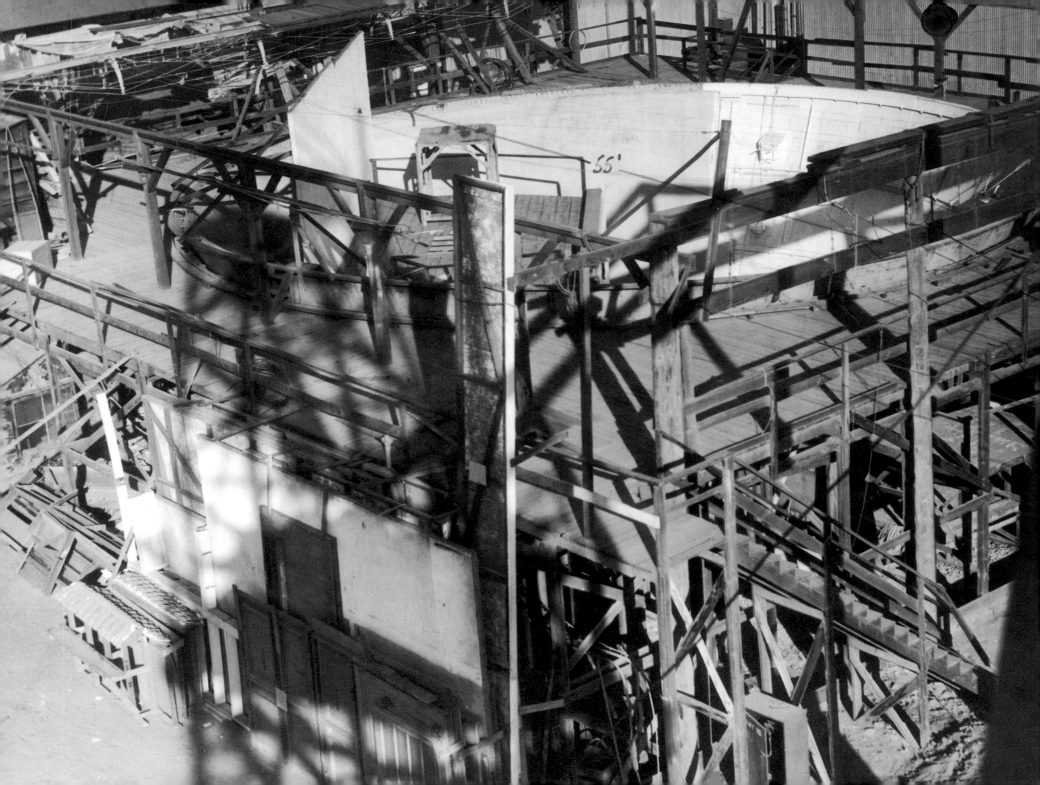

Left: The Mill Complex is housed in a relocated original glass stage once used for the filming of silent films (1935).
Right: The Mill Complex and an assortment of lumber prepped to be used in the art of movie making (1927).
Opposite: This never before seen photo was surely taken to document the set constructed here for *Red Dust* (1932). But it's Jean Harlow that makes it unforgettable.

Along the back end of the lot, parallel with Culver Boulevard, there survived—quite remarkably until early in the 21st century—several remnants of original stages from the Silent Era. The longevity of these massive glass structures was due to their occupation by more than a dozen studio departments after the coming of sound made them impractical as a location. This sector would become known as the Mill Complex. Here, during the studio's salad days and beyond, could be found the carpenter, machine, paint, furniture, sign (which included a magical workshop dedicated to the creation of neon), print,

39 MILL COMPLEX

prop (construction), sheet metal, tin, and rubber shops. Nearby were the Upholstery, Drapery, and Air Conditioning departments, the Electrical Department, a tool room, a foundry and blacksmith's shop, a chemical lab, and the Welding, Plumbing, and Fixtures departments.

The studio nursery, the lathe shop, and the staff shop—where molds were used to create architectural detailing—were considered part of the Mill Complex as well, although geographically they were outside the glass walls enclosing the complex.

Inside, some 3,200 artisans, craftsmen, laborers, and techni-

Above: Studio Mill carpenters create set "flats" and an elaborate staircase in 1940.

Left: The Marx Brothers nod off waiting for their studio pass outside the Construction Complex (1941).
Right: With a selection surpassing any hardware store, the Fixtures Department offers doorknobs, door latches, drawer pulls, and hinges from any style or historic period.

cians could be observed going on about their unpublicized tasks. On a normal day (if the phrase "normal" is at all applicable), this could include some 500 carpenters, 20 scenic artists, 15 plumbers, 50 plasterers, and so on.

The size, the immensity, and the sheer self-sufficiency of Metro Goldwyn Mayer were wonders to behold. "There was an aura about Metro in those early years," recalled art director Jack Martin Smith. "If you needed a chimpanzee tomorrow, it was sitting there. If you needed an alligator, it was there. If you needed a couple of lions, they were there. There were three or four men in the leather shop who did nothing but repair carriages and harnesses. Whatever you wanted, whatever you needed, it was there. And if it wasn't already there, someone would make it for you. "

"We had a tremendous number of top technical people avail-

Above: A set for *Little Women* is created off the drawings (found on the sawhorses in the lower left corner) of the Art Department (1949).
Opposite Top Left: The pipes going up to the ceiling rafters in the Mill are sawdust vacuum tubes (1936).
Opposite Top Right: The Sign Shop creates neon signage by heating glass tubes and bending them to form letters and then adding gas to create the magical glow (1951).
Opposite Bottom Right: A labor dispute outside the Construction Complex in 1946.

Below: A poster for the boxing film *Right Cross* (1950) dries in the Print Shop. A prop poster from *Show Boat* (1951) hangs from above.

able to us," said Buddy Gillespie. "Naval architects and machinists and hydraulic engineers. They were all at MGM. And they were there year in and year out."

Employees used to joke that in the carpenter shop, the largest of the old glass stages, you could drag an entire tree inside and have a single chair come out.

Beginning in the late 1920s, the area behind this vast building was MGM's massive lumberyard, where rare woods of every type were laid in racks ready for studio artisans. The studio also had its own oil well here with underground storage tanks.

Most of this complex beehive of buildings and departments, including the last haunted remnants of those original glass stages, was leveled in 2008 to make way for the construction of two new office complexes designed to house employees of Sony Pictures Television, an all-new New York Street backlot, and a 1,000-car parking lot.

Left: Camera dollies, buses, all-terrain trucks, camera cars, and "Honey Wagons" (portable toilets) are some of the Transportation Department vehicles parked on Lot Two (1962).
Right: Western covered wagons are unloaded from *Westward the Women* (1951) on Lot Two. The sign on the truck proclaims "1951 As The Year Of QUO VADIS." Above the covered wagons is an awning with "PHILADELLPHIA" signage that was part of a train station set for the film *The Tall Target* (1951).

40   TRANSPORTATION DEPARTMENT

The Transportation Department provided a variety of services at Metro Goldwyn Mayer. A studio limousine service transported the stars around the vast acreage of MGM. Janet Leigh recalled that "each film company had a limousine, maybe two (and sometimes, each *star* had a limo), to take the performers from makeup to the stage, to lunch, to the restroom, to their dressing room. . . ."

However, most of the duties of the Transportation Department involved moving not stars, but productions and production vehicles around the lot and, later, to locations. Keeping prop automotive stock operating was also an important part of the department's duties—all managed out of a V-shaped building that was built near the grounds of a Goldwyn-constructed backlot castle set, behind which an open parking area for trucks and prop vehicles stretched all the way to distant Overland Avenue.

Left: One of the dozens of film vaults located on the lot, this particular one was long utilized as storage for stock footage (1950s).
Top Right: On the first day of photography for *Tell It to the Marines* (1928), in front of the original Projection, Editing, and Film Vault building, Marine Major J.P. Wilcox presents a flag to Mayer, Thalberg, Harry Rapf, and W.S. Van Dyke. Mingling with the Marines is Lon Chaney, also in uniform.
Bottom Right: Howard Keel hosts a segment of *That's Entertainment! III* (1994), from inside a film vault.

The sum total of everything that ever happened at the studio and everything observed on the lot eventually ended up in these bunker-like sheds stored along the fenceline of a parking lot leased to the studio for the Transportation Department's usage. These vaults, and others around the lot and elsewhere, were used to store film elements, stock footage, and release prints that had been shipped back to the studio

41   FILM VAULTS

for storage. Until mid-century, highly flammable nitrate stock was what most movies were printed on. After safer film stocks were developed, many older nitrate-based prints were destroyed for safety reasons, often before a copy negative on safety stock could be produced. Untold treasures from the studios vaults were lost forever due to these practices.

THE SOUNDSTAGES

Left: (left to right) Jim Adamson with actors Bert Roach, Marceline Day, and Conrad Nagel on the site of the old glass "Stage 1," which had been torn down to make room for a new "talking movie" stage. Adamson, at the time of the photo, was the Studio's oldest employee (1930s).
Right: The world famous Metro Goldwyn Mayer Studios neon sign sits atop Stage 6, the tallest stage on the lot (1944).

Stretching west across the entire studio were the soundstages—a concrete jungle that both literally and figuratively erased the leisurely air of the studio's silent era. The very name "soundstages" bespoke an overnight change in every aspect of production in the late 1920s. The industry was forced to change how pictures had been shot for decades. Never again could three or four films be made in the corners of a single glass stage lit by the sun. These original stages, which obviously were not soundproof, now all had to be destroyed or converted to other uses.

With them would have to go the broad green lawns and garden paths so carefully designed by Sam Goldwyn. "Tony, the unhappy studio gardener, removed his prize rose bushes to a fenced in area on the backlot where he could maintain a greenery to ornament future films," recalled Samuel Marx. "Often, he dug feverishly at blossoming vegetation marked for removal, barely raising the roots from the soil before monster bulldozers growled at his heels."

Although Leo the Lion roared onscreen for the first time in *White Shadows of the South Seas* (1928), MGM's first all-talkie effort was *Alias Jimmy Valentine* (1928), starring William Haines and Lionel Barrymore. Because the soundstages and sound apparatus were not

Left: Jean Harlow and an assistant walk past a sound stage on Lot One (1930s).
Right: A studio street scene from above the East Gate in 1950. The Art Deco Studio Commissary is on the right.

ready, the MGM crew filmed the talking portions at Paramount's studios. The studio's last silent film was Greta Garbo's *The Kiss* in 1929.

By the time the massive construction project had been finished "on Lot One with 9,000 stages," as television director George Fenady used to marvel, there were supposedly 30 stages—although doubled stages with removable walls, temporary stages, sound recording stages, and the conspicuous absence of the number 13 accounted for variant numbers going up to 37 during different eras.

Here, on these dark and ugly soundstages, as clean and bare a slate as an artist could wish, MGM cameramen worked their wiz-ardry. Here, entire worlds could be created with the studio's 40 cameras and 60 sound machines. Indeed, many studio films never required the shooting of a single shot on the backlot. *The Wizard of Oz* (1939) is a good example.

At 41,985 square feet (310 feet long, 133 feet wide), Stage 15 was the world's largest. (A title it retained until 1977, when the UK's Pinewood Studios constructed the 45,000-square-foot 007 Stage for the James Bond picture *The Spy Who Loved Me*.)

For the 1936 production of *Romeo and Juliet*, Thalberg chose to build Juliet's quiet expansive garden (his most expensive set to date) not

THE SOUNDSTAGES

SIZE OF STAGES - M·G·M· STUDIOS
INSIDE DIMENSIONS

STAGE NO.	WIDTH	LENGTH	HEIGHT	HEIGHT TO KNEE BRACES	POSTS	TANK OR PIT	FLOOR
1	66-9	93-0	27-0	NONE	NONE	NONE	WOOD OVER CEM'T
2	66-8	93-3	26-6	NONE	NONE	NONE	WOOD OVER CEM'T
3	79-2	93-3	29-10	25-10	NONE	YES	WOOD
4	79-0	99-6	29-10	25-10	NONE	NONE	WOOD
5	78-10	127-5	44-5	41-3	NONE	NONE	WOOD
6	81-6	73-10	80-0	NONE	NONE	YES	WOOD
7	76-2	102-6	26-3	NONE	YES 4	YES	WOOD
8	74-8	102-9	26-10	NONE	YES 4	YES	WOOD BL'KS OVER CEM'T
9	73-4	153-0	33-11	27-5	NONE	NONE	WOOD BL'KS OVER CEM'T
10	87-8	149-7	30-0	23-0	NONE	NONE	WOOD
11	68-9+35-3 / 104-0	189-2	35-0	26-7 / 22-1	YES 8'	NONE	WOOD
12	101-8	177-2	37-9	30-2	NONE	NONE	CEMENT
14	89-3	179-6	35-0	28-9	NONE	YES	CEMENT
15	133-6	310-6	40-0	2-4 DROP IN FL AT 96-10	NONE	YES	WOOD & WOOD/CEM'T
16	103-0	131-10+64-10 / 196-8	20-0 / 24-0		YES 2	YES 2	WOOD
18	105-2	141-4	25-7 / 28-0	20-7	YES 3	YES	WOOD
19	106-5	159-11	25-7 / 28-1	27-4	YES 4	YES	WOOD
21	102-3	152-9	26-11 / 29-10	NONE	YES 4	NONE	WOOD
22	102-3	157-0	27-4 / 29-10	NONE	YES 4	NONE	WOOD
23	102-0	157-0	35-0	27-0	NONE	NONE	WOOD
24	102-0	157-0	35-0	27-0	NONE	NONE	WOOD
25	116-10	193-8½	40-0	NONE	NONE	NONE	WOOD
26	117-7	193-8½	40-0	NONE	NONE	NONE	WOOD
27	133-7½	236-10½	50-0 / 80-0	NONE	NONE	NONE	WOOD
28	116-11	196-8½	40-0	NONE	NONE	NONE	WOOD
29	117-10	196-8½	40-0	NONE	NONE	NONE	WOOD
30	131-10	236-10	50-0	NONE	NONE	YES	WOOD & CEMENT
BLDG. 144 LOT 2	68-6	210-0	28-6	24-4	NONE	NONE	ASPHALT
"A" REH HALL	70	58	20		0	0	WOOD
"B" "	52	70	20		0	0	WOOD

A highly detailed soundstage chart, with hand-written annotations. Most of these figures still accurately describe the property's soundstages today. Note that Soundstages 1 and 2 were actually a scoring stage and a screening room, respectively, and do not appear labeled on the map.

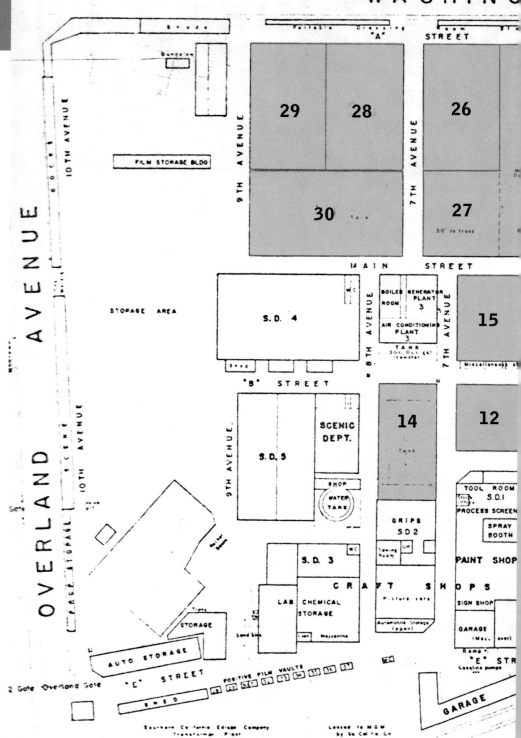

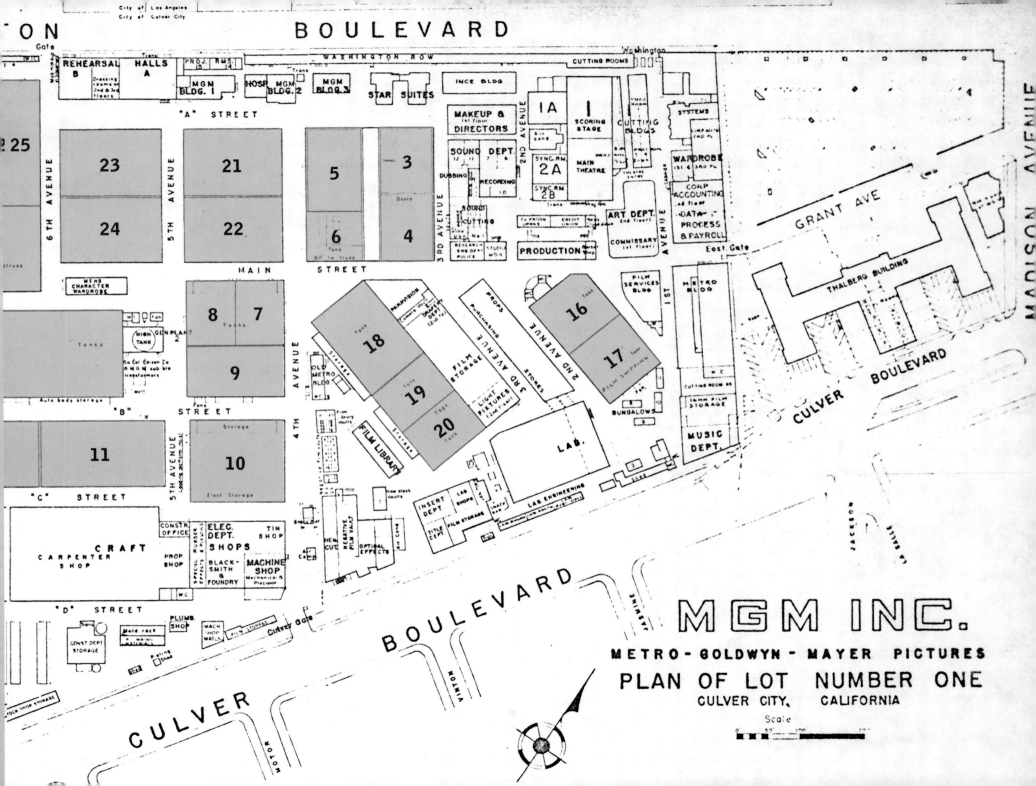

in Lot Two's Cohn Park, which was at the mercy of the weather, but indoors. The result was one of the studio's most elaborate and beautiful sets, running the entire length of Stage 15. Leslie Howard (as Romeo) and Norma Shearer (as Juliet) performed the famous balcony love scene here for four days under the direction of George Cukor.

Most films used more than one stage. *The Wizard of Oz* (1939) was filmed on Stages 14, 15, 25, 26, 27 (Munchkinland), and 29 (where the Technicolor poppy field was laid). The Yellow Brick Road actually snaked from Stage 27 across the studio's Main Street to Stage 15. Stage 27 (the next largest stage to Stage 15) was also used in *Forbidden*

Planet (1956), *The Wonderful World of the Brothers Grimm* (1962), and *The Unsinkable Molly Brown* (1964). The all-star Arthur Freed musical *Words and Music* (1948) was filmed on Stages 3, 4, 5, 9, 10, 15, and 27. Alfred Hitchcock's *North by Northwest* (1959) was shot on Stages 5, 18, 22, and 26, and Marlon Brando's remake of Thalberg's classic, *Mutiny on the Bounty* (1962), was shot on Stages 12, 14, 28, and 30.

Most of the stages, as alluded to above, had the sets inside removed between projects so that new sets could be constructed there. One exception, however: the connected Stages 5 and 6 were different because they contained a permanent "theatre set" for Metro's glorious

Opposite: The top of Stage 15 in 1950.
Center: On Lot One the tallest sound stage was Stage 6, with a legitimate theatre stage and backstage area. Almost all of MGM's musicals, and many dramas and comedies, used this stage as a Broadway theatre or Opera House through the decades (1950).
Left: The cast of *A Tale of Two Cities* (1935) strolls past sound stages on Lot One: (left to right) Claude Gillingwater, Henry B. Walthal, Elizabeth Allan, director Jack Conway, Edna May Oliver, and Ronald Colman.
Right: Actress Julie Christie walks to the set of *Demon Seed* in 1977.

musicals. Built in 1925 for *Pretty Ladies*, Stage 5 contained the seats and balconies for the audiences of well-dressed extras. Stage 6 contained the proscenium-arched raised stage—larger than any actually on Broadway—where the studio's best dancers and unrivaled warblers performed. The stage set contained an intricate series of hydraulic lifts and water tanks so that players could disappear under the stage or appear at any point on it. On the walls, elaborate gilded opera boxes could be folded out and populated with dress extras as needed for the current production.

The *Great Ziegfeld* and *Rose-Marie* (1936); *Maytime* (1937);

Babes in Arms (1939); *Ziegfeld Girl* (1941); *For Me and My Gal* (1942); *Broadway Rhythm* (1944); *Ziegfeld Follies* (1945); *Till the Clouds Roll By* (1946); *Easter Parade* and *Words and Music* (1948); *The Barkleys of Broadway* (1949); *Three Little Words* (1950); *Grounds for Marriage*, *Strictly Dishonorable*, *Royal Wedding*, and *An American in Paris* (1951); *Singin' in the Rain* (as Grauman's Chinese Theatre) and *The Belle of New York* (1952); *The Band Wagon* and *Kiss Me Kate* (1953); *Love Me or Leave Me* (1955); and *Silk Stockings* (1957) are only but a scant handful of the pictures shot here using a theatre setting. Martin Scorsese's *New York, New York* (1977) was probably one of the last pictures to use this

Left: Stages 11 and 15 on Lot One. The long storage facility running alongside Stage 15 housed the "breakaway" automobile interiors used for rear projection process shots (1940s).
Right: A lunch break includes a multitude of employees from every department of the studio (1941).

set in this fashion.

The theatre set was also used in *Scaramouche* (1952) for the longest, most spectacular swordfight ever undertaken, during which Stewart Granger and Mel Ferrer dueled across the stage and the auditorium and into the wings. The exciting duel clocks in at just less than six-and-a-half minutes.

At 80 feet high, Stage 6 is also the tallest on the lot—the 105-foot-wide, 15-ton "Metro Goldwyn Mayer" sign (complete with a roaring Leo the Lion) stood for decades on the roof of this building.

The first recorded fatalities at MGM occurred inside Stage 6, as well. Electrician Carl C. Barlow was on a lighting platform being moved across the stage in 1925 when one of the supports broke loose, plummeting Barlow and another technician onto the stage floor.

Whether or not these stages are haunted by more than memories have been cause for much speculation over the decades. Stories about a spectral worker wearing white overalls in the catwalks seem to be more persistent than ghostly visitations by actual stars. In her memoirs, Esther Williams reported hearing noises coming from Stage 5 in 1953 and, upon entering the darkened set, seeing not a ghost, but something perhaps even more haunting: actress Joan Crawford, back on the lot after 12 years, standing on the dark stage set wailing to an audience that wasn't there, "Why have you left me? Why don't you

come to my movies? What did I do? What did I say? Don't turn your back on me!"

Some places, and some people, are haunted by more than actual ghosts.

Stage 14 is two blocks down the street and was once known as the studio's Process Stage. If a backlot area did not exist for a production crew that needed actors in outdoor locales either mundane (driving a taxi or walking down Fifth Avenue) or exotic (Tarzan's jungle or the India of *Kim* [1950]), the production would come here.

Inside, actors would stand or act or walk in front of a giant screen on which film of the desired locale was projected. For example

Top Left: "On your marks, get set, go…" MGM's members of the fairer sex, Jane Powell, Debbie Reynolds, Cecile Rogers, Jane Fischer, Virginia Gibson, Nancy Kilgas, and Dolores Starr are ready to race.

Top Right: Debbie Reynolds selects a custom, deluxe bicycle befitting a MGM star on the rise (1953).

Above: Actor Stuart Whitman bikes to the *Signpost to Murder* set in 1965.

Left: Debbie Reynolds and Gene Kelly enter a soundstage door for *Singin' in the Rain* (1952).
Right: The construction of Stage 6, the "Theater Stage," was built to look like a Broadway playhouse, which, at 80 feet to the ceiling, is still one of the tallest in the world (1925). The building was eventually divided and became, among other spaces, the office of actor Danny DeVito.
Opposite: Stage 6, the stage constructed with a permanent theatre inside, is dressed for the lengthy duel between Steward Granger and Mel Ferrer for *Scaramouche* (1952).

in the *Tarzan* films, when Johnny Weissmuller or Maureen O'Sullivan are high up in the jungle trees, they are actually on this stage, on a prop branch with aerial jungle footage projected behind them.

Perhaps this stage's most common use was for those innumerable dialogue scenes within a "moving" automobile. Years later, historian Leonard Maltin expressed the opinion that MGM, inexplicably, shot these scenes more incompetently than any other studio. Perhaps, although even at their best, these shots were problematic. The studio probably realized that audiences of the era were trained to accept such sequences, like the movies they were in, as *symbolic* of the actual experience—a skill we, as modern audiences, have largely lost.

Only one soundstage can truly be said to be one star's alone: the 32,160-square-foot Stage 30, built in 1938 on top of the ruins of a backlot temple set. The studio's third largest stage, it was modified in

1944 to include four different plateaus of intricate underwater tanks, all of which were added that year for *Bathing Beauty*. Esther Williams recalled her first visit to the stage to film the spectacular finale for that picture as causing her mouth to drop open in amazement. Even today, visitors to the lot who see the pools—which are still used on occasion—tend to behave the same way.

The outer pool—90 × 90 feet across, up to 20 feet deep, and containing 721,000 gallons of water (the tank typically takes seven days to fill)—was the site of many of Williams's most famous water ballets, from *This Time for Keeps* (1947) with Jimmy Durante to *Million Dollar Mermaid* (1952) with Victor Mature.

The stage, either with a removable floor covering the emptied pool, or with sets built inside the vast, empty basins, was also used for hundreds of more landlocked productions, including the epic Glenn

Left: Part of the 1934 film *Student Tour* was set aboard an ocean liner with a swimming pool. All of it was constructed on a stage.
Right: *Bathing Beauty* (1944) being filmed in the giant Stage 30 pool.

Ford Western *Cimarron* (1960), Debbie Reynolds's jubilant *The Unsinkable Molly Brown* (1964), the Antarctic-set *Quick Before It Melts* (1964), and Elvis Presley's *Girl Happy* (1965). Talk about strange bedfellows.

A visitor exiting Stage 30 and wandering amongst its dozens of sisters across Lot One would find it hard not to marvel at the odd juxtaposition of projects shot in each and every one of them: *Conquest* (1937, starring Greta Garbo and Charles Boyer), *Three Little Words* (1950, starring Fred Astaire and Vera-Ellen), *Kismet* (1955, starring Howard Keel and Ann Blyth), *Lust for Life* (1956, starring Kirk Douglas), *Cat on a Hot Tin Roof* (1958, starring Elizabeth Taylor and Paul Newman), and the television series *Dallas* (1978–1991) were all shot on Stages 18 and 23. Stage 23 contained a matching recreation of *Dallas*'s Southfork Ranch exterior, including the swimming pool.

On Stage 25, Jeanette MacDonald and Nelson Eddy's *Sweet-hearts* (1938), Ingrid Bergman's Oscar-winning *Gaslight* (1944), Judy Garland's *The Harvey Girls* (1946), Esther Williams's *Million Dollar Mermaid* (1952), Roy Orbison's *Fastest Guitar Alive* (1967), and even the television series *Knot's Landing* (1979–1993) all battle for our memories and our attention.

Throughout the decades, you could have watched the Marx Brothers perform for *A Day at the Races* (1937) on Stage 4; you could laugh as Jean Harlow and Myrna Loy fought over potential groom William Powell in *Libeled Lady* (1936) on Stage 8; or you could check out the latest of the *Thin Man* series on Stage 9. On Stage 11, you could see for yourself if Robert Taylor was beefing up his pretty boy image in the boxing ring of *The Crowd Roars* (1938), or gape in amazement as Clark Gable (of all people) sang "Puttin' on the Ritz" on Stage 29 for *Idiot's Delight* in 1939. Spencer Tracy was introduced to newcomer

Left: A rear projection screen on Stage 14 being used for the filming of an unidentified MGM production.
Right: Gene Kelly dancing in the film *Invitation to the Dance* (1956), which was filmed in both England and Culver City.

Hedy Lamarr in her first American film, *I Take This Woman* (1940), on Stage 10. You could witness a star rising (Elizabeth Taylor confiding her dreams of horse racing to Mickey Rooney in *National Velvet* [1944]) on Stage 26 and falling (Joan Crawford skating on awfully thin ice in *The Ice Follies of 1939*) on Stage 12.

In 1943, the fantasy sets for Spencer Tracy's classic *A Guy Named Joe* made way for the Chinese sets of Katharine Hepburn's *Dragon Seed* (1944) on Stage 15. Ann-Margret strutted her stuff in *Made in Paris* (1966) on Stage 26. On Stage 15, Cyd Charisse was at her loveliest, dancing in her *Silk Stockings* (1957), and Grace Kelly was

romanced by Bing Crosby and Frank Sinatra in *High Society* (1956). Maurice Chevalier serenaded Hermione Gingold with "I Remember It Well" in *Gigi* (1958) on Stage 11.

Stage 29 could be a sinister London for the studio's rare foray into the dark world of Oscar Wilde in *The Picture of Dorian Gray* (1945), and then became the big, wide, beautiful outdoors of Oregon in Howard Keel and Jane Powell's *Seven Brides for Seven Brothers* (1954).

Like *The Wizard of Oz*, Arthur Freed's lavish *Brigadoon* (1954) was made entirely within these soundstages. Under the direction of George Gibson, who had executed the extraordinary backdrops for the

Left: A Concord, Massachusetts, mansion constructed on stage for *Little Women* (1949).
Right: *Little Women* stars (from left to right) Margaret O'Brien, June Allyson, Janet Leigh, and Elizabeth Taylor strolling through a snowy soundstage (1949).
Opposite: This big production number from the film *Rosalie* (1937) could be a metaphor for MGM's slogan: "Do it right…do it big…give it class!"

American in Paris ballet, the multi-hued Scottish highlands and their distant lakes and mountains came alive with a painted backdrop 600 feet wide and 60 feet high. Besides the rolling hills of real and painted heather, mountains, and distant lakes, a village was constructed beside a bridge and running stream. In all, the world of *Brigadoon* stretched 40,000 square feet across Stage 15 for a cost of $382,280.

The exteriors of the soundstages—in fact most of Lot One—have been captured on film for posterity since the studio's inception. Over the decades, some of the most memorable films using the studio *as* a studio have included a 1925 promotional film (for studio exhibitors), Buster Keaton's *Free and Easy* (1930), *Bombshell* (1933), *Anchors Aweigh* (1945), *Abbott and Costello in Hollywood* (1945), *The Bad and the Beautiful* (1952), *Singin' in the Rain* (1952), *The Loved One* (1965), the *That's Entertainment!* trilogy (1974, 1976, 1994), the TV movie *James Dean* (2001), and Martin Scorsese's *The Aviator* (2004).

As we depart from the soundstages, perhaps it is appropriate to point out the stages where three of MGM's most beautiful leading ladies made their final bows. Esther Williams would complete her career with *Jupiter's Darling* (1955) on her own Stage 30, Lana Turner provided a poignant (and underrated) farewell with pre-James Bond Roger Moore in *Diane* (1956) on 24 and 27, and soon-to-be-Princess Grace Kelly bid adieu to movie audiences, and turned down film suitor Louis Jourdan, in *The Swan* (1956) on Stage 1.

"It's always been wonderful to work in a studio like MGM because you realize you're in a national shrine—that on these dusty soundstages, these icons of American culture have been made, and you're sitting in dressing rooms where great stars have sat," recalled actor Michael York at about the time he was appearing in *Logan's Run* in 1976. Those words might be the ones to remember when exiting this vast, haunted, remarkable area.

Above: The undeveloped backlot area of Lot One in 1925.
Opposite: Lot One's mysterious and foreboding backlot as it looked in the late 1920s.

One corner of the lot remains unexplored: at Overland Avenue and Washington Boulevard. Since the 1980s, this area has been dominated by one of the most common of 21st century sights: a multi-level parking lot. But from 1924, and even beyond the expansion of studio facilities, this cramped smear of real estate was MGM's primary backlot—an amazingly varied and interesting conglomeration of outdoor sets dating from Ince and Goldwyn and through Metro Goldwyn Mayer's halcyon days. Hence, our tour of MGM's first backlot is a compact summation of the studio's early film output.

Few records exist of the sets that were built on this L-shaped parcel, making them as difficult to document as many lost silent films, sadly. MGM tossed away most records of its various Lot One backlots

nearly 30 years ago. However, a dozen yellowing folders, originally used for reference by the Art Department, have survived. These files were merged with the studio's Research Department, perhaps by a sympathetic employee (and there were many employees in the 1970s and 1980s that secretly saved material they were told to destroy). These folders give us a peek through the keyhole of a door otherwise forever locked, and illuminate some of the secrets of this most "lost" of all backlots.

Each file is labeled with a set name and stuffed with numbered location photos of that identified set. There are few people depicted in any of the photographs, except for an occasional blurred technician ducking out of the way of the camera. In one haunting photo, however,

Above: The circus comes to Lot One for *The Great Love* (1925), complete with an elephant surrounded by spectators.
Opposite: Looking north through a hole in the studio fence on Washington Boulevard, a pedestrian in 1925 would have seen this inexplicable tangle of architecture and edifice.

a black cat can be seen walking right down the middle of a French-looking boulevard. Its eyes are the only thing in any of the prints that actually seems to look out across the years at the modern viewer. Otherwise, the pictures represent a one-way mirror looking into a celluloid ghost town.

Some of the photos are slated for specific projects, and identified with production numbers, which were checked against MGM's master title list. Aerial photographs of the studio during that time, existing landmarks, and a powerful magnifying glass were used to try to ascertain each still's approximate location on the lot. Eventually, a fair idea of what was shot where emerged from the phantom past. The authors identified the sets on the following pages (and created the map on the next page) in order to help bring to life what previously only existed in the surviving films for which the sets were originally designed.

THE LOST LOT ONE BACKLOT SETS

1 Lot One Lake
2 Castle
3 Cabbage Patch
4 Lot One New York Streets
5 Warehouse Section
6 Church Alley
7 French District
8 Escarpment Rocks
9 Leper Rocks
10 Waterfront Street
11 Irish Street
12 Small Town
13 Spanish Hacienda
14 Ben-Hur Set
(Located off the backlot
at La Cienega and Venice
Boulevards)

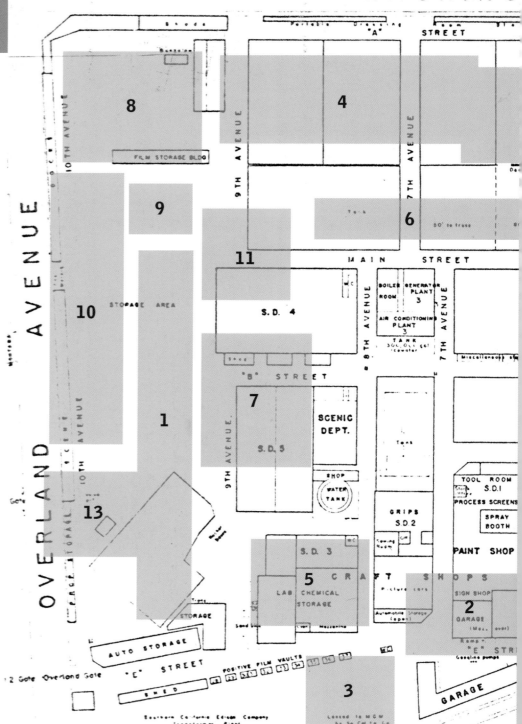

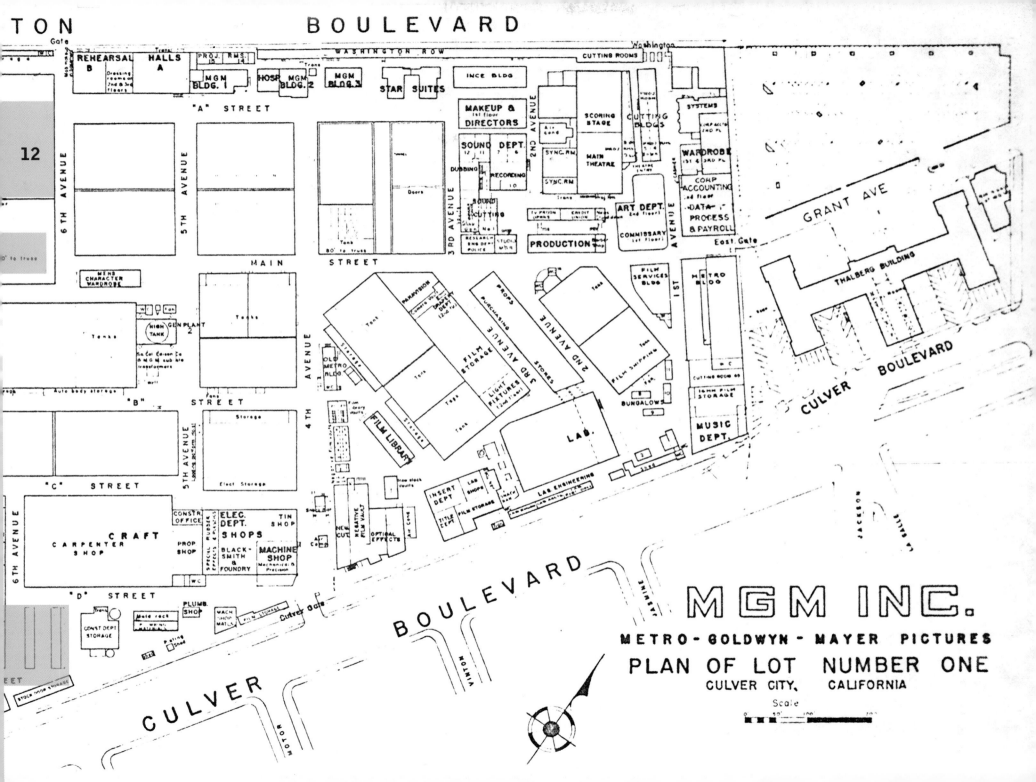

Left: Lot One Lake and a portion of Waterfront Street.

Right: Lot One Lake dressed as darkest Africa, however, the telephone poles and wires in the background did not appear in the finished film (1932).

T he Lot One backlot's primary exterior set was a half-acre lake. This cement-bottomed body of water possessed the chameleon-like ability to mutate or vanish outright as needed. In some early aerial photos it is there; in others, it seems to have changed shape, relocated, or disappeared entirely—only to startlingly materialize once more in later photos and in later films. This *Flying Dutchman* quality characterizes the entire Lot One backlot experience.

Throughout the 1920s and 1930s, the assorted sections of Ince and Goldwyn's city sets gave way to new ones usually constructed

1   LOT ONE LAKE

around this body of water. *Tell It to the Marines* (1926), *The Single Standard* (1929), *Tugboat Annie* (1933), *Min and Bill* (1930), *Peg o' My Heart* (1933), *Treasure Island* (1934), *Lazy River* (1934), *Riffraff* (1936), *David Copperfield* (1935), *The Winning Ticket* (1935), *China Seas* (1935), and *Exclusive Story* (1936) all used the man-made coastline and/or the several full-size ships that were constructed on or around the lake.

In 1931, cinematographers Harold Rosson and Clyde De Vinna shot portions of *Tarzan the Ape Man* (1932), the first in the studio's fabulously successful series, on the lake. *Red Dust* (1932) and later

Left: Lot One Lake dressed as the Netherlands for *The Red Mill* (1927).
Right: Lot One Lake and a rustic Waterfront Street along side it (1935).

Strange Cargo (1940) also created most convincing jungle ports here. In contrast, *A Tale of Two Cities* (1935) featured the set as both the Paris and London waterfront. A few of these venerable façades would be moved across the street the following year and continue to see duty for decades as "Waterfront Street."

These sets were the lucky ones. In November of 1940, because of falling high-tension wires, fire raged through the area, destroying much of the set and threatening the old *Tugboat Annie* tugboat. The heat was so intense, and aggravated by a stiff ocean breeze, that windows in the studio's Cartoon Department across Overland Avenue were shattered. The 12-man studio fire department was forced to call on the Los Angeles Fire Department to put out the blaze. The tugboat survived, however, and would finally be secured on the Lot Three lake.

The artificial lake was still being used for films in the late 1940s, but activity in the area steadily decreased in tandem with the deteriorating financial state of the studio. By the 1960s, the lakebed was being used to store sawdust from the studio's carpenter shop. Today, a parking lot covers most of the area.

Left: *Annie Laurie* simulates a snowy day on the Castle set (1927).
Right: The battlements of the Castle set could be seen towering behind less exotic façades in 1926.

2 CASTLE

The formable battlements of a castle stood just beyond the banks of the lake. Built for the Goldwyn-produced *In the Palace of the King* (1923), which itself later had its sets cannibalized for *Bardelys the Magnificent* in 1926, the façade was ransacked to create Lot Two's Castle Finckenstein set over the course of several years. Some pictures, like *Maytime* (1937), seem to have used parts of both castles on both lots interchangeably.

3 CABBAGE PATCH

Several acres of Lot One's backlot housed a none-too-glamorous trash dump, containing everything the studio could no longer use, but hadn't bothered to cart away yet. This refuse heap was dressed into an unlikely backlot set at least once. For the film *Lovey Mary* (1926), a Bessie Love/William Haines vehicle, it portrayed the ramshackle village of Cabbage Patch. Decades later, long after Lot One's backlot had disappeared, this area—a parking lot for the company's automobiles and trucks—was still being called called "Cabbage Patch" by studio employees.

Above: The Lot One New York Streets covered with posters and patriotic bunting for the film *Possessed* (1931).
According to the posters, the "King," Clark Gable, abdicates to become a mere governor.

ext door was the studio's first residential district: Brown-stone Street, which included a row of New York-style brownstones that cut up into the front lot going east and ran roughly parallel with Washington Boulevard. The western end, however, although still identified by the same name, seemed to mutate and corkscrew into a morass of battling architectural styles

4   LOT ONE NEW YORK STREETS

before finally settling into a vaguely American residential street.

This brownstone district can be seen in *Old Clothes* (1925); *The Guardsman* (1931), starring Alfred Lunt and Lynne Fontanne; *New Morals for Old, Night Court,* and *Are You Listening?* (1932, the latter dusted with an artificial winter's snow); and *Another Language, Beauty for Sale, The Secret of Madame Blanche, Day*

Left: "Step right up! See the 25 Beauties!" The naughty, seedier side of New York Street.
Right: The Max Brecht Deli façade made for the film *Beauty For Sale* (1933).
Opposite Top Left: Night falls on New York Street in *Sidewalks of New York* (1931).
Opposite Bottom Left: New York Street/Brownstone Street (1931).
Opposite Right: A tong war breaks out in the middle of New York Street in *The Cameraman* (1928), and Buster Keaton captures it all on film.

of Reckoning, Looking Forward, and *Stage Mother* (1933). *Forsaking All Others* and the Seine bridge exteriors of *Paris Interlude* (1934); *Baby Face Harrington* and *Kind Lady* (1935); and *The Garden Murder Case* and *The Unguarded Hour* (1936) are also identified as having been shot on these sets.

In the early, pre-merger days, there once stood an impressive-looking courthouse façade bracketed with wide white columns at the axis of these streets—it was later removed when the street expanded farther west.

The more residential, tree-lined boulevard on the western side of Brownstone Street hosted titles like *Arsène Lupin, Divorce in the Family, Strange Interlude,* and *Smilin' Through* (all 1932); *The White Sister* and *The Day of Reckoning* (1933); and *The Mystery of Mr. X* (1934). One of these houses played the minister's home in *This Side of Heaven* (also 1934). There was such a crush of production during these early, boom years that it should be emphasized that for every title mentioned, there were probably a dozen from the same year, maybe the same *month,* which shot on the same street.

It was on these modest New York-style streets that the studio's earliest comedians ran rampant, including Laurel and Hardy and

Charley Chase. Laurel and Hardy, the most famous of these (both then and today), actually have a tenuous connection with MGM, however. Their films were produced by filmmaker Hal Roach, who also made the *Our Gang* series at his nearby Culver City studio at 8822 Washington Boulevard, and both were distributed by MGM. But, like the *Our Gang* kids, who occasionally appeared in MGM films like *General*

Spanky (1936), the comics did appear in a few MGM extravaganzas like *The Hollywood Revue of 1929* and *Hollywood Party* (1934). Roach's studio would be torn down in 1963.

Although his best work was behind him, Buster Keaton would create his last masterpieces at MGM such as *The Cameraman* in 1928 and *Spite Marriage* in 1929. In fact, Keaton would be a permanent,

Above: The New York Taxicab Co. façade from the film *Here Comes the Band* (1935) on New York Street. This street of narrow false fronts was attached to the side of a sound stage to maximize space, a practice still used today.

unhappy fixture here on the backlot in his waning days of stardom. His talent, like that of fellow MGM directors Erich von Stroheim and Rex Ingram, and actors John Gilbert and Karl Dane, wilted under the hot lights of studio supervision. "You studio people warp my character," he complained to Thalberg. With his professional life in a slump, and a pending divorce from his wife, Natalie Talmadge, he camped out on this backlot in his deluxe dressing room trailer and held a series of parties here with his fellow comedians and assorted "actresses." Mayer, fearing scandal, put an end to them by firing Keaton. "I can't make stars as fast as L. B. can fire them," Thalberg was heard to complain.

5 WAREHOUSE SECTION

Nearby, the Warehouse Section was just that: a short, downscale strip of real estate that terminated in an alley, encasing a couple of dirty basement windows built at street level, and a loading dock. Look for it in Ramon Novarro and Helen Hayes's ill-fated *The Son-Daughter* (1932), as well as *The Bishop Misbehaves* (1935) and *The Great Waltz* (1938).

Left: A shiny new Lincoln is parked in front of a house of worship façade on Church Alley.
Right: Church Alley and Brownstone Street.

6 CHURCH ALLEY

Church Alley, as seen in *Looking Forward* (1933) and *Kind Lady* (1935), included not only the front and side of a church—complete with tree-lined rectory, park benches, and wrought-iron fences—but also incorporated some dressable storefronts that stood adjacent to the chapel. Amusingly, *The Winning Ticket* (1935) cast one of these buildings memorably as "Salome's Tonsorial Palace." Most of the sets were later moved or replaced by Church Street on Lot Two.

Left: **Storybook French architecture on display on Lot One's French Street (1936).**
Opposite Top Left: **French Street (1936).**
Opposite Top Right: **A feral cat roams a back alley of French Street (1936).**
Opposite Bottom Left: **A redress of French Street in 1936.**
Opposite Bottom Right: **"Cobblestones" are half-buried in the street for easy removal and reuse (1936).**

7 FRENCH DISTRICT

The French Farmhouse District, later known simply as the "French District," apparently started out as a single structure that was expanded into an entire Gallic-themed village as production warranted it. It was overdressed with atmospheric little touches: thatched or shingled rooftops, courtyards, and balconied avenues with winding exterior staircases and gabled windows. One side faced the aforementioned lake; the other side of the avenue included several shops with actual interiors. Look for it most memorably in *The Big Pa-*

rade (1925) as the spot where John Gilbert and Renée Adorée first meet and fall in love. Other titles in which these façades saw duty include *Flesh and the Devil* (1926); *The Student Prince in Old Heidelberg* (1927); *The Sin of Madelon Claudet* (1931); *The Merry Widow* (1934); *The Perfect Gentleman*, *Mutiny on the Bounty*, *Naughty Marietta*, *Vanessa: Her Love Story*, *The Night Is Young*, *A Tale of Two Cities* (1935); and *The Firefly* (1937). For Garbo's *The Painted Veil* (1934), a church was constructed that could be seen in most films made on the location thereafter.

Left: Tarzan (Johnny Weissmuller) and "Boy" (Johnny Sheffield) lead the way up the Escarpment Rocks in *Tarzan's Secret Treasure* (1941).
Right: Maureen O'Sullivan and Neil Hamilton take a break from filming *Tarzan the Ape Man* (1932) at the Escarpment Rocks.

8   ESCARPMENT ROCKS

"Escarpment Rocks" was the name for a narrow strip of outdoor sets that rimmed the fenceline of the studio and included wooded trails, with both real and simulated trees, towering snow-capped mountains, at least one precariously bridged ravine, and several man-made structures. This was the "Mutia Escarpment," a mountain barrier protecting the realm of Tarzan and the Elephant Graveyard, referenced in the studio's *Tarzan* series. Other titles at least partially lensed here include Clark Gable's *Hell Divers* (1931); *Fugitive Lovers* (1934), for a snowbound bus crash; and *Tough Guy*, featuring a breakaway bridge that did just that in 1936.

The most notorious and famous film shot here is the cult classic *The Mask of Fu Manchu* (1932), featuring Boris Karloff. All-American, Montana-born Myrna Loy played his evil Oriental daughter as, to quote the lady herself, "a sadistic nymphomaniac." Although she admitted she "looked about as Chinese as Raggedy Ann," audiences of the time seemed more interested in Loy's exotic demeanor than in her ethnic makeup.

9   LEPER ROCKS

A nearby cliffside of artificial rocky ledges known as "Leper Rocks" was constructed for *Ben-Hur* (1925). An assortment of buildings were gradually built within its shadows, including a miner's shack, assayer's office, and corral that variously played both period-Europe and, on occasion, the American West. Pictures shot in this area included *Queen Christina* and *Clear All Wires!* (1933) and *Sequoia* (1934). The area was eventually replaced by the Rock Formation set on Lot Three.

Left: Waterfront Street in *The Captain Is a Lady* (1940).
Top Right: Waterfront Street dressed as "Chili Port" for the film *Adventure* (1945).
Bottom Right: Waterfront Street (1949).

10 WATERFRONT STREET

Waterfront Street, a (usually) European district on the western side of the lake, ran south along the studio's western fence-line and terminated on the banks of Escarpment Rocks. This street frequently depicted France, particularly after the actual French Street to the east started looking more like Bristol than Bordeaux.

The Passionate Plumber and *Rasputin and the Empress* (1932); *The Stranger's Return*, *Turn Back the Clock*, *Gabriel Over the White House*, *The Secret of Madame Blanche*, and *What! No Beer?* (1933); and *Paris Interlude* (1934) are but a few filmic examples of this versatile set in action.

Many of the façades that made up this street were uprooted and moved across the street to Lot Two starting in 1935. The name "Waterfront Street" crossed the lot as well, although there was no nearby water on the new set.

11 IRISH STREET

Irish Street was actually a holdover from a Scottish village constructed in 1920 for one of the pre-merger Goldwyn pictures, *Bunty Pulls the Strings* (1921). Pieces of it show up in *The Big Parade* (1925); *Storm at Daybreak* (1933); and *The Bishop Misbehaves* and *The Casino Murder Case* (1935).

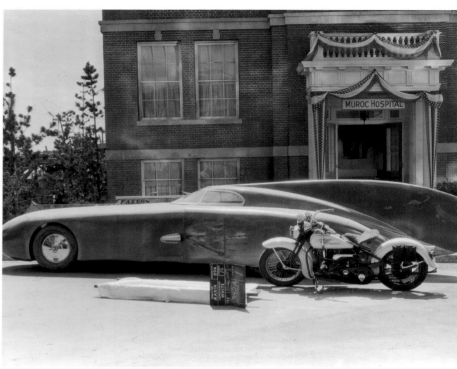

Left: Small Town dressed for *Pursuit* (1935). This photo was taken as some of the façades on Lot One were being moved to Lot Two.
Right: Small Town in *Speed* (1936). The featured Indianapolis 500 race car could be an early prototype of the Batmobile!

12   SMALL TOWN

Other freestanding buildings pockmarked the edges of these sets or were constructed over the front of soundstages or technical buildings. Notably, a sort of prototypical American small town was constructed very early on in an open area behind Washington Boulevard—approximately where Stages 25 and 26 later rose. *Peck's Bad Girl* (1918) is one Goldwyn title known to have used these sets.

Left: Spanish Hacienda as seen in 1926's *Torrent.*
Right: Spanish Hacienda in 1924. The chimney in the center is the studio's incinerator.

13 SPANISH HACIENDA

The Spanish Hacienda was constructed for Garbo's *The Temptress* in 1926, and adapted for *Flesh* and *Fast Life* (1932). An ice cream factory with an imposing front gate was built here for *Have a Heart* (1934) and can be seen in *Fugitive Lovers* made the same year.

Most of these piecemeal sets, and eventually all of the structures described above, were torn down or moved. By the late 1930s, only the lake was still being regularly used.

Left: The Roman Circus Maximus set for the 1925 production of *Ben-Hur*.
Top Right: The Roman Circus Maximus set was constructed on a lot at La Cienega and Venice Boulevards in Culver City, CA.
Bottom Right: The building and parking lot seen in this photo sits on the land that once housed the Lot One backlot. The structure has been used over the years by MGM, United Artists, Tri-Star, Columbia, and Sony.
Opposite: A publicity composite photo of the chariot race and spectators from *Ben-Hur* (1925).

14 BEN-HUR SET

In 1925, after the three-way merger that had created the company, Thalberg was forced to shut down production on Fred Niblo's spectacularly out-of-control *Ben-Hur*. The entire unwieldy project then limped back home to Culver City to await redemption and completion. But once cast and crew had been transplanted onto the lot, Thalberg (with Mayer looking over his shoulder, no doubt) realized that the Lot One backlot was too small and already too congested with standing sets to contain the massive coliseum which, Griffith-like, would have to be built for the picture's chariot-race climax.

The solution was an abandoned lot several miles up the road at the intersection of La Cienega and Venice boulevards. Unfortunately, in a potentially disastrous oversight, no one bothered to actually rent the property from anyone, and when a city bulldozer started to disassemble the still-unfinished set for a county construction project, it took a great deal of pleading and probably the greasing of more than

a few outreached palms in order to postpone the project so set construction could continue. At a cost of $300,000, a most generous budget for an entire picture at the time, the Roman Circus Maximus was eventually recreated and thousands of extras (including then-unknowns Myrna Loy and Marion Davies) were called upon to watch several dozen gladiators (actually local cowboys) tear around the track as recorded by an unprecedented 42 cameras.

When the dust had settled on the spectacle, and the cameras and the cowboys and the crew had been sent back to the studio, Mayer and Thalberg realized, sadly, that they could not keep the magnificent set, and, in fact, it was soon bulldozed. Knowing they would need area to shoot equally epic scenes for the forthcoming *The Big Parade* (1925), the idea of a second, expanded backlot, a *magnum opus* of backlots—Lot Two—was born.

PART TWO:

POTEMKIN'S VILLAGES

Under the moon, the backlot was 30 acres of fairyland—not because the locations really looked like African jungles and French châteaux and schooners at anchor and Broadway by night, but because they looked like the torn picture books of childhood, like fragments of stories dancing in an open fire. I never lived in a house with an attic, but a backlot must be something like that, and at night of course in an enchanted distorted way, it all comes true.

—F. SCOTT FITZGERALD,
The Love of the Last Tycoon

"FALSE FRONTS"

We walked out past the soundstages and the machine shops and the labor gangs to the backlot. We walked past the New York street and up through the Latin quarter of Paris until we came to a South Seas island and a little beach leading down to real water. We crossed the little bridge to the island and sat down on the sand in front of a native hut. The hot April sun was just what the set designer ordered. I dug my hands into the warm sand and lay on my back looking up through a palm tree supported with piano wire and a cloudless sky.

"Where are we?" I said.

"This used to be Hollywood," she said with a poker face and voice, "before the depression."

—BUDD SCHULBERG, *What Makes Sammy Run?*

Expanding MGM's backlot across Overland Avenue from the honeycomb of outdoor façades on Lot One was easy, but politically problematic. The proposed real estate was the property of Loew's co-founder Joseph Schenck (brother of Nicholas). In 1927, a deal was worked out to purchase 25 acres of land from Schenck at $375 an acre, with the provision that additional acreage could be added later. Eventually it was, after further acquisitions in 1935, 1937, and 1939, to total 37 acres. Additionally, for many years the studio continued to purchase residential tracts northeast of the property, hoping for another expansion that would never come.

There was one problem: The land Mayer bought from Schenck wasn't land at all; it was actually a gravel pit—a gaping, unseemly hole in the earth some 40 feet deep, choked with black mud, leafless tree trunks, and oily industrial waste. Surely Harry Culver, showing off his planned utopia to prospective investors, stayed away from *this* neighborhood.

Obviously, this acreage would have to be filled in before it would be usable. The solution was provided by the City of Los Angeles, which was excavating the La Brea Tar Pits on Wilshire Boulevard. Earth from this ancient and storied resting place for prehistoric beasts

was dumped into what became known as Lot Two. Later landfill was provided by the discarded sets themselves. The lot was used almost immediately for the final, climactic battlefield scenes for King Vidor's celebrated *The Big Parade* (1925).

Mayer and Thalberg now required a man to design the new backlots. They agreed that Goldwyn's art director, Cedric Gibbons, understood the job and its unique qualifications perhaps better than anyone in the industry. Ultimately, it would be Gibbons who would find a look and physicality for the MGM backlot—for backlots in general—and for the physical look for the entire 20th century.

According to his official studio biography, Gibbons was born in 1893 (although some sources have claimed 1890). He joined Goldwyn as an assistant art director in New York before making the trip to California to head the Art Department in 1919. From the very beginning, even before he picked up the habit of marrying movie stars, Gibbons had an affinity for attracting personal publicity. As early as 1920, *American Architect* magazine ran a feature story about Gibbons's masterful recreation of a Scottish village for the previously mentioned *Bunty Pulls the Strings* (1921).

Gibbons was not immediately attuned to Thalberg's wish to

Above: **Cedric Gibbons (center), flanked by his art directors Edwin Willis and Fred Hope, inspects blueprints on the Verona Square set for *Romeo and Juliet* (1936).**

extend the backlot. "Because Thalberg wanted his pictures made where he could watch them, the art department had to design sets of foreign locales at a furious rate and paint backdrops of famous places, although Cedric Gibbons thought they should be photographed on their actual sites," recalled Sam Marx. "His fine sense of authenticity was outraged when the scenario of [*The Latest from*] *Paris* called for a love scene in that city with a moonlit ocean in the background. He went to Thalberg with a sheaf of photographs to prove that no large body of water was anywhere in that vicinity. Thalberg's reply represented the studio's—and the industry's—argument for the need of backlots: 'We can't cater to a handful of people who know Paris,' he told the annoyed art director." After *Paris* was released, Thalberg asked Gibbons if he received many letters that pointed out the scenic error. Gibbons had to admit there was not a one.

Gibbons's second wife, Hazel Brooks (his first was actress Dolores Del Rio), recalled that "his best years were with Thalberg. He got what he wanted and had fun."

Ever the company man, Gibbons saved everything that he ever used and dutifully cataloged and stored his treasures away. "Metro operated like a little old lady, saving pieces of string and tinfoil and storing it. I always wondered where and how they stored so many things," remembered television producer George M. Lehr. "Those staircases they stored were used over and over and over. If backlot sets had any interiors, they were frequently filled with miscellaneous stuff from over the years." Producer Buck Houghton agreed. "I knew it had the best storehouse of sets in town. MGM traditionally kept everything they ever made."

For this kingdom of make-believe, it helped that Gibbons grasped that designing for the screen was different than designing for the stage or for life. "Perhaps the most important thing for the movie designer to remember," Gibbons lectured in 1937, "is that he can never visualize a setting from just one angle—as the stage designer can, and must. He must build each set in his mind and then go around it. One must not concentrate on one fine picture, forgetting entirely that a moving picture is . . . a *moving* picture."

Gibbons designed his sets to accommodate not just one viewpoint, but an infinite number of viewpoints and combinations, both in the current film and for future productions yet unimagined. An interior set designed for a Marx Brothers comedy could be rotated and

PARCELIZATION & ZONING MAP

CULVER CITY

METRO-GOLDWYN-MAYER, INC.

Legend:

- M-G-M PROPERTIES
- RESIDENTIAL
- MULTIPLE
- COMMERCIAL
- INDUSTRIAL

0' 500' 1000' 1500'

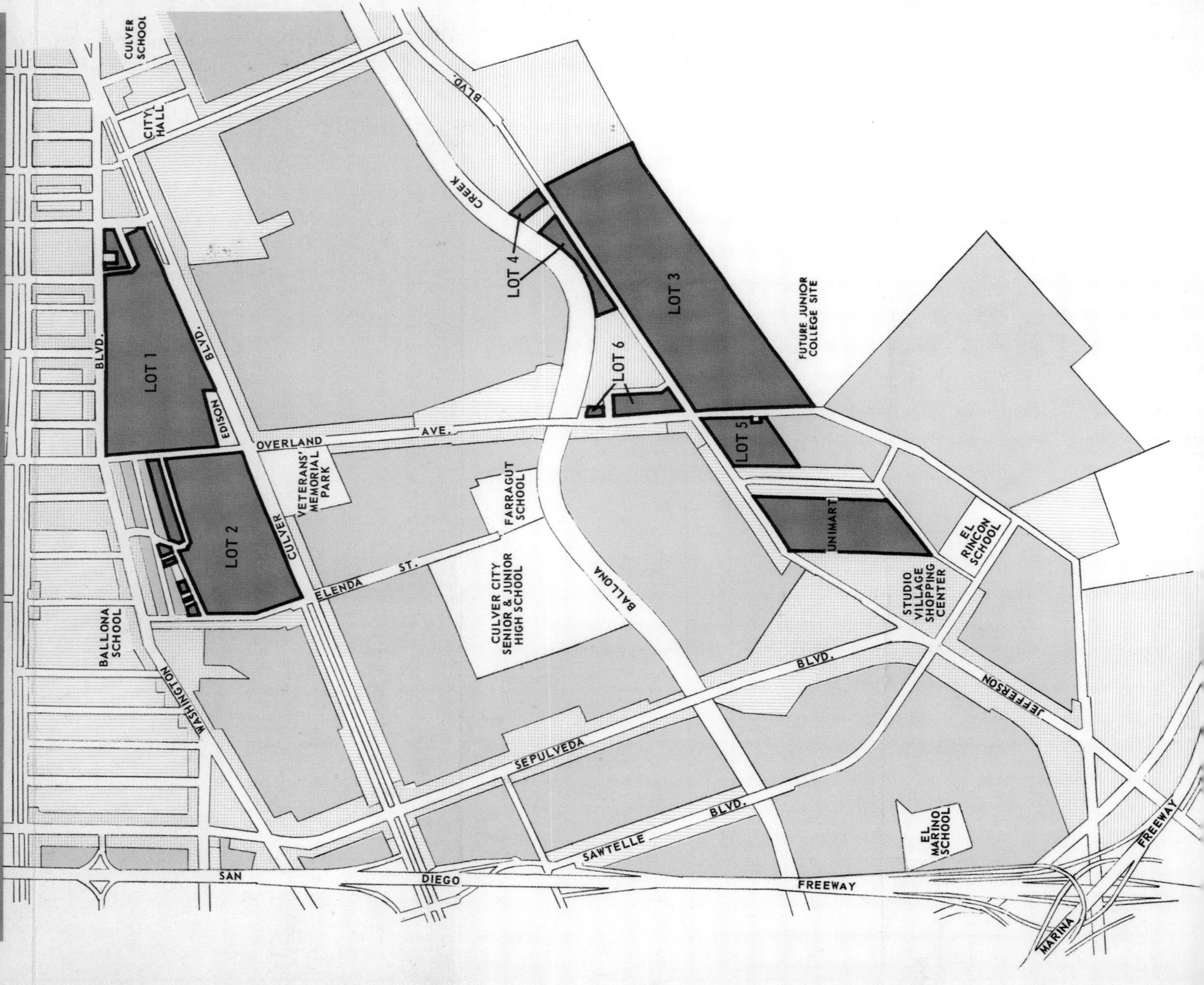

Prepared by

Real Estate Research Corporation, 1967

N

LOT 1

LOT 2

LOT 3

LOT 4

LOT 5

LOT 6

UNIHART

CULVER SCHOOL

CITY HALL

CULVER BLVD.

CREEK

FUTURE JUNIOR COLLEGE SITE

EDISON BLVD.

OVERLAND AVE.

CULVER BLVD.

VETERANS' MEMORIAL PARK

FARRAGUT SCHOOL

ELENDA ST.

BALLONA SCHOOL

WASHINGTON BLVD.

CULVER CITY SENIOR & JUNIOR HIGH SCHOOL

BALLONA

BLVD.

STUDIO VILLAGE SHOPPING CENTER

EL RINCON SCHOOL

JEFFERSON

SEPULVEDA BLVD.

SAWTELLE BLVD.

EL MARINO SCHOOL

SAN DIEGO FREEWAY

MARINA FREEWAY

reassembled in a different combination for a hair-tearing Greta Garbo epic. Streets Gibbons designed on the backlot could play Normandy one week and Waxahachie, Texas, the next. Note, for example, how often Gibbons re-used the expensive interior sets from *Marie Antoinette* (1938). Studio researchers had spent an unprecedented year in France, studying period architecture and sending back some 12,000 photographs from which Gibbons's staff built, in the words of *Architectural Digest*, "an improved version of Versailles, with a grand staircase that was unaccountably omitted from the original. The authentic stucco moldings were too delicate to look impressive on film, so they were reproduced more boldly on the sets in order to achieve a convincing illusion of reality."

Yet these beautifully crafted vistas, typical of the MGM extravagance not found at any other studio, with their intricate, gilt-edged scrollwork and painted murals, can be seen not only in the picture they were obstinately designed for, but in films made virtually every year after that, from *The Earl of Chicago* in 1940 through *Du Barry Was a Lady* (1943), *Anchors Aweigh* (1945), and *Lovely to Look At* in 1952. In fact, these same "Versailles walls" could still be recognized as late as 1963 as the interior of a luxury liner in a *Twilight Zone* episode. Similarly in 1943, screenwriters assigned to write an Abbott and Costello feature were told to base it on the *Arabian Nights* so the *Kismet* (1944) sets could be used. Thus, *Lost in a Harem* (1944) was born.

Oddly, certainly unintentionally, this admittedly spendthrift tactic resulted in a consistency in design and sensibilities that would span the entire studio era. As much an auteur as any director, Gibbons's sets became recognizable as a house style long before any "filmmakers" achieved that status.

Gibbons's sets generally tended to be over-lit, so as to show off their craftsmanship; whites, rather than shadow, tended to predominate. His influences were American by way of the 1925 Exposition Internationale des Arts Decoratifs et Industriels Modernes—which introduced him, and the world, what would become known as Art Deco—as opposed to the Grimm's Fairy Tale horrors or Teutonic expressionist shadows flickering on the dark sets of studios like Universal. His 1930s Deco and later streamlined-Moderne stylings created, if not the actual look of an era itself, then certainly our later perceptions of what that era looked like.

By the mid-1930s, Culver City's growth now entirely surrounded MGM's existing property and further expansion of the increasingly crowded Lot Two was looking unlikely. In 1936, in the search for more production room, Mayer looked to another 60-acre parcel Joe Schenck owned further south, a half-dozen blocks past Ballona Creek on Overland Avenue. "Mayer called me in and said, 'There's a piece of property for sale on the corner of Jefferson and Overland, take a look at it,'" recalled J. J. Cohn.

Right: The Staff Shop creates a gamut of items made from an indestructible plastic compound called "Greutert's plastic" (1939).
Opposite: This parcelization map, used by the studio to sell of their real estate in 1969, shows all of the companies' properties in relation to one another.

Cohn recalled going out to see the property with Gibbons, who wanted something with terrain, however—rolling hills, valleys, trees, and water. It happened that there was a parcel of land in the San Fernando Valley that perfectly fit the bill, and at $75 an acre, this land, known as the Agoura Ranch, was considerably cheaper than the Culver City property.

Mysteriously, though, pressure was brought to buy the Schenck property instead. Cohn remembered Mayer instructing him to buy the more expensive property—and at $275 an acre. "And that's what we paid for it."

That unusual purchase created the massive Lot Three, which did contain its own small forest—for which Schenck charged them an additional 25 cents per tree.

Lot Three was quickly followed and surrounded by the smaller Lots Four (1940, original cost: $13,129.97), Five (1940, original cost: $9,550.00), Six (acquired in parcels over nine years starting in 1940, total cost: $13,267.73), and even Seven (in 1945, for $38,496.70). The company's empire eventually even included an entire second studio in Great Britain, MGM Borehamwood, equipped with seven soundstages of its own and sprawling over nearly a hundred acres.

The studio vistas expanded so far and so wide that when producer Dore Schary was visiting former actress Grace Kelly and her husband, Prince Ranier of Monaco, in the 1950s, Schary is said to have asked the prince how big Monaco was. Rainier told the studio executive that it was five square miles and Schary said, "Jesus, that's not even as big as our backlot."

Gibbons's department would continue to build and refine this ersatz fairyland for the next quarter century. But without Thalberg, his professional life became a struggle. Gibbons was never able to respect the bombastic Mayer in quite the same way he had Thalberg. Mayer, for his part, secretly resented Gibbons's affected elitism. He was inexplicably bothered by Gibbons's habit of wearing uncuffed pants and white slipper-like shoes. Mayer's more conservative view of the American scene allowed for less satire, less exaggeration, and more tasteful

vulgarity in its interpretations and did not allow for the flights of architectural fantasy that Thalberg had indulged in. So a bigger-than-life Versailles gave way to ever more variations on Andy Hardy Street, with only occasional forays into history, science fiction, satire, and sex to liven up Gibbons's world.

Mayer was, however, very loyal to Gibbons, as he was prone to be to anyone who exhibited loyalty to MGM. If finances are a mark of esteem, then Gibbons's $91,000 salary in 1941 certainly signified a level of appreciation. (Mayer, of course, made $704,000 that year.) The mogul realized that Gibbons, more than anyone else, had created the physical look for both the films and the studio where they were being created. If Mayer walked across his lot through the lakes and soundstages and castles, or sat in his white Art Deco office, or dined at his commissary, it was Gibbons's work he saw. Watching a film in a screening room at night, it was Gibbons's—not Mayer's—sensibilities and taste on display. In fact, the very walls of the theatre in which the picture was being screened had all been designed by Gibbons.

Eventually, that title—"art director"—was oft-times replaced by the more comprehensive label "production designer," an on-screen

Right: Staff Shop workers are seen here fabricating "realistic" stone walls and ornamentation (1930s). Vacuum form machines have made the process quicker today, although some of the techniques on display here are still employed daily in the 21st century motion picture industry.

credit first used to describe William Cameron Menzies for his all-inclusive, jaw-dropping work on *Gone with the Wind* (1939). The duties inherent in the position have varied greatly over the years. Gibbons, unsurprisingly, interpreted his job in the widest possible context. His influence over the physical look of each production always extended well beyond his sets.

"Even though there was a separate Wardrobe Department, he often was involved in costumes," recalled Buddy Gillespie. "There was another separate department, the set dressers under Ed Willis. But Gibbons was over all of them, too. Later on, a Matte Painting Department headed by Warren Newcome was also under his jurisdiction. And when I became the head of the Special Effects Department, unlike all the other studios, it was still part of the Art Department and I was under Gibbons. But he was smart enough to give all his men, including me, almost total control."

In 1943, it was estimated that 70% of the 4,500 employees on payroll were affected by this department's practices in one way or another. "[Gibbons] was the most influential person on the lot except for the owners," director Elia Kazan said.

Just how much did Gibbons contribute to the cinematic works of MGM? Gibbons never seriously claimed to have personally designed every setting for which he took credit. It was a common practice at that time, in that pre-union era, for the department head to be the only person credited for a specific job. Contractually, as Art Department head, Gibbons was required to receive a credit for every MGM picture produced in the United States. In a 1932 *Los Angeles Times* article, Gibbons claimed 936 credits. In 1953, Gibbons reported to *Daily Variety* that the "recently completed *Julius Caesar* was his 2,200th film for Metro, including features and shorts." A 1948 *Hollywood Reporter* article claimed 1,500 films. *Let's Go to the Movies* by Lester Gordon parrots this figure, as does the reference work *Film Facts* by Patrick Robinson. The Internet Movie Database, however, credits Gibbons with a mere 1,100 titles, including his one (partial) directorial credit (1934's *Tarzan and His Mate*), but omits some of his short subjects.

Members of his staff probably resented their relative anonymity, however, in spite of Buddy Gillespie's assertion that "Gibbons was so admired by the people on his staff, I don't think they ever felt any resentment that he would get the acclaim for a picture." Duncan Cramer, former head of the Art Department at 20th Century Fox, had nothing good to say about Gibbons as a person. In an unpublished 1970 reminiscence to Michael Grace, he referred to him as being "terribly pompous" and remarked that "Bill Horning was his assistant. He was a very bright and capable architect and art director. Cedric Gibbons surrounded himself with men of this caliber to protect his own interests. Horning was said to be the brains behind the operation." It should be noted here that Horning won two Oscars himself, for *Gigi* (1958) and *Ben-Hur* (1959), both projects created after Gibbons's departure.

No one ever voiced any objections to Gibbons's own 40 Academy Award nominations or his 11 wins, however. In 1958, he was awarded a lifetime membership in the Academy. That was, after all, appropriate since it was Gibbons who, with sculptor George Stanley, designed the Oscar statuette for the Academy of Motion Picture Arts and Sciences.

Following a natural progression, Gibbons eventually assimilated his gift for three-dimensional set design to actual homes. Both Mayer and Thalberg had Gibbons design homes for them, evocative of the Art Deco fantasies Gibbons created for them onscreen. Gibbons's own home contained some unique only-in-Hollywood touches as well. With the assistance of MGM architect Douglas Honnold, he installed water sprinklers above his bedroom that sprayed water on his copper roof to imitate rain, a secret trap door in the floor, and light projectors to create moonlight.

On the backlot, the studio's exterior sets were made of assorted materials, all treated and aged to simulate wood or marble or steel or stucco. Plaster of Paris was a popular and inexpensive substitute for just about any architectural detailing, but never lasted long, even on a soundstage, and was nearly useless under the elements on a backlot. Early on, wood was the most popular building supply and could be fashioned to look like anything—at least until World War II when Law L14 restricted how much money ($5,000) and what materials (no new lumber) could be spent on sets, and Gibbons's old habit of saving old flats paid off in unexpected ways.

Studio sculptor Henry Greutert eventually developed an early plastic compound that could simulate just about any solid object that could be produced by man or nature. This mystery substance could be molded into various architectural decorative patterns and fastened onto the sets, or used to sculpt everything from music boxes to forests full of artificial trees. "Greutert's plastic," as it was called, not only made

formally heavy objects mobile, but was also nearly impervious to weather. Celotex, an insulation compound made of sugar cane, was also popular.

Once crafted, walls and entire buildings could be towed onto the backlot and were then fastened to tar-treated telephone polls that had been purchased from the city and secured into the ground. Sets tended to be constructed, whenever possible, facing north-south, so that the best sun would strike the façades later in the day, when they were most likely to be in use. Streets were usually horseshoe or T-shaped to maximize the possible number of usable camera angles. When the sets needed to be modified or redressed over the years, new flats would be brought out and attached to the older ones, eventually creating a sort of archeological history of the productions shot at a specific building. Oft-times in the doorways or window sills, it was possible to see the edges of a half dozen or more walls of artificial brick, stone, or glass peeking through, waiting to be opened up and studied like one would fell a tree for the purpose of counting the rings.

Rooftops (even though optics would often extend a building's actual height), landscaping, and the appropriate sidewalks or street detailing were installed next. Window dressings, parking meters, or hitching posts were added later by the Property Department depending on the location the set would need to play that day. The next day, or even that afternoon, the whole ordeal would be repeated for another project.

In the mid-1950s, the construction, if not the face of the backlots, changed again with the introduction of fiberglass. Although this wondrous composite material had actually been invented in 1938, the Hollywood miracle makers were slow in realizing its potential in mim-

METRO·GOLDWYN·MAYER STUDIOS

LOT 3

LOT 2

LOT 1

icking both architecture and nature. Many sets in the 1950s used fiberglass sparingly, although today, much of the detailing on surviving backlots is created using this substance that, as its name implies, is created using extremely fine glass strands.

Remarkably, these structures would prove to be uncommonly durable. Many of the sets constructed in the '30s were still usable for production in the late '70s when they were dismantled. Surprisingly, despite Los Angeles's reputation for earthquakes, little backlot damage was reported over the years.

An urban legend about backlots, perpetuated on the Universal Studios studio tour, maintains that sets were constructed in varying scales in order to make actors look bigger or smaller as needed, the reasoning being that the camera naturally enlarges what it sees. This is partially true. Doors were often built slightly smaller than full scale. Second or third floors, if they existed, tended to be smaller than first floors, with the scale actually diminishing within the same building as it spiraled up. A modern visit to Disneyland, where a castle can look much taller than it really is, reveals the same trick in effect. Incidentally, Disneyland and Hollywood's backlots share an interesting symbiotic relationship. Among the park's architects were such former MGM art department professionals as Herb Ryman, Ken Anderson, and Mary Blair.

Not everyone appreciated all of this artificial reality, although it's hard to say if Ethel Barrymore was referring to Hollywood or to her backlots when she complained, "This whole place is a set. A glaring, gaudy, nightmarish set built up in the desert!" Similarly, Nicholas Schenck was once heard to wail, "False fronts! False fronts! Nothing behind them. They are like Hollywood people." False fronts they may have been, yet nowhere else in the world was there anything else quite like Gibbons's phantom towns of Lot Two.

Above: **MGM publicists created this geographical abstraction of their major properties in the 1940s, as a way of illustrating to the public their peculiar "city with a fence around it."**
Opposite: **The fully utilized Lot Two in 1949.**

Look at this street, all cardboard, all phony, all done with mirrors.
I like it better than any street in the world.

—*Sunset Blvd.* (1950)

Left: Lot Two in 1936 with Culver Boulevard running parallel along the bottom.
Opposite: The recently completed New York Street set dominates this aerial view of Lot Two (1938).

If the weed-woven, chain-link fence encircling the 37-acre Lot Two, hung with "Keep Out" signs featuring the studio's roaring Leo the Lion in a decidedly unglamorous context, managed to discourage you from entering the lot—as it did most of the curious—an alternate method of seeing the stars existed for a time. Beginning in 1952, you could ascend a 15-story observation tower in the Veteran's Memorial Auditorium, across the street at the corner of Overland Avenue and Culver Boulevard, for 25 cents and view Metro's moviemaking magic.

"There was a short time that the city was trying to make it profitable," recalls Culver City engineer Webb Phelps. "They even had a movie museum (more an exhibit of cinema memorabilia) in the rotunda room of the auditorium." Production was already tailing off even in the early '50s, though, so on many days there was little to see even from this God-like vantage point. The tower tours lasted less than a year, although today the virtually abandoned tower remains a city landmark to Culver City's movie past as the "Heart of Screenland."

LOT TWO

REET

HOUSE

HOT HOUSE

SHED

SHED

GATE

30

27

MONTANA AVENUE

GREEN SPRAY SHED

33 COPPERFIELD COURT

472 467 466 465

463 462 455

35 STREET

36 FILMWAYS BUILDING

750

446

31

34 WIMPOLE STREET

WATERFRONT STREET

37

CARTOON ST.

751

PARK 461

43 PARK AVENUE

BROWNSTONE STREET

419 438

419A

ROAD

DIRT PILE

CHURCH STREET

40

454 414

418 487

9

SLOPE

DN DN

477

42 CULLEM STREET

480 479

444

453 405A 413

417 483

10 734

49

470 434

407

406 WAREHOUSE ALLEY

452 39

402 404B

411

HESTER ST.

8

423 474

404A

410 WC

38

405B

476

408

LAKE

BRIDGE 735

WC

41 FIFTH AVENUE

476

CAFE STORAGE SHED

SCENE DOCK 6

ELEC. TRAN

7

736

737

492 491 490 482 471A 477 495 494 493 424 445 403

PROP STORAGE

74

32

UNPAVED

1 GATE

SMALL TOWN SQ

STOCK STORAGE 3 STOCK STORAGE

TRAIN STORAGE

WAREHOUSE 2

160

M.G.M. LOT 2

MAIN ROAD

2 ROAD

GATE M.G.M. LOT I

STORAGE SPACE

159

6 R.R. STA.

PROP STORAGE TEXTILE

STORAGE SHED

DRAPERY WC

OVERLAND AVENUE

37 36 38 35 39 154

156

ROAD

144 BOAT DOCK 4

STORAGE

ROAD

ROAD

5

155

STOCK STORAGE

STORAGE SHED

NEW ENGLAND STREET

20

32 31 30

PAVED STOCK STORAGE

1647.50

VER BLVD.

N

SCALE 1" = 100'

0 50 100 200 300

Top Left: The Lot Two Entrance Gate in *The Phantom of Hollywood* (1974).
Bottom Left: In 1952, Culver City's Veteran's Memorial Auditorium charged tourists 25 cents to ride the tower's elevator to view backlot filming on Lot Two. The business venture did not last a year (2009).
Right: New York Streets' Eastside district in 1978, with the tower still looming in the background.

1   LOT TWO ENTRANCE GATE

A guard shack with an office to the right of the entrance stood on the southwestern side of Overland Avenue. For years, the intention had been to build a bridge spanning the street to connect Lot One to Lot Two, but this was never done.

Left: A crew loads props and lumber for the off-lot shoot of the 1960 western *Cimarron.*
Below: The Warehouse District is in disarray in *The Phantom of Hollywood* (1974).

Passing the gate and guard shack, a paved road curved south through a hodgepodge of warehouses and sheds. These were mostly used by the Prop Department to store the treasures that the studio had accumulated. Some of these buildings were well used as a set for an episode of *The Outer Limits* called "The Invisibles" in 1964. An annex commissary also stands here.

Two of these warehouses were

2 WAREHOUSE DISTRICT

counted by the studio as soundstages and advertised as such, particularly when MGM began to lease its backlot to outsiders. They are large enough to film in, and may indeed have been used for hastily scheduled interior shooting while backlot casts and crew waited out one of those supposedly rare Southern California downpours. As late as the 1970s, at the very end of the studio's life, this location was still being used to shoot interiors for *Logan's Run* (1976).

Above: **Kirk Douglas finds the perfect staircase among many from the Lot Two Scene Docks in *The Bad and The Beautiful* (1952).**

O pposite these padlocked and non-descript sheds can be glimpsed yet more of the company's seemingly endless supply of scene docks. A peek inside the shadowy, cavernous interiors revealed not only hundreds of stored flats, or interior set walls, but other, sometimes inexplicable items like rocky cliffsides, or submarine fuselages. All of which, however ornate on the camera-out

3 **LOT TWO SCENE DOCKS**

side, invariably had ratty plywood backs. Part of this district can be seen as an on-camera set in *The Bad and the Beautiful* (1952) and *The Loved One* (1965).

Stored nearby was the studio's impressive inventory of staircases, several facing Culver Boulevard, providing an odd view of the studio to passing motorists.

Above: The Ocean Liner façade was part of the New York Dock set.

Opposite this building sat an ocean liner that never saw port. The side facing Culver Boulevard was just an empty shell, impossible to discern from the street as anything other than a jumble of plywood 2 × 4s, all jutting rafters and eccentric construction. But from inside the lot, it looked like a midsection for the RMS *Lusitania* or the RMS *Titanic* (both of

4 NEW YORK DOCK AND OCEAN LINER

which it had played). Its massive plywood face included a dozen portholes and its hundreds of rivets were painted with "rust" as a perceived result of the salt air. Full-size metal funnels loomed up from the partial deck. Metal gangplanks reached over a cement pool to a railroad warehouse that doubled as a pier.

Top Left: Louis Calhern & Betty Hutton walk the gangplank of the Ocean Liner façade in *Annie Get Your Gun* (1950).
Top Right: A well staged publicity photo of Dawn Addams preparing to board the Ocean Liner (1952).
Bottom Left: The Ocean Liner, after years of neglect and vandalism, seen in *The Phantom of Hollywood* (1974).
Opposite: Groucho Marx offers brother Harpo Marx a much-needed helping hand as the two hang from the side of the Ocean Liner in *A Night at the Opera* (1935).

The large sheds opposite the ship set, usually equipped with gangplanks so as to portray docking platforms, were cavernous enough to double as impromptu soundstages inside. *The Naked Spur* (1953) used this area as the inside of a cave and *The Long, Long Trailer* (1953) shot interiors of the title vehicle here. *The White Cliffs of Dover* (1944) and *The Tall Target* (1951) even used the outside of these warehouses, which paralleled the studio railroad lines, as a train shed/station set.

A study in contrasts: Mickey Rooney was as lonely (disembarking as Lorenz Hart in *Words and Music* [1948]) as Mario Lanza was triumphant (arriving in New York in a crowd for his Metropolitan debut as Enrico Caruso in *The Great Caruso* [1951]). The effervescent Jane Powell arrived here twice, first in *Three Daring Daughters* (1948) and again later that same year when the ship played the title role in her musical *Luxury Liner*. The elephants from *Billy Rose's Jumbo* (1962) were

housed here and nearly wrecked the place.

The titles are legion. At least until *Double Trouble* (1967) with Elvis Presley, which was in fact one of the last verifiable feature titles for this set, making it the first location stricken with the alleged "Elvis Presley curse"—so named because virtually *every* set at the studio featured a Presley vehicle as its last, or virtually its last, screen credit—al-though this particular set would cameo several times on television.

By the time producer George M. Lehr scouted the set for television's *Combat!* (1962–1967), however, there apparently was not much left to shoot. "The big ship dock was pretty ratty," he recalled. "We couldn't use it."

The studio road termi-
nated in a clump of
trees. Behind it was New
England Street—one of the most famous and recognizable film sets
in the world. The houses, the church, the small businesses—including
a folksy malt shop exterior, a filling station, and winding tree-lined
square—were photographed so much that they resembled a snapshot
in a shared family album.

When *Ah, Wilderness!* went into production in 1935 (starring
Lionel Barrymore, Spring Byington, and a young star named Mickey
Rooney), director Clarence Brown suggested that Gibbons's wizards
construct a street of homes based on his own home town of Clinton,
Massachusetts. This was done, although some of the houses were actually redressed sets from earlier films like *Polly of the Circus* (1932) and
David Copperfield (1935). J. J. Cohn recalled, "When we made *David
Copperfield*, we built a bit of old England down near the beach. When it
was over, we took those build-
ings and brought them back to
the lot and that—with some
changes—became our New England Street, the Andy Hardy town."

"Creating this New England utopia was all part of L. B. Mayer's master plan to reinvent America," said Mickey Rooney. "In most of
his movies that came under his control, Mr. Mayer knew that he was
'confecting, not reflecting' America. . . . He wanted values to be instilled
in the country and knew how influential films could be. . . . The picture
helped Mr. Mayer cast a spell on America, on its values and attitudes
and images."

To reap the profits of another *Ah, Wilderness!*-type hit, Sam
Marx purchased a New York play called *Skidding* for $5,000. Re-imag-
ining the world of Eugene O'Neill, screenwriters Frances Goodrich and
Albert Hackett developed *A Family Affair* (1937), an unabashedly sentimental family comedy for the studio's pint-sized star, Mickey Rooney.

MAR 2

Top: A panoramic view of Andy Hardy/New England Street (1950).
Bottom Left: The Andy Hardy/New England Street houses were created as sets and contained no interiors (1965).
Bottom Right: With Andy Hardy/New England Street in the background, the Transportation Department loads a wagon used for the production of *Cimarron* (1960).

Left: **Andy Hardy/New England Street in 1944, with the steeple removed from the Chapel at the end of the street.**
Right: **The Chapel on the east corner of Andy Hardy/New England Street in 1965 with its steeple restored.**
Opposite: **The house on the left was the Andy Hardy home from 1936 to 1958 (1944).**

Rooney was cast to type as an excitable, good-hearted, girl-chasing teenager named Andy Hardy. After this little, decidedly un-ambitious picture grossed more than half a million dollars, Mayer commissioned a second film, *You're Only Young Once*, which was released in 1937.

After minor tweaking on the studio's part (for instance, the studio's venerable star, Lewis Stone, replaced Lionel Barrymore as Andy's wise father, Judge Hardy), the franchise was on its way. In all, 17 Andy Hardy films would be made at Metro Goldwyn Mayer. In 1942, the Academy of Motion Picture Arts and Sciences recognized the series's extraordinarily positive influence by awarding it a special Oscar statue for "its achievement in representing the American way of life."

The familiar patterns of the Hardy family lives became so ingrained into the American psyche that we've never really shaken them off, despite of the fact that generations have grown up since who have never actually seen a picture in the series. The prototype had been created, and we know the Hardy family today by innumerable television spin-offs like *Father Knows Best* (1954–1960), *Leave It to Beaver* (1957–1963), *The Partridge Family* (1970–1973), *The Brady Bunch* (1969–1974), *Eight Is Enough* (1977–1981), and *7th Heaven* (1996–2007).

"The Andy Hardy movies didn't tell it 'like it is,'" said Mickey Rooney. "They told it the way we'd like it to be, describing an ideal that needs constant reinvention. That is why we will always need Hollywood, the Hollywood that keeps manufacturing dreams."

"There were 24 Andy Hardy movies," exaggerates Howard Strickling. "I call them the forerunners of *Peyton Place*." Thus, New England Street became synonymous, indeed inseparable, from Andy Hardy's hometown of Carvel, population 25,000.

The street returned to its *Ah, Wilderness!* roots in 1946 when producer Arthur Freed remade the film as a musical called *Summer Holiday* (1948), starring (again) Mickey Rooney.

Of course, the studio did cast this street in other films, but filmmakers were forced to devise clever ways to disguise one of America's—indeed, the world's—most famous streets. Mickey Rooney found

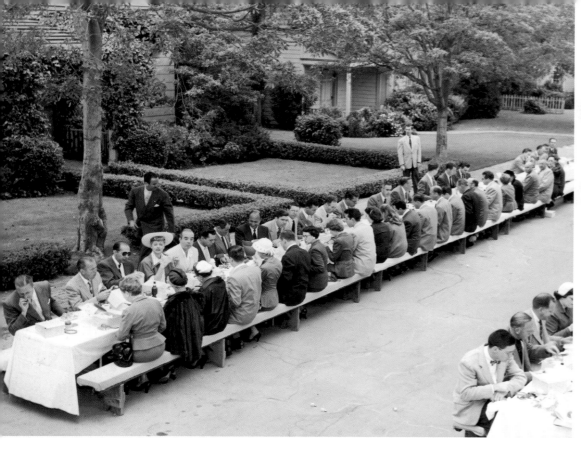

Left: Lucille Ball, Vincente Minnelli, and Desi Arnaz share a publicity lunch for *The Long, Long Trailer* (1954).
Right: Bobby Van hops all over Andy Hardy/New England Street in *Small Town Girl* (1953).

time between Hardy pictures to shoot scenes here for *Babes in Arms* (1939) and *Strike Up the Band* (1940). In both, he appeared opposite Judy Garland, who also played neighbor Betsy Booth in the Hardy pictures, and whose house stands to the right of the Hardy homestead. Today, these "let's put on a show!" musicals appear as slightly more lavish Andy Hardy adventures, with their use of interchangeable Hardy attitudes, sets, and stars.

Judy Garland was not the only one reared to stardom by the Hardy family. Throughout the 1930s and 1940s, Andy Hardy's up-and-coming girlfriends included Lana Turner, Kathryn Grayson, Esther Williams, and Donna Reed. Suffering through Andy's flings with these temporary residents of Carvel was longtime girlfriend Polly Benedict, played by Ann Rutherford, who reflected years after the fact that, "I knew Andy Hardy's street better than my own, right down to

the doorknobs of 'my'—Polly's—house. It was a beautiful street."

Almost as common a tenant on this street as the Hardy family was Lew Ayres, in an almost parallel series, as the earnest, but chronically unlucky Dr. Kildare. Andy Hardy/New England Street usually played the good doctor's idyllic hometown, where his folksy general practitioner father (Samuel S. Hinds) dispensed medicine and cracker-barrel wisdom that would have made Judge Hardy proud.

Similarly, the cast and crew of the popular, urbane *Thin Man* series made a stop on the set for *The Thin Man Goes Home* (1945) when William Powell's Nick Charles character visited his inexplicably rural parents in folksy "Sycamore Springs."

The street's resume continued to rack up titles throughout the 1950s. In 1950, Elizabeth Taylor was memorably married off in the church at the end of the street in *Father of the Bride*, while just around

Left: A parade along Andy Hardy/New England Street with "local" children supporting the war effort by selling Defense Saving Stamps.
Right: "Andy Hardy" made his last recorded visit to "Carvel" in 1974 for *That's Entertainment!* The curved shed behind Mickey Rooney is part of the nearby New York Dock set.

the block, at the corner of "Sunset and Camden," Debbie Reynolds dropped Gene Kelly off in Beverly Hills for *Singin' in the Rain* (1952). The roadster she drives is, in fact, Andy's first car from *Love Finds Andy Hardy* (1938). Contract dancer Bobby Van showed off the street from end to end in his memorable "Take Me to Broadway" number for *Small Town Girl* (1953). In that picture, Jane Powell was the girl and Andy Hardy/New England Street played the small town.

In 1957, rock and roll echoed from the malt shop jukebox out into the streets for the first time as Elvis Presley made his MGM debut here in *Jailhouse Rock*. The last Andy Hardy picture *Andy Hardy Comes Home* (1958) was made here the following year and made little money. Audiences found it too old-fashioned in an era and a place that had been introduced to teenage angst. Those audiences, now joined by their children and grandchildren, were more interested in the shady dealings

of Frank Sinatra and Shirley MacLaine in *Some Came Running* (1958). Ironically, Frank lived in the house next door to the Hardys in that one.

A 1975 lot fire (one of two that year) destroyed some of the street, including the church. Andy and Polly's house survived the blaze, but now their days appeared numbered.

Yet when Universal rented the space for *Sgt. Pepper's Lonely Hearts Club Band* (1978), the set came gloriously back to life with the aid of that studio's staff of carpenters and painters. "It was so beautiful," preservationist Robert Nudelman recalled. "I expected Mickey Rooney and Judy Garland to come out and greet Peter Frampton and the Gibb brothers while they filmed there. That proved that the sets could yet be saved and still held value as rentals. Commercials were always being shot there—particularly because the lot held no union restrictions. But I could never convince the studio of this. . . ."

Top Left: The "Bridgewood" Small Town Railroad Depot in *Singin' in the Rain* (1952).
Bottom Left: The "Baltimore" Small Town Railroad Depot in *The Tall Target* (1951).
Right: Small Town Railroad Depot seen in *Meet Me in St Louis* (1944).
Opposite: The Small Town Railroad Depot hosts a typical small town station greeting in *Strike up the Band* (1940), with (left to right): Judy Garland, Milton Kibbee, Virginia Brissac, Mickey Rooney, George Lessey, June Preisser, and Ann Shoemaker.

6 SMALL TOWN RAILROAD DEPOT

At the end of the street, behind the houses, stood a railroad terminal, one of at least three located on Lot Two during various eras. This quaint-looking building sat between Andy Hardy/New England Street and the interchangeable Small Town Square, which circles north. It looked exactly like a thousand real-life railroad stations from which a thousand real-life Andy Hardys or Dr. Kildares left home to seek their fortunes in the big city. Besides the Hardy and Kildare series (and the *Maisie* series for that matter), look for it as Port Huron in Mickey Rooney's *Young Tom Edison* (1940), as well as in *Blossoms in the Dust* (1941), *For Me and My Gal* (1942), and *Girl Crazy* (1943). In *Singin' in the Rain*, it can be seen in the opening montage narrated, with tongue-firmly-in-cheek, by Gene Kelly. This was also the depot where a little Catholic orphan (Donna Corcoran) was dropped off, inflaming the ire of the little town of Scourie when she was adopted by a Protestant couple played by Greer Garson and Walter Pidgeon in *Scandal at Scourie* (1953).

The Trouble With Girls (1969) starring Elvis Presley was the symbolic end of the tracks for this set.

Left: Small Town Square in *Night Must Fall* (1937), starring Robert Montgomery (with bike).
Right: Small Town Square in its inaugural picture *Fury* (1936).
Opposite: Small Town Square dressed for *The Trouble with Girls* (1969).

7   SMALL TOWN SQUARE

The railroad depot faced Town Square proper, which of course was largely yet another facet of that well-known town of Carvel. This square, however, has a parallel (if slightly different) history. It originated in 1936 as part of the set for Fritz Lang's *Fury*, depicting a much more cynical—and violent—view of small-town life. Some of the façades for this set were eventually built right up against the back of Andy Hardy's street. The Comber Home, which was to the immediate left of the venerable Hardy House, turned out to have a bank where its backyard should be. The Hardy home itself was actually made up of storefronts on its northern side, which faces the square. Were you to enter the front door of either house or business, you would find yourself trapped in a jigsaw jumble of false fronts and plywood walls, designed to block one side of the house from the view of the other.

Yet the set was remarkably versatile. It appeared as an 18th century village in *Northwest Passage* (1940); a Civil War-era town in *A Southern Yankee* (1948) and *Raintree County* (1957); a 1920s hangout for college kids in *Good News* (1947); *Two Loves* (1961) used it as New Zealand; it briefly played sedate 1940s Philadelphia for *The Philadelphia Story* (1940); and *High Barbaree* (1947) used the set for flashback scenes nostalgically remembered by soldier Van Johnson, who spent most of the film adrift in the South Pacific. His memories of the location aptly summed up the idealized, unreality of the location.

This area continued to be used through the 1960s. The set was dressed in "snow," which was actually bleached cornflakes, for *Period of*

Adjustment (1962). The same year, for the Elvis Presley vehicle *Follow That Dream*, it played sunny Florida and hosted some engaging musical numbers that must have reminded the thinning ranks of old-time employees of bygone days. Later films included soap operas like *Joy in the Morning* (1965) and exploitation fare like *Hot Rods to Hell* (1967) and *They Only Kill Their Masters* (1972).

Late in the set's long lifetime, MGM took to claiming (wrongly, as it turned out) that this street marked the first MGM appearance of Clark Gable, playing a milkman in *The Easiest Way* (1931)—actually, Gable played a laundryman in that film. But this story is so famous that even Jackie Gleason mentioned it in an episode of *The Honeymooners*—although, perhaps intentionally, he also got Gable's occupation wrong, claiming that the future superstar had played a bus driver.

Television offered a sort of 11th hour reprieve for the set in its sunset years. It was perfectly cast in *Twilight Zone* episodes like "Nick of Time" (1960), featuring William Shatner, and "Stopover in a Quiet Town" (1964), penned by Earl Hamner Jr. The latter's plot concerns a bickering couple who discover they have been kidnapped into an alien child's playset.

"I was always very impressed by the backlot," Hamner explained. "Everything was made of papier mâché and was a false front. It suddenly came to me: What if someone woke in this surrounding and there was nothing but false labels on everything, and if you dropped a lighted match on the grass it would catch fire, and if you got on a train, it would come all the way around to where it started from?"

Actor Rod Taylor once remarked that the street made a different, but similarly eerie impression on him, "It was unreal how large the backlots were. I couldn't get over the miles of picket fences. . . ."

Top: A panoramic view of the Small Town Square in 1960. From left to right: the business district, the courthouse, and the railroad station. Waterloo Bridge can be seen in the background to the right.
Inset: The business district of the Small Town Square hosted a display of military vehicles during the MGM auction in 1970.
Opposite Top Left: Small Town Square is given a decidedly French ambiance in *Gigi* (1958). Louis Jourdan and Maurice Chevalier are waiting in the carriage.
Opposite Bottom Left: Leaving the set of *The Three Musketeers* (1948), Lana Turner sashays past the northern tip of Small Town Square.
Opposite Top Right: Elvis bids a fond farewell at the Small Town Railroad Station in *The Trouble with Girls* (1969).
Opposite Bottom Right: Small Town Square being prepped, supposedly for the last time, in *They Only Kill Their Masters* (1972).

Above: The Cemetery set in *Times Square Lady* (1935) . . .
Below: . . . and more than 40 years later in *Logan's Run* (1976).

8 CEMETERY

Nearby, and up a very familiar and well-traveled road could be found one of at least two cemeteries that were more-or-less permanent fixtures. This set usually portrayed a pleasant small-town graveyard, photographed more often to evoke Veterans Day than Halloween. The gravestones, unlike those found at the real thing, were largely portable and interchangeable.

Above: Johnny Weissmuller (center) seems nonchalant as an "ape" takes off his head to cool down between scenes for *Tarzan and His Mate* (1934).

utting north, a visitor would arrive at the edge of a vast-seeming lake. A heavy stone bridge looms ahead that, truth be told, would look a little odd in person, as anyone wishing to cross the lake could merely walk a few feet and circle around the shore, rendering the existence of the bridge superfluous. Of course, the relative nearness of the shore wouldn't be visible onscreen. Likewise, if one were to walk up to the bridge and look at the walkway spanning the water, the bare wooden railroad ties that hold her in place would be visible on the bridge floor—but again, not to the camera. A backlot is architecture created for selected and two-dimensional vantage points. Real people,

9	**LOT TWO (TARZAN) LAKE AND LOT TWO JUNGLE**
10	**WATERLOO BRIDGE**

with their ever-changing points of reference and perspective, are not intended to be part of the equation.

Lot Two's Tarzan Lake, so named because of the MGM series that was filmed here, was constructed of poured concrete. At its deepest, it contained only about four feet of water. A bank of trees, both natural eucalyptus and imported jungle foliage (supplemented as needed by their artificial cousins), lined the northeast bank. The other exposed areas of shoreline included beaches with imported sand, docks, and grassy waterfront lawns that could be rolled up and removed as needed. To one side, often obscured by foliage, stood an odd, almost other-

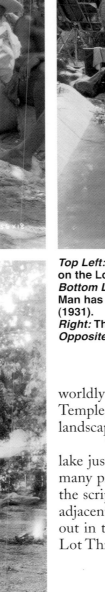

Top Left: The cast from *Tarzan the Ape Man* (1931) enjoys a much needed break on the Lot Two Lake and Jungle set.
Bottom Left: A ghostly visit from Tarzan to the Lake and Jungle set. The Ape Man has been superimposed onto the shot due to an error made in the lab (1931).
Right: The Lake and Jungle set provide a tropical setting (1933).
Opposite: The Rock Temple façade on the shore of the Lot Two Lake (1965).

worldly grouping of stacked, artificial boulders known as the Rock Temple, which was rarely visible onscreen, but the construction and landscaping of it must have been expensive.

The lake was a solution to the problem of the original Lot One lake just not being big enough to adequately service the needs of the many productions that needed a body of water—either as required by the script, or as a pictorial backdrop for whatever was going on in the adjacent sets. The set's use as a jungle or tropical location was phased out in the late 1930s by the creation of a similar, even bigger lake on Lot Three.

The bridge, one of two on the lake, was sometimes referred to

Left: Jane Powell cools her feet in front of the Waterloo Bridge (1947).
Right: The lawns in front of the Waterloo Bridge are a tip-off as to how small the "lake" actually was (1965).
Opposite Top Left: Waterloo Bridge combined with an optical matte painting for *The Three Musketeers* (1948).
Opposite Top Right: Eva Marie Saint and James Garner enjoy a picnic near the Waterloo Bridge in *36 Hours* (1965).
Opposite Bottom Left: Bing Crosby reminisces about the Lot Two backlot while standing in front of the Waterloo Bridge in *That's Entertainment!* (1974).
Opposite Bottom Right: Joan Fontaine and Charles Drake enjoy a romantic moment in front of the Waterloo Bridge in *Until They Sail* (1957).

as the Waterloo Bridge—which, regardless of what the old-timers in the '60s were telling their friends, was not the setting for that memorable picture of the same name—and was part of a Scottish village in *Hills of Home* (1948) and *Challenge to Lassie* (1949). It was English for Jane Powell and Peter Lawford in *Royal Wedding* (1951), part of New Zealand for *Until They Sail* (1957), French in *Young and Pretty* (1951), and Transylvanian for *Young Frankenstein* (1974). It was much-captured by the Germans, or the Allies, depending on which episode of the first four seasons of the *Combat!* (1962–1967) TV series a viewer happened to tune into.

Romance bloomed along the lakeshore for decades. In 1931, Norma Shearer and Chester Morris played their opening love scene here in *The Divorcee* (1930). In *Cass Timberlane* (1947), Lana Turner and Spencer Tracy fell in love here during a picnic. Peter Lawford

and June Allyson cavorted along the lake bank in the 1949 remake of *Little Women*.

Moving forward into the future, this is perhaps a good time to note the bridge's last appearances in a feature film, as well. In 1974, Bing Crosby stood here to eulogize the movie musical on camera for the documentary *That's Entertainment!* (1974). The film was a eulogy for the backlot as well, delivered before it was even gone.

"It seems to me that the backlot reflects the personality and character of its studio and this was the biggest and, I think, perhaps the best backlot in all of Hollywood," Crosby said in his patented, easygoing style. "Course the old backlot looks a little shabby right now, sort of scruffy. Kind of an illusion on an illusion. But that's because most Hollywood filmmakers, they don't use backlots anymore. They prefer the real thing."

Left: The Three Musketeers Court (1951).
Right: Three Musketeers Court is combined with an optical matte painting for *The Three Musketeers* (1948).

Q uality Street, French Court-yard, Three Musketeers Court, and Copperfield Street have the oldest and most convoluted and intertwined history of any set on Lot Two. Quality Street was in fact the first major street built on Lot Two during the studio's expansion in 1927. The set (which included remnants of Lot One's French District was built over a mound of debris left over from the special-effects-laden *The Big Parade* (1925). Trees and grass were planted, and the area had to be carefully landscaped; grassy berms were built and the boulevards were paved with real cobblestones.

The first picture to use this area was aptly named *Quality Street*

11	**FRENCH COURTYARD**
12	**THREE MUSKETEERS COURT**
13	**COPPERFIELD STREET**
14	**QUALITY STREET**

(1927), starring Marion Davies. The cost of constructing this charming, evocative outdoor setting was probably absorbed by Cosmopolitan Pictures, the production company financed and run by Davies's famous lover, newspaper tycoon William Randolph Hearst.

Quality Street (a.k.a. Green Dolphin Street, after a much later project) was vaguely British, but segued so well into the French Courtyard that the two districts could be used interchangeably. The northern end of this street sloped up a hill and terminated at a very large, four-sided "house," apparently built for the Austrian-set Luise Rainer film *Escapade* (1935). The house was typecast as Viennese from then on, representing the same general location in *The Emperor's Candlesticks*

Left: Three Musketeers Court in *Scaramouche* (1952) starring Janet Leigh, Nina Foch, and Mel Ferrer.
Right: Copperfield Street as it appeared onscreen for the first time in *David Copperfield* (1935).

(1937), *The Great Waltz* (1938), and *Bitter Sweet* (1940). Years later in 1954, it was seen as Elizabeth Taylor's mansion in *The Last Time I Saw Paris.* The house faces a district sometimes identified as Christina Court, probably an echo of the Garbo classic *Queen Christina* (1933).

The producers of *A Tale of Two Cities* (1935) and *Marie Antoinette* (1938) used the neighboring French Courtyard set—a very Gallic-looking row of buildings complete with courtyard, ornate shops, and alleys—as Paris. The entire district was silently guarded by Hotel Tréville, a towered, castle-like fortress still hauntingly recognizable to insomniacs addicted to the late show.

Nearby was another set of façades, representing real estate found on the other side of the English Channel. Dating from the 1935 Dickens adaptation of *David Copperfield*, and rightfully called Copperfield Street, the set shared an origin and a similar name, if not a

geographic location, with Copperfield Court, which was constructed at the same time on the other side of the lot, acres away.

Years later, in 1948, Three Musketeers Court would be added to the already-gigantic complex for that picture, which would use it well as a setting for the swashbuckling antics of Gene Kelly. The set would be largely rebuilt in 1962 for *The Wonderful World of the Brothers Grimm.* Although no one knew it at the time, Three Musketeers Court would be the last major permanent standing set constructed anywhere on the backlot.

Not surprisingly, an Elvis Presley vehicle, *Double Trouble* (1967), would be one of the last MGM pictures shot on any of these districts, and by that time, the street was really showing its age. (Although black-and-white cinematography, horror-movie fog, and Marty Feldman's humped-back managed to conceal these flaws pretty well as

Left: A section of Quality Street is dressed for *The Secret of Madame Blanche* (1933).
Top Right: Thanks to neglect, vandals, and the *Combat!* television series, the south side of the French Courtyard was in shambles in the early 1970s when historian Julie Lugo Cerra took this badly damaged, yet somehow evocative snapshot.
Bottom Right: Quality Street in *An American in Paris* (1951) starring Gene Kelly.
Opposite: The cast and crew of *The Three Musketeers* (1948) takes a break while filming on Quality Street.

late as 1974 in Mel Brooks's *Young Frankenstein*. "MGM had one of the greatest backlots of all time. They had like four giant backlots in which they built everything," Brooks remembered.

Quality Street's actual destruction in 1978 was filmed as part of a mock battle scene with a WWI tank for the Fox picture *The Stunt Man* (1980). Director Richard Rush said that the set was "scheduled to be torn down and they said we could tear it down with the tank without replacing it—which was a real boon in our picture."

Left: Railroad Terminal #2 dressed for the Norma Shearer vehicle *Smilin' Through* (1932).
Right: The same set, this time dusted with "snow," for *Anna Karenina* (1935).

T he southernmost tip of Quality Street's enormous and complicated tangle of sets was actually designed to block our view—or, more accurately, the camera's view of a second railroad depot, built along the same ribbon of track in Small Town Square. Many early 1930s pictures completed before the construction of the depot, like *Smilin' Through* (1932) and *Sequoia* (1934), used this second depot that was actually built first—and which eventually took its name from employees' verbal reference to another, "second choice" railroad station. This depot is not

15 **RAILROAD TERMINAL #2**
16 **GRAND CENTRAL STATION**

too different from its younger sister and can usually be picked out onscreen by a smaller, even more rural look that distinguishes this Railroad Terminal #2 from its near twin up the tracks. This depot also doubled as a working loading dock for removing heavy sets and camera equipment transported aboard the real trains. A visitor to Railroad Terminal #2 probably could hardly help but remember its most memorable onscreen appearance, which occurred when Fredric March approached Greta Garbo while she stood alone in the snow in *Anna Karenina* (1935), staring at her with undis-

Above: The soon-to-be-demolished Western Street in *The Champ* (1931).

guised longing, and whispered, "I'll never forget *anything* of you."

The open space between the two stations was used for projects that needed an open countryside and the nearby railroad tracks. The first Western Street was located here, used for such early studio Westerns as *Billy the Kid* (1930) and Cecil B. DeMille's sound remake of *The Squaw Man* in 1931. The façades were redressed into modern storefronts for *A Free Soul* (1931), *The Champ* (1931), *Prosperity* (1932), *What! No Beer?* (1933), *Tugboat Annie* (1933), *Operator 13* (1934), and *Laughing Boy* (1934). Some of the buildings were later incorporated into parts of Andy Hardy/New England Street and Small Town

Square. By the 1960s, the area was empty except for some ruins.

This railroad track terminated in a third, Grand Central Station-inspired railroad depot, used for a hundred teary, sentimental scenes. Built in 1933 and eventually including both terminal and outdoor track sections, it was as the St. Petersburg Train Station (its official name, although the Grand Central moniker is the one that sticks) that Greta Garbo stepped onto the tracks and perished as *Anna Karenina* (1935). (Yet Garbo was back as *Ninotchka* in 1939. Only in the movies.)

For the melodramatic classic that earned her a Best Actress Oscar, *Gaslight* (1944), Ingrid Bergman was luckier in love than Gar-

Top: Grand Central Station in
Anna Karenina (1935).
Bottom Left: Railroad Station
#2 is on the left; on the right is
an entrance to nearby Quality
Street (1950).
Bottom Center: Grand Central
Station in 1935.
Bottom Right: An early version
of the Grand Central Station set
in 1933.

Left: Greer Garson and Ronald Coleman say good-bye on the Grand Central Station set in *Random Harvest* (1942).
Right: The working interior of Grand Central Station was used in *North by Northwest* (1959).
Below: The ruins of Grand Central Station serve as a backdrop for this publicity still of Fred Astaire and Gene Kelly in *That's Entertainment!* (1974).

bo, but remembered shooting a kissing scene here with leading man Charles Boyer while the diminutive Frenchman was "perched up on a ridiculous little box since I was quite a few inches taller than he."

In the 1940s, this place was also identifiable in two weepy Margaret O'Brien wartime classics, *Journey for Margaret* (1942) and *Music for Millions* (1944). Her search for costar June Allyson in *Millions* offers movie fans a great look at the expansive set.

In the station's last decades, it hosted Fred Astaire's memorable "By Myself" number in *The Band Wagon* (1953); Cary Grant and Eva Marie Saint made a hurried stop here while racing *North by Northwest* (1959); Marilyn Monroe received a wolf-whistle from a steam locomotive here in United Artists' *Some Like it Hot* (1959); and Paul Newman hopped a train here in *The Outrage* (1964).

Fred Astaire returned one last time for *That's Entertainment!* in 1974, but in that picture, the set was so ramshackle that the adjacent Chinese Street could be glimpsed through the holes in the walls.

The very last project the set hosted was also one of the first of an emerging and very influential new hybrid of cinema and music (and marketing) that would dominate popular taste in coming decades. In 1977, the phenomenally successful Australian musical group the Bee Gees, took an afternoon off while filming *Sgt. Pepper's Lonely Hearts Club Band* on nearby Small Town Square to shoot a "music video" (although the name had not yet actually been coined), primarily on the Grand Central Station set. The number they were amateurishly filmed lip-syncing to that day—using the same technology Fred Astaire had used much better, much earlier, and on the same spot—would become one of the biggest hits of the 1970s when featured in Paramount's *Saturday Night Fever*; it was called "Stayin' Alive."

The title, in this case, was ironic.

Left: Chinese Street in *Thirty Seconds Over Tokyo* (1944).
Right: Chinese Street dressed for *Dragon Seed* (1944).
Opposite: Chinese Street was flooded with water for a scene in *Green Dolphin Street* (1947).

17 CHINESE STREET

Chinese Street—four acres of pagodas and statuary, gates and palaces, and even a section of the Great Wall of China—lay just south and slightly west of Copperfield Street. Gibbons and associate art directors Harry Oliver, Buddy Gillespie, and Edwin B. Willis designed the set for Thalberg's *The Good Earth* in 1937, although parts of it seemed to have existed around the lot before that. For that movie's biggest scenes, up to 600 extras crammed onto the set's streets.

The set was seldom used after *Earth* until World War II, and a rebirth of interest in our Chinese allies. *They Met in Bombay* (1941) brought Clark Gable and Rosalind Russell here. *Dragon Seed* (1944) featured Katharine Hepburn as the screen's most unlikely Chinese woman, and *Thirty Seconds over Tokyo* (also 1944) cast the area as WWII China. In a change of pace, the versatile boulevard played Italy in *Jupiter's Darling* and ancient Egypt for *The Prodigal* in the same year—1955.

Universal's *Flower Drum Song* (1961) brought the set full circle, playing (once again) China. *The Hook* (1963) cast the area as Korea. Beginning in the 1960s, this set, like so many others on the MGM backlot, was often used for exotic locations in television shows like *The Man from U.N.C.L.E.* (1964–1968).

Left: Castle Finckenstein (left) and Chinese Street (right) as they looked in *They Met in Bombay* (1941).
Right: A construction photo of Joppa Square from *The Prodigal* (1955).
Opposite Top: A newly remodeled Joppa Square for *The Prodigal* (1955).
Opposite Bottom: A scene from the film *Plymouth Adventure* (1952). Van Johnson is visible to the right of one of Culver City's most peculiar architectural oddities.

18 | JOPPA SQUARE AND CASTLE FINCKENSTEIN

The neighboring, ancient-looking relic known as Joppa Square is always identified as being built for the 1925 silent *Ben-Hur*. Yet mysteriously, the spectacular sequences from that film involving the square and gates are now known to actually be among the few shot in Italy visible in the finished film. However, it's likely that *something* from *Ben-Hur* was shot on sets built on Lot One and later repositioned here. Actually, the set might have dated back even farther—to the Lot One castle set discussed earlier. The walls here were reluctant indeed to give up their secrets.

The towering side of the edifice, which resembled a medieval castle, was, of course, only a front. This castle's turrets and walls, its stone and mortar, its towers and spires, were all constructed on top of a wooden skeleton of yellow 2 × 4s and plywood. The back side—and it only had one where it needed to face the set behind it—revealed this particular castle as a warrior's lair that could never endure a real war. Grigori Potemkin, the Russian speculator who built artificial castles and villages to impress Catherine the Great, would certainly have understood the subterfuge.

According to studio publicity, this edifice was "Castle Finck-

enstein, in Prussia" in the film *Conquest* (1937), although the castle onscreen was mostly a matte painting. In 1948, it was used as the home of the musketeers in *The Three Musketeer*s, and in 1952, it was seen in *Scaramouche* and *Prisoner of Zenda*. In 1955, an expensive rebuild of the set and the surrounding grounds resulted in a convincing replica of ancient Damascus for *The Prodigal*. What was still left in 1974 toppled spectacularly for *The Phantom of Hollywood*, its humiliating fall at the blades of a tractor symbolizing the end of the whole studio era. The set took all her secrets with her.

Research has taught us that a combination "New Orleans–Mexican border town" was also built in this area. We know that *Pursuit, Rendezvous, Naughty Marietta* (all 1935), and *Speed* (1936) were filmed here. Other titles are lost in the battlements of Hollywood history.

Above: Verona Square under construction for *Romeo and Juliet* (1936).

In 1936, Thalberg asked Cedric Gibbons to build Verona here for *Romeo and Juliet*. It was an assignment Gibbons was uniquely qualified for, having designed a previous three-dimensional Verona set for Goldwyn's 1921 production of *Doubling for Romeo*. "Cedric Gibbons painstakingly created a replica of the square in Verona, assisted by brilliant Oliver Messel, who came from England to work on it," recalled Samuel Marx. "Thalberg was often on the set, an unusual action, but indicative of how much the picture meant to him. He saw it as a monu-

ment to his career."

Having Thalberg make a rare appearance on your set was unsettling, as actress Maureen O'Sullivan recalled. "I think he was rather frightening. He didn't talk much, and when he spoke it had meaning. I found him intimidating. He was a little awe-inspiring. . . . He was a remote figure, and when he came on a set, there was really silence."

The Verona Square section shared many titles with Spanish Street. The set was designed to be completely four-sided, like a true

courtyard, which would have made camera placement difficult had the set not been so large. It featured a truly dazzling array of fountains, statuary, churches, and colonnades. Every imaginable detail, from the cobblestone streets and the icon niches to the mosaics on the stucco walls, contributed to the conviction that this really was just what it was built to be. "The workmanship was phenomenal. The detail was just incredible," Todd Fisher, who spent his childhood on the lot, remembered.

An odd press release the studio would issue in 1972, just as the caterpillar tractors were fueling up to tear the set down, stated that at one time, "a few sentimentalists prayed that the set could be preserved as a monument to the care exerted by movie technicians."

Despite the prayers of those aforementioned sentimentalists, the set's very last appearance would be in the 1974 TV movie *The Phantom of Hollywood*, where the venerable old courtyard finally played itself: a crumbling, haunted old movie set slated for demolition, and vandalized by local kids. How far it had come from the glorious silvery images of Thalberg's favorite film.

Top Row: The Production department used to systematically photograph the backlot to make identification and utilization of the sets easier, in this case Verona Square.
Bottom Right: A massive wall (seen in the background) was built to seal off Verona Square from Spanish Street to create the courtyard used in the 1956 film *Diane*.

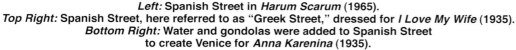

Left: Spanish Street in *Harum Scarum* (1965).
Top Right: Spanish Street, here referred to as "Greek Street," dressed for *I Love My Wife* (1935).
Bottom Right: Water and gondolas were added to Spanish Street
to create Venice for *Anna Karenina* (1935).

20 SPANISH STREET

Nearby beckoned the Moorish spires of Spanish Street, which actually curved in a gigantic horseshoe shape to become Verona Square/Verona Hall on its southwestern bank. Spanish Street was, at various times over the years, also called Greek Street, New Orleans Street, and Cuban Street. It was built in 1931 and consisted of two blocks of archways, open stairways, colonnades, and balconies built along a wide cobblestone street. The name of the street seems to have come from an Eddie Cantor vehicle, *The Kid from Spain* (1932). Al-

though, the stucco-covered façades also played Cuba in *The Cuban Love Song* (1931) and Greece in Garbo's *As You Desire Me* (1932).

In the mid-thirties, the street was flooded and used as Venice, complete with floating gondolas, in both *Student Tour* (1934) and *Anna Karenina* (1935). In the 1950s, it doubled for Spanish California in *Callaway Went Thataway* (1951) and was seen to good advantage in a colorful 1954 *Student Prince* remake. In 1965, Elvis showed up for *Harum Scarum*.

Above: English Home dressed for *Arsène Lupin (*1932*)*.

Left: The grand façade of the English Home in 1937.
Right: Ronald Colman and Susan Peters rehearse a scene from *Random Harvest* (1942) for director Mervyn LeRoy on the front patio of English Home.

"It's like out of Ivanhoe.*"*
"Oh, I'm afraid it's much older than that."
"Why is it so big?"
"Because we couldn't afford anything smaller."

21   ENGLISH HOME

The above dialog is from 1960's *Please Don't Eat the Daisies.* The house that stars David Niven and Doris Day are referring to had, by this point, been a backlot fixture for almost 30 years.

The Art Department once nicknamed this place the "C. Aubrey Smith Home" because it often played, or looked like it should have played, the "*veddy* English" character actor's domicile. (The same department occasionally referred to the same set as the "Tudor House," as well.) White columns could be placed in front of the entrance and the entire structure was sometimes repositioned under a staircase for visual variety.

Behind the façade's door, pieces of furniture, candlesticks, silverware, and cobweb-dappled wine glasses sat scattered in the elements, upended and ransacked like some cache of lost pirate booty.

Seeing this, one is reminded not of anything from *David Copperfield* (1935)—which actually did shoot here—but of a scene from another Dickens novel, *Great Expectations*, of Miss Havisham's house, heavy with rotting furniture, memories, and decay.

Another picture that did film here, *The Canterville Ghost* (1944), always held special memories for contract star Robert Young, not from the house (here turned into a castle with the help of a matte painting), but about child star Margaret O'Brien. "The fact that she stole scenes from me cannot be disputed," he admits. "This pain was eased only by my knowledge of her great talent, and the lovely surprise that she was such a very nice person. . . . I cannot help remembering how I ran across a downcast Charles Laughton on the set after he had been bested by little Margaret. 'What's the matter, Charles?' I asked. Charles sighed and looked at me forlornly. 'I really must kill that child,' he said."

Exiting through the front door of this haunted set, it's impossible not to hear Laughton's words echoing through the peeling, storied façades.

Above: The Eucy Grove area dressed for *The White Sister* (1933).

22 EUCY GROVE

ucy Grove or, rather, "Eucalyptus Grove," was a different sort of backlot. There were no permanent buildings there; the "set" consisted of a wooded area above Verona Courtyard, honeycombed with varied vegetation and plant life. Unlike the more fantastical jungles on Lot Three, most of the trees (not all of them eucalyptus) here were real. Yet, they were just as arranged and art-directed as any of the towns and buildings that were its neighbors.

The set had a strange affinity for tropical locations. In 1935, scenes supplementing the Tahitian sequences filmed on Catalina Island for *Mutiny on the Bounty* were shot here. Another film the same year,

Last of the Pagans, redressed these sets (slightly) as approximately the same tiki-laden location.

Years later, the set hosted yet another return to the South Seas when in May of 1976, Paramount Pictures rented the area to construct a spectacular 47-foot-high, 800-foot-long bamboo wall for its 1976 remake of *King Kong*. The wall was constructed over telephone poles driven deep into the earth and secured with concrete blocks. Additional trees imported from Mexico surrounded it, although once again, these same, sad, much-photographed eucalyptus trees helped stand in for the vegetation of the South Seas. Later, for the same film, the wall was redressed with aluminum to play

Left: Eucy Grove hosts a Polynesian-themed setting for *Last of the Pagans* (1935). *Right:* Construction of the Great Wall for the 1976 Dino DeLaurentiis re-make of *King Kong.*

New York's Shea Stadium.

Gary Martin, who today is the president of studio operations at Sony Pictures, was the construction coordinator on *King Kong* in 1976. Two years later, he was back to supervise the demolition of the wall for a housing development. "I wanted to pull up the cement moorings the poles were embedded in," he remembered, "but they told me to just cut the poles away at ground level. The wall came right down, but when they came in later with the tractors, the blades would dig into that buried cement and break right off. We lost two D-9 cats that way!" A little backlot revenge perhaps?

Eucy Grove in the 1960s also still contained a "Quonset Village" of hut-like structures and was bordered on one side by another massive scene dock. Roofless, but encircled on three sides by walls (some of which were actually the backside flats for Verona Square), it was a miniature version of the property warehouses on Lot One and elsewhere. Within were numerous wall units, staircases, Western stockades, stately Greek columns, and other ephemera of the filmmaking process.

Above: Camille Cottage as it looked in its debut film *Camille* (1937).

Nearby, on the grove's other, vaguely northern side, bordered by more trees, was the so-called "Camille Cottage." This charming setting was reached by crossing a tiny carriage bridge built for the 1936 Greta Garbo classic, *Camille*. Its formidable size contradicted its modest name: its walls were almost hidden from view, its appearance, forlorn and ragged—like a classic haunted estate.

The château's onscreen appearances have been comparatively few. The place was cast as another French country home in *Love on the Run*, the same year as *Camille*, hosting none other than Clark Gable

and Joan Crawford. It can be glimpsed as set dressing in *The Kid From Texas* (1939) with Dennis O'Keefe, as well, and was the residence of composer Jerome Kern (played by Robert Walker) in *Till the Clouds Roll By* (1946). *The Prisoner of Zenda* (1952) would be the most recent title the set has on its resume for many a year. By 1960, like a cottage from a Brothers Grimm fairytale, the set had been almost completely forgotten, only the studio's oldest or most adventurous residents would even be able to locate it, so obscured and overgrown by vegetation has the set become.

Left: The Formal Garden in *Scarmouche* (1952).
Right: The Formal Garden gets a swashbuckling workout in this scene from *Scarmouche* (1952).

The Formal Garden was a large, impeccably manicured estate lawn dotted with terraces and fountains and flowers and walkways. It was actually part of an even larger parkland dubbed "Cohn Park" by employees. In a talk with historian Rudy Behlmer, J. J. Cohn, the studio's general manager, and the area's namesake recalled:

> When I suggested building a park on the lot, people told me I was crazy. They would refer to it as "Cohn's folly." But I went ahead. They said, "Oh, it would take 10 years before the trees grow." People think negatively. And I said, "Well, we'll buy big trees then, as much as we could." Cedric Gibbons laid it out and it cost about $8,000, as I remember. No one used it for a while, ex-

cept for some of the extras who did their 'courting' there, but eventually a director [Cecil B. DeMille] decided to shoot at the 'park' instead of spending three days in Pasadena, and what he saved by working on the lot made a big impression. . . . [After that,] we used to listen to what I call a lot of crap. Directors would say, "Oh, you can't shoot that. They don't grow eucalyptus trees in Connecticut!" And I used to say, "Who the hell knows what that tree is 200 feet from the camera? Or if it was right under your nose!"

There was never any hard and fast rule about location work. Sometimes, it was called for. Sometimes, it was merely an extravagance. Even in the 1920s, if you took the company to Sherwood Forest [an area north of Los Angeles] you'd spend $1,800 before you got outside the studio gates. And if there was bad weather, that day was lost. But at the studio, if you had bad weather—and a day's shooting often represented an outlay of $25,000 in the 1930s—you could move into a stage and save some of the money.

Garbo made an appearance here playing croquet with Fredric March in *Anna Karenina* (1935). In *Camille* (1936), she ran amongst the shrubbery to the larger park site to find out if Robert Taylor (as Armand) had been shot in a duel.

Ever since *Gone with the Wind* (1939), MGM studio tour guides—indeed tour guides throughout the United States (particularly in the South)—have claimed that scenes were filmed right in their backyard. But in fact, former MGM executive David O. Selznick, who became an independent producer in 1937, oversaw most of the filming at his own studio (the former Ince Studio-RKO lot further down Washington Boulevard). MGM was only the distributor of that picture and provided financing, contract star Clark Gable, and the use of its unrivaled technical departments.

Yet some of the film was indeed shot on this lot. Battle scenes, mostly unused, were filmed at MGM and, in the Formal Garden, the death of Rhett Butler and Scarlett O'Hara's child, Bonnie Butler, was filmed. The garden was the lavish backyard of the Butlers' extravagant Atlanta home.

David O. Selznick had determined that the film would be his own personal production rather than another product of the vast MGM assembly line. Consequently, he made sure that when the cameras rolled, it was mostly at his own plant, away from Mayer's overpowering influence. (In addition to being Selznick's former boss, Mayer was also his father-in-law.) Eventually, the film became as

identified with MGM as with Selznick—either as an individual or a company. Today, film buffs and even historians tend to forget that *Gone with the Wind*—the ultimate example of the Hollywood studio system in its golden years—was actually made as an independent!

By the 1960s, the name "Cohn Park," which had at one time been a synonym for the entire backlot—indeed, for the very idea of shooting on a backlot—was sadly little used. The moniker "Formal Garden"—originally only an elaborate section of "Cohn Park"—is now the name on the official studio map. Yet old-timers still remembered it by its original name.

Below: The Formal Garden in *Gone with the Wind* (1939). The house behind Clark Gable and company is a clever matte painting.
Opposite: A short lived but intriguing staircase tucked away in a corner of Cohn Park (1933).

Left: Katharine Hepburn dives into the Esther Williams Pool in *The Philadelphia Story* (1940).
Right: The Esther Williams Pool dressed for *Living In a Big Way* (1947).

25 ESTHER WILLIAMS POOL

swimming pool stood behind the square where these impressive gardens presided. A diving board was on the western side and a footpath led away from that end into Eucy Grove.

Built in about 1935, Esther Williams didn't take her inaugural dip here until 1942, swimming in this pool for the first time in *Andy Hardy's Double Life*. She also performed her first starring role here, in a spectacular Technicolor-pink swimming suit in *Bathing Beauty* (1944). A few of her subsequent film roles kept her close to this corner of the lot, but as her popularity and box office receipts soared, so did the budgets of her films and the much-larger underground tank in the cavernous Stage 30 was used instead.

The pool was used in non-Williams vehicles over the years, including the Clark Gable-starrer *The Hucksters* (1947), *Invitation* (1952), *Jailhouse Rock* (1957) and, memorably, *The Wings of Eagles* (1957), in which John Wayne belly-flopped an airplane here, disrupting a garden party. Paul Newman swam here in 1962 for a hotel sequence from *Sweet Bird of Youth*.

Incidentally, a second, smaller (but more ornate) and little-seen circular pool was built near the Lord Home set.

Top Left: Cameras roll at the Esther Williams Pool for *Everybody Sing* (1938).
Top Right: The Esther Williams Pool being utilized for *Jailhouse Rock* (1957). Jennifer Holden is hugging Elvis.
Bottom Left: A smaller prototype of the Esther Williams Pool dressed for *It's In the Air* (1935).
Bottom Right: Donald O'Conner reminisces about the MGM film career of Esther Williams in front of the now derelict Esther Williams Pool in *That's Entertainment!* (1974).

Left: The Southern Mansion in 1961's *Ada*, with Spanish moss hand placed in the surrounding trees. *Right:* Katharine Hepburn relaxes on the steps of the Southern Mansion behind the scenes of *Undercurrent* (1946).

26   SOUTHERN MANSION

The Southern Mansion stood north of the swimming pool and in front of the lathe house, greenhouse, hothouse, and nursery that hid against the studio fence on Arizona Boulevard.

The mansion looked like nothing so much as one of the plantations in *Gone with the Wind* (1939), and was oft-mistakenly or misleadingly referred to as either Tara or Twelve Oaks Plantation by company employees. Although it resembles the Wilkes home from that seminal film (and although it was in fact built while *Gone with the Wind* was in pre-production), the imposing edifice was actually created for *The Toy*

Wife (1938). This film, like *Jezebel* (1938) at Warner Bros., was made to take advantage of the unparalleled interest in *Gone with the Wind* and the rebirth of interest in the Civil War.

The mansion was actually called "Twelve Oaks" onscreen as Arlene Dahl's home in Red Skelton's 1948 Civil War spy spoof, *A Southern Yankee*, which might account for the confusion, as well.

In 1978, right after the mansion was torn down, the *Los Angeles Times* reported that a Pasadena couple, William and Linda Holland, had seen a photograph of this house (taken during its demolition) in

Left: The Southern Mansion plays host to a hoedown in *Hootenanny Hoot* (1963).
Top Right: An early 1930s prototype of the Southern Mansion as used in *Reckless* (1935).
Bottom Right: From this angle of the Southern Mansion, it is apparent that the "Greek columns" are actually rolled paper tubes (1935).

the paper—identified as being Tara from *Gone with the Wind*—and decided to construct their own home as a duplicate. Irate film fans flooded the *Times* offices with letters pointing out that the pictured set was most certainly not the plantation used as Tara in the movie. The paper dutifully printed a retraction, stating that the mansion was actually that picture's Twelve Oaks Plantation, instead. Although, of course, the set was neither! In the years since, the Holland home has oft-been identified, however, in guidebooks and local history as a house—sometimes Twelve Oaks and sometimes Tara—actually used in the production of the movie. No wonder people were confused.

Views of the familiar façade were occasionally obscured by foliage or a bandstand (as in *The Great Sinner* or *In the Good Old Summertime*, both from 1949) in order to expand the nearby Girl's School campus setting, or to offer less Dixie-oriented views.

An earlier version of this mansion, built in approximately the same place, can be seen in *Operator 13* (1934), *Reckless* (1935), *Naughty Marietta* (1935), *Saratoga* (1937), and *Man-Proof* (1938).

Left: The front of Vinegar Tree House (1953).
Right: The backyard and patio of Vinegar Tree House. This set was one of the few backlot sets that had a working front and back (1965).

27 VINEGAR TREE HOUSE

Vinegar House (a.k.a. Vinegar Tree House) was so-named for the large vinegar tree whose branches spread across the yard. Built for *Rich Man, Poor Girl* (1938), it notably lists *National Velvet* (1945) among its film credits, in which it played young Elizabeth Taylor's home. The more intimate backside of the house—inexplicably known as the "Bransom Cottage"—was the backside of the *Please Don't Eat the Daisies* (1960) house, and the campus home inhabited by lovebirds Richard Chamberlain and Yvette Mimieux in *Joy in the Morning* (1965).

Left: The Stable set contained working interiors, as seen here in this snapshot from *Undercurrent* (1946), starring Robert Mitchum and Robert Taylor.
Right: Elizabeth Taylor and Mickey Rooney in front of the Stable set exterior in *National Velvet* (1944).

28 STABLE

A tree-lined path led to a stable, complete with sheds, tack-barn, and corrals. The district was probably built in 1939 for *Stand Up and Fight* and was seen most famously in *National Velvet* (1944). This set was destroyed in the same mysterious 1975 studio fire that leveled the nearby Girl's School set.

Left: The Girl's School, seen here with its original rooftop, dressed for *The Cobweb* (1955).
Right: The Girl's School and surrounding buildings when shot as a group made an ideal Campus setting. *Waterloo Bridge* can be seen to the far right (1965).

The Williamsburg-styled Girl's School was designed to overlook the Formal Garden and Cohn Park so that the two sets could be used interchangeably with or without one another. *Forty Little Mothers* (1940) is usually credited as being the picture for which the set was constructed, yet a viewing of the film reveals a very different-looking school house indeed. Production records for that film indicate that a "faculty wing" was constructed at a cost of $10,000—the largest single construction expense on the picture—yet are not otherwise explicit on the subject.

Regardless of its origins, a T-shaped roadway intersects in front of the main building, which has a spectacular clock tower added to the original Victorian rooftop by art director Edward Carfagno for Deborah Kerr's tour-de-force *Tea and Sympathy* in 1956. A French church was built behind the façade.

Most projects between the mysterious *Forty Little Mothers* and *Tea and Sympathy* similarly cast the area as some sort of collegiate or academic setting. In 1955, the set was altered by Carfagno to portray a sanitarium for *The Cobweb*. From this point on, and right through the *Tea and Sympathy* facelift, a gabled roof and Victorian porch would be a permanent part of the set. With these renovations, the structure continued to be a popular location. *Logan's Run* (1976) utilized this set just days before it mysteriously burned down on July 28, 1975.

Top Left: The Girl's School, with the addition of snow and Elizabeth Taylor, made an ideal Campus setting for 1947's *Cynthia*.

Bottom Left: Seen in the background of this set for 1975's *Hearts of the West* is the Girl's School campus.

Top Right: The Girl's School in *Logan's Run* (1976). Shortly after this scene was filmed, the set was destroyed by arson.

Center Right: "This building, or what's left of it, was, among other things, Tate College in *Good News*," recalls Peter Lawford in *That's Entertainment!* (1974).

Bottom Right: Elvis Presley passes a football on the front lawn of the Girl's School during a break from filming *The Trouble with Girls* (1969).

Left: Old Mill House, built for the 1941 film *When Ladies Meet*, seen here in 1965.
Top Right: The piping for the water supply to the Old Mill House pond is visible in the lower right-hand corner.
Bottom Right: Jack Cassidy as *The Phantom of Hollywood* haunts a slightly reconfigured Old Mill House in 1974.

30   OLD MILL HOUSE

Crossing around to the back of the stables, and past a church—which was actually built into the back of the defunct stable—is another view of the Lot Two Lake. Further north along its banks was the Old Mill House. This structure, which looked like a converted gristmill, made its debut in 1941 for *When Ladies Meet*. The set caused something of a sensation with viewers. Audiences were enchanted with the idyllic image of a mill being used as a house, and the waterwheel powered by a delightful "natural" swimming pool. It all made an especially salacious setting for the onscreen love match between stars Joan Crawford and Greer Garson over debonair Robert Taylor. How sophisticated. And, at the same time, how rustic! After the film opened, Gibbons's office was reportedly flooded with inquiries about the set, in answer to which he created blueprints and reportedly mailed them off by the thousands to future mill-dwellers around the world. Whether or not any would-be Joan Crawfords actually tried to build a home from these nonfunctioning set blueprints could only make for interesting speculation.

Not surprisingly, the popularity of the set didn't stop it from being recycled in wildly different contexts in the ensuing years. But alas, it was never done with the same popular results, perhaps proving that some performers, real or carpentered together, are really only one-picture stars.

Above: Lord Home was built for the 1940 film *The Philadelphia Story*. The front door, visible here, is remembered for a scene in which Cary Grant pushes Katharine Hepburn through it after she breaks his golf club.

East of the Old Mill House was the green-shuttered Lord Home—the house of Katharine Hepburn, as Tracy Lord, and her family in *The Philadelphia Story* (1940). Actually, this home has a slightly different pedigree than most of the houses on the backlot in that it was constructed on a Lot One soundstage and carefully moved where (with the addition of structural reinforcements, landscaping and a driveway) it could be preserved and used for other productions. It was.

Other titles that used this location included *Dr. Kildare's Wedding Day* (1941) with Lew Ayres, of course; *Killer McCoy* (1947) with Mickey Rooney; *Athena* (1954) with Jane Powell; and at least two epi-

| 31 | **LORD HOME** |

sodes of *The Twilight Zone* (1959–1963). Publicity issued by the studio indicated that *High Society*, a 1956 musical remake of *The Philadelphia Story* with winsome Grace Kelly in the Hepburn role, used the house as well. This is true. But as befitting the new title, the remake used the more lavish Southern Mansion set as its primary location.

Exiting the Lord Home and heading northeast, one would pass the little-seen Davis Home and an equally mysterious set only identified as the Palace Court and arrive at a four-way fork in the road where Copperfield Court, Wimpole Street, and New York Street's Park Avenue and Cullem Street intersect.

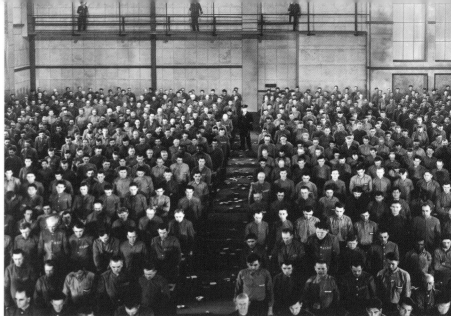

Left: The bared front gate of the Prison set built for *The Big House* (1930).
Right: An interior set, photographed on a soundstage, of the Prison in *The Big House* (1930).
Below: A poster for *Pardon Us* (1931), which was filmed on the Prison set.
Opposite: The reconfigured/redressed Prison set becomes the Bastille in *A Tale of Two Cities* (1935). Parts of this sequence were also filmed on Lot One.

32 PRISON

Across the street from the fork in the road described above was the site where once lay a prison set constructed in 1929 for *The Big House* (1930). This early talkie was a prototype for every prison picture that would ever end up doing hard time—but great box office returns—in cinemas. This huge set, with its high walls and vast courtyard, was frequently prison-populated in the 1930s, and can be seen in viewings of Laurel and Hardy's well-titled *Pardon Us* (1931), *Public Hero #1* (1935), *Exclusive Story* (1936) and, naturally enough, as the debtors prison in 1935's *David Copperfield*.

The set was reconstructed on a massive scale to play a key role in *A Tale of Two Cities* (1935) for the legendary storming of the Bastille sequence (although a copy of the massive drawbridge was constructed on Lot One). But the following year, it was demolished to make way for an expansion of New York Street. Afterwards, the towering Fifth Avenue façades rising from the site would provide little clue to the casual visitor of the area's past life as the movies' most famous prison.

In at least one way, the destruction of the set would turn out to be regrettable. A few months later, Thalberg, in one of his last projects, would film the story of *Marie Antoinette* (1938). Although, as in *A Tale of Two Cities*, no expense would be spared in recreating 18th century France, one detail—the storming of the Bastille, although talked about in the script—could now no longer be shown.

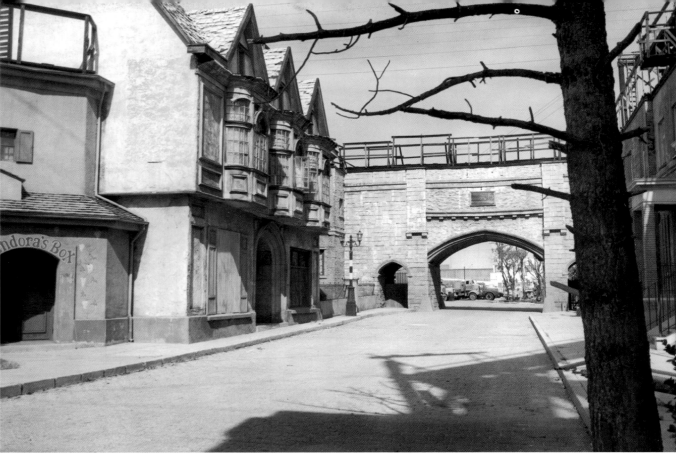

Top Left: The archway joining Copperfield Court to Waterfront Street (1968).
Bottom Left: A scale miniature of Copperfield Court is destroyed in *The Time Machine* (1960).
Right: Copperfield Court in 1968.

33 COPPERFIELD COURT

Copperfield Court (not to be confused with Copperfield Street) was constructed in 1934 for Selznick's *David Copperfield*. It featured a block of English townhouses and shops, and sloped upward at the northern end before melding into Waterfront Street, a different set sometimes used interchangeably.

Dividing the two sets was an impressive "brick" entranceway that made the set easily identifiable—although a similar landmark stood on Lot Two's Quality Street. This particular archway is dimly visible in dozens of pictures, but finally graduated to co-star status in 1960's *The Time Machine*, where it provided a familiar touchstone throughout many of the time traveler's (Rod Taylor) adventures before finally being destroyed onscreen in a far-future calamity.

It was here legendary comic W. C. Fields—borrowed from Paramount—performed his key scenes for *David Copperfield*. After years of writing comedic lines for himself—or ad-libbing—Fields depended on offscreen cue cards at MGM. For director George Cukor, the result was worth it. "He was born to play the part . . . he realized he was working with something that was a classic and he behaved that way."

Prowling the street, it's hard not to imagine Fields's distinctively nasal voice ricocheting across the cobblestones. "Any friend of my friend Copperfield has a personal claim upon me. . . ." Is it possible, now, even with the better part of a century having slipped away, to read the above line and *not* imitate Fields while doing so?

Top: Wimpole Street looking west, and nearby Copperfield Court on the far right (1959).
Bottom Left: An actual photo of the front door of Edward Moulton-Barrett's house on 50 Wimpole Street in London, taken by Thalberg and Gibbons during an on-location trip (1934).
Bottom Right: The same doorway recreated in Culver City for *The Barrett's of Wimpole Street* (1934).

34   WIMPOLE STEEET

Just south of this real estate was Wimpole Street. Wimpole Street was a more affluent version of Copperfield Street—more Baker Street than Whitechapel, more Henry Higgins than Eliza Doolittle. At its peak, the street contained a park area, sidewalks, gaslights, trees, and fences. Even undressed, it was a perfect representation of the British Empire, over which the sun never set. All that's missing is the clip-clop of the hansom cabs and the swirl of the fog.

This set was what it was because Irving Thalberg wanted it that way for one of his wife's most fondly remembered films, *The Barretts of Wimpole Street* (1934). Designed by Gibbons with Henry McAfee and Edwin B. Willis, the resultant set was a perfect backdrop for the unforgettably ferocious portrait of parental abuse on display in Charles Laughton's performance as Papa Barrett. This place of stiff upper lip resolve is also proudly on display in *Waterloo Bridge* (1940), *Dr. Jekyll and Mr. Hyde* (1941), *Gaslight* (1944), *The Picture of Dorian Gray* (1945), and *Mrs. Parkington* (1944).

After World War II, when continuing Anglo-American relations were no longer as crucial to the cause of global peace, the set fell in to relative disuse. In 1962, when production problems plagued the Paris location shoot for *The 4 Horsemen of the Apocalypse*, the crew returned to Lot Two to use both Wimpole Street and Waterfront Street. In order to match footage with the scenes shot on location in Paris, the park was removed and a church façade built, greatly increasing the usable set space. Although, sadly, the district was seldom used afterwards.

Top: A panoramic view of Waterfront Street looking west (1944).
Bottom: The top side of Waterfront Street and the entrance to Copperfield Court, visible on the left (1959).

In the skewered way of Hollywood, the neighboring Waterfront Street set did not contain any water. The origins of the name may lie in the fact that some of the façades were moved here from their original home beside the artificial lake on Lot One in 1935. Most of these appeared European in origin—indeed one of the first features utilizing these relocated façades was *A Tale of Two Cities* in 1935—although American film noir settings (like *Scene of the Crime* in 1949) were not beyond this set's scope, as the street was modified many times over the decades. The original designers were Gibbons, Henry McAfee, and Edwin B. Willis.

Joan Crawford fans may remember the set from scenes in *Above Suspicion* (1943)—an unhappy experience for the star. Joan was increasingly frustrated with scripts like this one by the 1940s. It was probably evident when she made this picture that MGM executives were looking for new, younger talent.

To most movie buffs, Waterfront Street is best known for its transformation into Paris for the studio's Academy Award-winning musical *An American in Paris* (1951). "MGM agreed to let us shoot in Paris," recalled star Gene Kelly. "It was the French officials who wouldn't let us. And mighty MGM, who would never admit they weren't allowed to do anything, put out the publicity that we preferred the backlot, and 'Kelly can't dance on cobblestone.' So we had to do it on the backlot, and we did a good job of it. We had just two establishing shots of Paris."

Vincente Minnelli and art director Preston Ames spent hours of research before transforming this section of the lot. "I must have spent a month on Waterfront Street alone," said Ames. "I tried to figure out what I could do and what angles I should use to make all this look like Paris. But when I thought I had come up with a solution, I

Left: Waterfront Street as it actually looked in 1951 during the production of *An American in Paris* . . .
Right: . . . and again, as the set looked to audiences in the finished film. The rooftops, the chimneys, and the sky have all been optically painted in.
Below: Waterfront Street portrays the other side of the English Channel for *Random Harvest* (1942).

had not taken into consideration choreography, movement, and music." Ultimately, Ames would create Paris by combining Waterfront Street, French Courtyard, and Quality Street. Another of the "exteriors" necessary was a quay on the Seine, which was built on Stage 30.

Alfred Gilks, the cinematographer, remembered the café set for that picture, for which he wanted to show action in the background. "A building was cleared here and the café interior built in conjunction with a real street—in fact, three streets. Directly across from the wide entrance of the café, a street extended straight away for a block to another cross street, parallel to our foreground street, which extended a full block from the café on one side and a half block on the other."

Additionally on this set, in order to

control sunlight, diffusion silks or black duvetyn tarps were wired over the tops of the sets, which could be folded or extended as needed in order to subdue light or create darkness.

So potent, and so French was this remarkable set in this remarkable movie that decades and generations later in Universal's *Forget Paris* (1995), Billy Crystal stood on a real French street, thousands of miles from Culver City, and rhapsodized to Debra Winger that *this*, indeed, was the spot where Gene Kelly had likewise fallen in love with Leslie Caron.

In actuality, a studio fire on March 12, 1967, destroyed this entire set and robbed the industry of one of its most popular backlot settings.

In the northeast corner of Lot Two, behind Waterfront Street and facing Overland Boulevard, stood MGM's Cartoon Department. Accessed by a New York Street road known as "Cartoon Alley," this was home for 20 years to the crazy antics of Tom and Jerry, Droopy, Barney Bear, and a host of other memorable characters created by such animation greats as William Hanna, Joseph Barbera, and Tex Avery. After sub-contracting to former Disney animators such as Ub Iwerks (who produced the now-forgotten *Flip the Frog* cartoon shorts between 1930 and 1933) and Hugh Harman and Rudy Ising (who would produce the memorable anti-war Oscar-winner *Peace on Earth* in 1939), L. B. Mayer established the studio's own cartoon department in 1937 with former salesman Fred Quimby in charge. By 1940, the department had earned its first Oscar for the short *The Milky Way* (1940). But it was another short made that year, titled *Puss Gets the Boot*, that would literally save the animation studio.

Joe Barbera recalled decades later that the short, with its battling cat and mouse protagonists, was "the most unoriginal, stupid idea, but we went ahead with *Puss Gets the Boot* anyway—and were nominated for an Academy Award!"

A $50 bonus was offered to the studio employee who came up with the character names. Animator John Kerr earned it for choosing Tom and Jerry. The new characters would bring seven Oscars to MGM. (In contrast, Mickey Mouse over at Disney and Bugs Bunny at Warner Bros. have, to date, only won a single competitive Oscar each.) "Joe was a great artist," recalled Hanna. "I was a lousy artist. I concentrated on the

direction and timing of the cartoons while Joe animated them. We worked that way for many years." The pair also supervised some classic melding of animation with live action in MGM films like *Anchors Aweigh* (1945) and *Dangerous When Wet* (1953).

When former Warner Bros. animator Tex Avery arrived, the studio's Cartoon Department burst with new creativity. Tom and Jerry were revitalized, and Avery's own wacky, racy cartoons such as *Blitz Wolf* (1942), *Red Hot Riding Hood* (1943), and *Swing Shift Cinderella* (1945) were immensely popular with movie audiences.

By 1957, Hanna and Barbera were virtually running the unit, and had doubled production with 17 artists on staff. "By any standard, we were on top of the world," said Barbera. "Then one day, we got a phone call—*a phone call*—from the Accounting Department to close the studio down and give everyone two weeks salary." Apparently, these accountants had discovered that *Tom and Jerry* made the same in reissues as they had originally. So from then on, the studio would only reissue older cartoons.

Hanna and Barbera and their staff subsequently turned to television, and created such classic series as *The Flintstones* (1960–1966), *The Jetsons* (1962–1988), and *Scooby-Doo, Where Are You!* (1969–1972).

The cartoon building was eventually rented as production offices to Filmways Television.

The M-G-M Cartoon Building, housing more than 150 artists and technicians who produce 18 cartoons in Technicolor annually.

Fred C. Quimby, right, head of the Cartoon Department and the man largely responsible for M-G-M being the first major producer to make its own cartoons, is shown above with C. G. Maxwell, production supervisor.

MEN WHO MAKE SHORTS

CARTOON DEPARTMENT...

1. After a story has been written the first step in making an animated cartoon is the sketching of the characters. Robert Allen uses live models.

2. Co-directors Joe Barbera and William Hanna develop the character to its full humorous possibilities, suggest expressions and tricks to humanize it.

3. Animator Lovell Norman draws the characters in many consecutive motions which, when filmed and run off, give them "life".

Inset: A page from a 1940 MGM distributor magazine showing the Cartoon Department building and staff—including a young William Hanna and Joseph Barbera (bottom center).

Top: A panoramic view of New York Street's Fifth Avenue (left) and Eastside Street (right) in 1944.
Bottom Left: Brownstone Street was the location of the secret headquarters in *The Man from U.N.C.L.E.* (1964–1968).
Bottom Right: Brownstone Street in *Somebody Up There Likes Me* (1956), starring Paul Newman and Pier Angeli.

The rest of Lot Two, almost 10 acres in all, was composed of an amazingly detailed recreation of New York City, including a backlot Park Avenue, Fifth Avenue, Eastside Street, Hester Street, Cullem Street, Church Street, Warehouse Alley, Cartoon Street, and Brownstone Street.

"Any actor or actress who made, say, more than one or two films at the studio sooner or later probably would find himself shooting a sequence here," Gene Kelly recounted in 1974's *That's Entertainment!* Indeed, a large part of our shared movie heritage originated here—the most-used section of the backlot.

	NEW YORK STREETS
37	BROWNSTONE STREET
38	EASTSIDE STREET
39	WAREHOUSE ALLEY
40	CHURCH STREET
41	FIFTH AVENUE
42	CULLEM STREET
43	PARK AVENUE

Overland Avenue.

The phrase "New York Street" actually referred to two separate construction projects built in the same place. Some of the buildings survived both phases, but many of the original structures were replaced when the area was widened and divided up into "districts" in 1935, starting with Fifth Avenue. This second phase construction was apparently initialized with the studio's purchase of seven acres of real estate extending that portion of the lot to

Fifth Avenue featured wider streets and taller buildings (up to five stories high) than any other commercial district façades on any

Top Left: Brownstone Street stands in for Moscow in 1940's *Comrade X*. However, the signs above camera range are still in English.

Top Right: Eastside Street dressed for *Boys Town* (1938).

Bottom Left: An aerial view looking southwest at the entire 10 acre New York Streets district as it looked in the 1950s.

Opposite: The same set on Fifth Avenue as used for three different projects.

Top Left: Fred Astaire in *Royal Wedding* (1951).

Top Right: Gene Kelly in *An American in Paris* (1951).

Bottom Left: Marshall Thompson, Mickey Rooney, and Tom Drake in *Words and Music* (1948).

backlot. The set was networked with piping for rain sequences and included permanent black duvetyn tarps that could be unfurled across the tops to simulate darkness. The first film to use this splendid new set was *Wife vs. Secretary* (1936), starring Myrna Loy and Jean Harlow in the title roles (guess who played who?) battling it out over a lucky Clark Gable.

The next year, the street had the title role in *San Francisco* because many of studio wizard Gillespie's special effects were full-scale. In fact, for the still-unrivaled 20-minute earthquake sequence, Gillespie fitted one of these buildings with breakaway walls and harmless "lite" bricks rigged to fall on 300 terrified extras.

At the same time San Francisco was tumbling into ruin, Jeanette McDonald and Nelson Eddy were crooning just up the boulevard in the opera house set in *Rose-Marie* (1936). Standing on the wide sidewalk and looking up at the sign in front of this formidable façade (and it was just a façade, there was no theatre inside), it's hard not to speculate that as many famous names have been emblazoned in lights on that marquee as any on Broadway. In fact, this *was* Broadway many, many times. And for generations who have never visited the real dis-

Left: Gene Kelly duets with the world's most famous lamppost on the corner of Waterfront and Eastside Streets in *Singin' in the Rain* (1952).
Right: Further down along the block, Eastside Street was dressed very differently in 1950's *The Yellow Cab Man.*

trict, and even many who have, this is the visual we conjure up when asked about the Great White Way.

For example, this was the theatre exterior that Fred Astaire got a memorable shine to his shoes in front of in *The Band Wagon* (1953). A couple years later, James Cagney discovered "Ten Cents a Dance" hoofer Doris Day (as Ruth Etting) in *Love Me or Leave Me* (1955) at the "dive" next door.

Unlike most of the sets on Lot Two, New York Street was seldom used for anything other than an urban American city. Exceptions did occur, however, and this included Hedy Lamarr's *Comrade X* (1940),

for which the familiar signs were translated into Russian and the area portrayed quite a convincing Moscow. The boulevard was dressed as Nazi Germany in *The Seventh Cross* (1944), Red Square in *Yolanda and the Thief* (1945), India in *They Met In Bombay* (1941), and as London for *Royal Wedding* (1951) and *Gaby* (1956).

Stateside, but far from the Big Apple, it was here on Eastside Street that *Singin' in the Rain* (1952) shot its title number. This time, the street played Hollywood with its signature lampposts. "They thought I was crazy," remembered Gene Kelly, "because I went to the set and had them dig holes in the ground to accumulate the rain water,

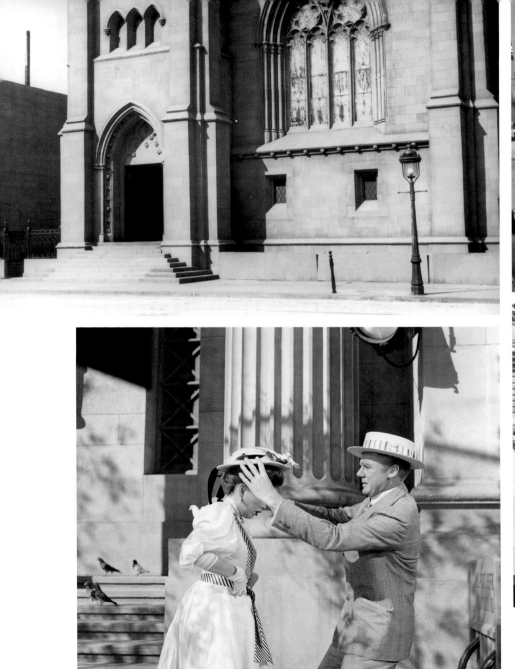

Top Left: A house of worship on Church Street.
Top Right: A dilapidated Fifth Avenue in *Soylent Green* (1973).
Bottom Left: The courthouse set seen here with Judy Garland and Van Johnson in the film *In the Good Old Summertime* (1949).
Bottom Right: Fifth Avenue hosts a lunch break for the cast, extras, and crew of *Cimarron* (1960), which was shooting nearby. The Lot One Water Tower can be seen in the distance.

to give me puddles that I would use for certain steps in my dance routine."

The number took a day and a half to complete, beginning on July 17, 1952. And although set at night, the whole number was shot on a sunny day with sprinkler heads simulating the rain and heavy black tarps keeping the sun out. Several people who were there have remembered that as Culver City residents came home around five o'clock, they would start to water their lawns, causing the water pressure on the set to suddenly drop. When it was discovered what was happening, the shoot was rescheduled and Gene Kelly's—indeed any musical's—most famous number was completed the following morning.

Oddly, the lamppost Kelly leapt onto in that number survived the set. In 1986, Bryan Goetzinger was clearing out a prop warehouse

Above: A Mardi Gras parade along Fifth Avenue in *Holiday For Sinners* (1952).
Below: Gene Kelly on roller skates in *It's Always Fair Weather* (1955).

and discovered it in the process of being thrown out. He verified that the lamppost was indeed used in the film by referencing the inventory number (thank you, Cedric Gibbons), and took his treasure home to Hermosa Beach—where it was sadly stolen from his yard and has never been recovered.

The elaborate network of rain piping that supplied the rain for this sequence could be easily assembled above Eastside Street to water many a famous movie scene below. Robert Taylor and Audrey Totter got a workout in the rain-soaked *High Wall* (1947). In *Words and Music* (1948), Mickey Rooney played his final scene under contract to Metro Goldwyn Mayer here as the critically ill—and wet—Lorenz Hart. Bosley Crowther of the *New York Times* called this soggy ending "among the most inadequate and embar-

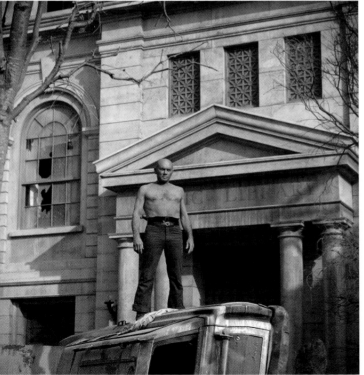

A great deal can be learned about studio history by tracing the rise and fall of a single façade, in this case the Embassy/School set located on the south end of Fifth Avenue. . .

Top Left: A reference photo of the set looking "bare"—no set dressing or special effects (1963).

Top Right: Glenn Ford catches up to Anne Francis in front of the newly snow covered façade in *Blackboard Jungle* (1955).

Bottom Left: In 1975, the set was still visible, this time co-staring with Yul Brynner in *The Ultimate Warrior*.

Bottom Center: John Divola's study of the set just before it was demolished (1980).

Bottom Right: The same set, far right, as the "Burma Empress Hotel" in *Never So Few* (1959).

Top: This townhouse façade at the intersection of Cullem and Wimple Streets was extensively used in *That Forsyte Woman* (1949).
Bottom: A panoramic view of the intersection of Fifth Avenue and Cullem Street. The townhouse in the above photograph is also visible here, in the top right-hand corner (1959).

Above: **The lonely intersection of Park Avenue and Cullem Street, between assignments, in 1959.**

rassing things this reviewer has ever watched.'"

Eastside Street ran approximately north-south, roughly parallel to Overland Avenue outside. Hester Street intersected it on its northern end and looked like it should run to the gate and have intersected with Overland Avenue. It didn't. Further south, Warehouse Alley branched off Eastside Street and sliced right through a triangular cluster of buildings at which all the New York streets roughly intersected. This narrow passageway of loading docks and fire escape-rimmed tenements actually widened as it cut toward the more exclusive neighborhoods, finally branching into a Y-shape and veering into Fifth Avenue on one side and Brownstone Street on the other. This district contained a three-sided church (Catholic, Jewish, and Protestant) and *Dr. Kildare*'s Blair Hospital.

On one side of this district was a large and very familiar hotel façade that has been seen in—among many, many others—*The Big Hangover* (1950), *Show Boat* (1951), *Royal Wedding* (1951), and *Just This Once* (1952).

Cameras would continue to turn on these streets until the late 1970s. A few examples of these latter-day pictures include *It's Always Fair Weather* (1955), a surprisingly cynical musical that did have a great roller-skating sequence on these wide boulevards; *North by Northwest* (1959) with Cary Grant disrupting an auction; *Period of Adjustment* (1962) with Jane Fonda and Tony Franciosa; *Joy in the Morning* (1965) with Richard Chamberlain; *Made in Paris* (1966) with Ann-Margret; and *Where Were You When the Lights Went Out* (1968) with Doris Day. Yet by this time, art directors were finding it increasingly hard to shoot around the peeling brick and potholed streets that the set was by now blighted with. In 1976, the studio even resorted to subleasing the street to the local police for use in training and tactical maneuvers.

By the 1970s, the set was in such a state of ruin that it was able to portray the apocalyptic vistas of *The Ultimate Warrior* (1975) and the New York City of 2022 in *Soylent Green* (1973) with very little set dressing. "It looked horrible," said *Soylent* producer Walter Seltzer, "and very sad."

PART THREE:

MYTHIC LANDSCAPES

The only bit of shade he could find was under an ocean liner made of painted canvas with real lifeboats hanging from its davits. He stood in its narrow shadow for a while, then went on toward a great 40-foot papier-mâché sphinx that loomed in the distance. He had to cross a desert to reach it, a desert that was continually being made larger by a fleet of trucks dumping white sand. He had gone only a few feet when a man with a megaphone ordered him off.

—NATHANIEL WEST,
The Day of the Locust

I think the best of it is still that lion; that roaring lion.
—LUISE RAINER

An efficient studio tram system could take you south on Overland Avenue to Lot Three. But on the way, a visitor would pass Lots Four, Five, Six, and Seven.

A studio zoo, stocked with every manner of beast or fowl, mostly collected for the studio's long-running *Tarzan* series, was originally established on Lot Three under the aegis of studio trainer George Emerson. Many a studio employee has fondly recalled seeing Emerson walking his assorted charges—chimps, lions, and elephants—peacefully across the lot in the late 1930s.

But Emerson and his menagerie were eventually forced off that property because his zoo was using too much real estate and the noise the exotic animals made interfered with production at the very urbane Victorian mansion sets next door. The Zoo ended up on the four-acre Lot Four, which was located between Jefferson Boulevard and Ballona Creek. It was there that the Zoo's population grew, although movie scenes involving animals were shot all over the various lots.

Naturally, MGM employees have many anecdotes about the studio's mascot and logo: "Leo the Lion." The supposed original Leo was—according to studio publicity, anyway—a placid, friendly beast that was sometimes allowed to wander free across the

Above: The Metro Goldwyn Mayer lion logo is the most recognizable logo in the world. This version was used until 1959.
Below: This is the logo that has opened most MGM pictures from 1959 to present. The only recent addition is the company's web address at the very bottom of the logo.

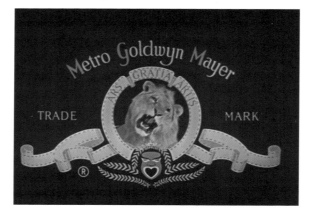

lot during the early years. Actually, "Leo" was several lions and their born names were Slats, Jackie, and Tanner.

Brainard Miller recalled watching the shooting of the studio's famous trademark, which still opens every MGM film, on Lot One. "They shot it outdoors. The lion roared on cue to the noise of a baby's toy through a huge cutout of the logo," he said. "It was shot again and again in all the theatrical aspect ratios—including Cinemascope and 16mm. The lion was very well behaved."

Culver City residents could, from the right vantage point, catch a glimpse of Leo in his cage from outside the property on Jefferson Boulevard. As a child, local James C. Christensen remembered his parents pointing out the Zoo's most famous resident. "'That's the lion at the beginning of the movie we saw last night,' they would tell me."

Over the decades, few movie buffs have noticed that in addition to dozens of versions of Leo's roar recorded over the years, the surrounding logo itself has changed as well. Once.

From 1928 to June of 1959, the logo around Leo's head was relatively consistent with the words "Metro Goldwyn Mayer" housed in a rectangular box beneath the fanfare. Inexplicably, beginning with *Never So*

Few (1959), the words "Metro Goldwyn Mayer" started appearing above Leo's head. With a few exceptions, including the sterile "computerized" version that was used for a few pictures starting in 1966, this is the version used even today. In 2008, the same image was digitally restored and the audio rerecorded for the James Bond picture *Quantum of Solace.*

The Zoo was quietly phased-out as the public's vogue for pictures with wild animals subsided and production in general diminished to the point where such a menagerie was no longer necessary, although the rodeo picture *Arena* (1953) used some of the livestock pens as part of its set.

Lot Four was originally designed for a more active roll in production, however. In 1938, company legers indicated an expenditure of $26,469.13 for "relocation of street sets from Lot One to Lot Four," and presumably the subsequent dressing and construction of these same sets. Lot Three eventually ended up fulfilling much of this mission instead.

Lot Five, which was 7.8 acres and located on the eastern corner of Jefferson and Overland, contained storage hangers, prop houses, stables for the horses of moguls and movie stars, craft shops, scene docks, and temporary backlot sets, which were usually taken down after production on whatever they were being used for had wrapped. Art director Jack Martin Smith once said that, "Lot Five was all carriages and buggies and rigs and harnesses, a storehouse where you could pick out a period hearse for your picture, or a Hungarian carriage, or a landau, a spring buggy, an army wagon, any kind of bridle or saddle. . . ."

For much of its life, Lot Five was also a depository for assorted storage and property items—most notably, a very large collection of airplanes. Most of these beached aircraft are not props, but real, almost-complete DC-6s and B-25s from *Thirty Seconds over Tokyo* (1944) and other WWII epics.

On May 27, 1957, actress Anne Francis learned how to ride a horse on Lot Five prior to her role in *The Hired Gun.* The same year, Elvis Presley was scheduled to report to Lot Five for lessons from forklift operator Chuck Hildner for a scene in *Jailhouse Rock.*

Lot Six, spanning across four acres, primarily contained the studio's nursery and sod farm, where hundreds of living plants needed for production were raised, cared for, and stored. But for a while in the late 1940s, Lot Six (occasionally along with Lot Five) reportedly contained the personal horse stables for Louis B. Mayer and Fred Astaire. Lot Seven, located near Jefferson and Sepulveda, contained whatever ephemera there was no room for anyplace else.

The night watchman moves his hand in the empty air toward the half-cities and the night. So many films were made here in all the long years. Extras moved in the streets in costumes. They talked a thousand tongues. . . . All those little things and big things stayed on. The sights of far places. The smells. The salt wind. The sea. It's all here tonight if you listen.

—RAY BRADBURY, "The Meadow"

Below: Lot Three in the late 1930s during its initial development phase. The Process Tank (before expansion) and the Zoo in nearby Lot Four are already visible.
Opposite: Lots Three, Four, Five, and Six in 1961.

"Lot Three was one of the greatest lots in the picture business," producer Ed Woehler remembered, "because we had a big backing out there. We had the big lake, we had the big waterfront street, we had the St. Louis street, and we had three Western streets."

"It just seemed like miles of old sets and jungles and seaports and city streets and tanks where they had sea battles. You could find lakes and trees, sidewalks and lawns and cozy suburban homes, a bandstand, a bridge, whatever you wanted. You could walk right in. It reminded me of those fairy-tale villages they built for children," Jane Powell once marveled.

Director Ralph Senesky agreed. "There were bridges, plantings, it was magical. Just pick your angle."

"People used to ask me if it was fun to travel to locations all over the world for *The Man from U.N.C.L.E.* I'd tell them we never left Culver City," recalled actor Robert Vaughn. In 1979, fellow performer William Le Massena remembered that "it was all in a semi-state of decay and rot and disintegration. But it was so beautiful, and I'd be there all by myself with all those ghosts of a thousand *Bounty*s. It was terrific."

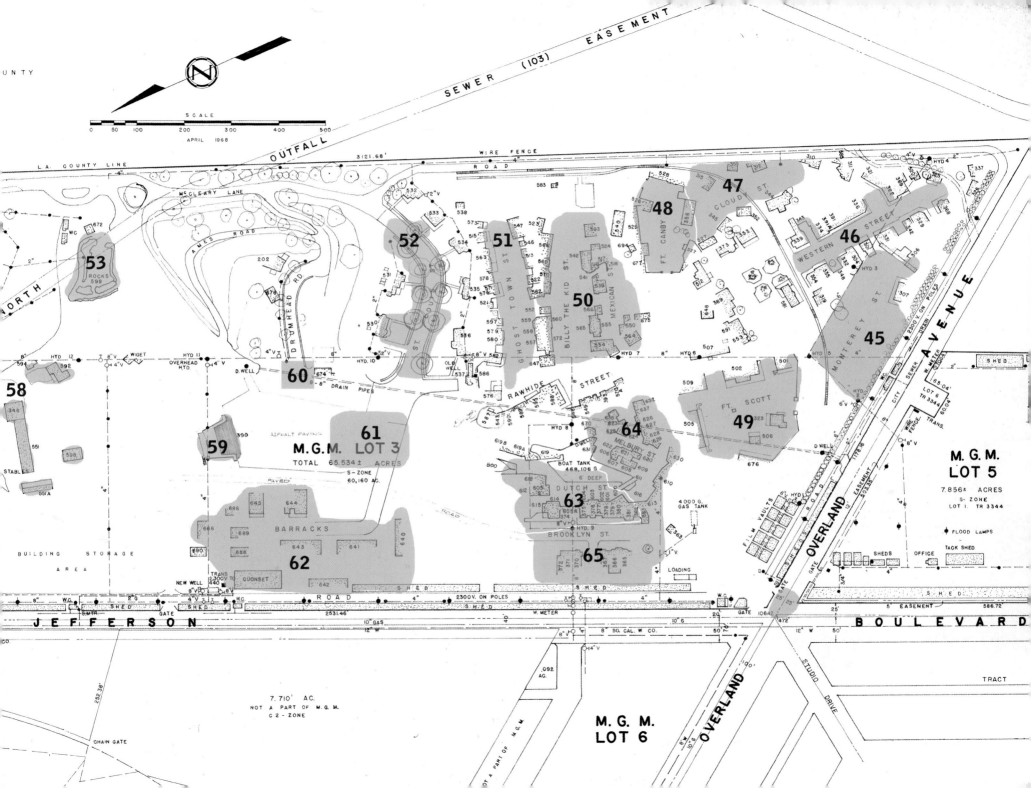

Above: Lot Three's entrance at the intersection of Jefferson Boulevard and Overland Avenue (1970).

Those who think seriously about the matter of images would have been near one gate.

T he entrance gate in the center of the green-painted fence-line, however, was even more anonymous than that for Lot Two. And the relatively remote location of the property insured that the tourists who tended to prowl the perimeter of the other lots were generally absent. This anonymity came at a price, however. George M. Lehr used to complain that "it took a lot of time to move everything down Overland to Lot Three." Therefore, fewer MGM films—particularly after 1960—were filmed there. Consequently, the property became almost exclusively the hangout of independent producers, and television and commercial productions. In fact, studio records from the era reveal that only 12 MGM features were shot on Lot Three in 1960. The independents, or other studios, could rent the jungle area at this time for around $250 a day, for ex-

ample—$463 if one wanted to shoot the well-maintained river as well.

The sad part is that few took advantage of it. Not many in Hollywood seemed to realize that audiences probably would not be able to tell the difference between an actual New York and a well-dressed backlot version—or wouldn't care if they could. The problem with films during this era was actually the people in the foreground, onscreen and off—the aging, out-of-touch performers (and the clueless executives who hired them)—not in the sets in the backgrounds. The stale smell of mildew coming from movie screens in the 1960s was from the front office, not the backlot.

The first substantial set a visitor would have seen inside Lot Three would be found beyond a tree-covered berm. . . .

Left: Monterey Street in *They Met in Bombay* (1941).
Right: Monterey Street in the 1950s

nevitably, because of MGM's lavish and urban house style, Western Street was more elaborate and civilized looking than most Western streets at other studios. Like its brethren at 20th Century Fox, Columbia, or Warner Bros., Western Street did come complete with familiar, frontier-era slat buildings, but it also included a beautifully manicured town square; a tall, steeple-crowned brick courthouse; and a section of railroad track. The reason for this truncated railroad was two-fold: Sequences involving locomotives could be shot on this track or, ingeniously, high boxcars could

| 45 | MONTEREY STREET |
| 46 | WESTERN STREET |

be placed here to hide the fancy courthouse and square from the rest of the more ordinary, Old West–looking town buildings.

Western Street was constructed in 1938 for *Stand up and Fight* (1939), a "buddy" war picture featuring that tried-and-true pairing of the grizzled veteran (Wallace Beery) and the cocky newcomer (Robert Taylor). The production of films like *Barbary Coast Gent* (1944), *Our Vines Have Tender Grapes* (1945), and *Scandal at Scourie* (1953) are typical of the quasi-Westerns that would keep the set busy. Big Western features like *Seven Brides for Seven Brothers* (1954)

Top: Western Street in *Cimarron* (1960).
Bottom Left: Western Street's distinctive brick courthouse (1970).
Bottom Right: A publicity shot for *Honeymoon Hotel* (1964) with Anne Helm and Robert Morse (left chariot) and Chris Noel and Robert Goulet (right chariot) in front of the brick courthouse façade on Western Street.

Left: The Atchison, Topeka, and Santa Fe train pulls into the town of "Sandrock" for *The Harvey Girls* (1946).
Top Right: A neglected Western Street set in the 1970s.
Bottom Bight: *Billy Rose's Jumbo* films on Western Street in 1962.

and *How the West Was Won* (1962) used the set only briefly, but the expensive 1960 *Cimarron* remake showed it to good advantage. Television also helped to keep the street busy into the 1960s.

Nearby, Monterey Street could be found. Although built for the production of Westerns, the set—consisting largely of two-story clapboard bunkers encircling an open courtyard—could be easily dressed to resemble a fort, prison, or POW compound, and memorably portrayed a haunted concentration camp in the infamous "Deaths-Head Revisited" episode (1961) of *The Twilight Zone*.

Above: Cloudy Street in *Song of Russia* (1944).

47 CLOUDY STREET

To the right of Western Street's belfry-capped town hall was the set employees long-referred to as Cloudy Street. This long, gently curved boulevard ran roughly parallel to Western Street, and was, according to later publicity, built for David O. Selznick's *Anna Karenina* (1935)—although, as MGM hadn't fully occupied Lot Three yet, this may be studio ballyhoo.

The set was probably named for *The Girl of the Golden West* (1938), but with its Russian-styled buildings carved from heavy wood and "distinctive touches of Russian folk art," as MGM historian George P. Erengis described it, it certainly looked like a proper hangout for doomed maidens and Cossacks. Other Russian projects filmed here include *Balalaika* (1939), and *Song of Russia* (1944), in which the set portrayed the town of Tschaikowskoye. Many of the buildings were destroyed for that film's memorable bombing sequences.

The street's icy, rustic look—with Pacific-Northwest modifications—made it perfect for *The Wild North* (1952), with Stewart Granger and Cyd Charisse, and that Royal Canadian Mounted Police perennial *Rose Marie* (the 1954 version). As the set aged and the paint on the wood peeled, taking with it even more of the original Russian architecture, the studio used the street as an alternative Western town for television.

Above: Fort Canby in *A Thunder of Drums* (1961).

eyond the Cossack-themed Cloudy Street could be found still more of the American West. Namely, Billy the Kid Street, Ghost Town Street, and a variety of frontier-themed annexes, outposts, and settlements.

All told, these sectors—including Western Street and Rawhide Street (built at the lower lip of Billy the Kid Street) and the neighboring cavalry sets Fort Scott and Fort Canby—consisted of more than 12 acres, the largest Western movie location in the world. The Cheviot Hills to the east, although spotted with oil derricks, provided a suitable background for all of this picturesque

48	**FORT CANBY**
49	**FORT SCOTT**
50	**BILLY THE KID STREET**
51	**GHOST TOWN STREET**

frontier real estate. The sets were used interchangeably and will be described thus, except where noted.

Ghost Town Street was constructed for the non-Western *Boom Town* (1940) and, indeed, was sometimes referred to as "Boom Town Street" internally. Billy the Kid Street was constructed in 1941 to portray New Mexico for *Billy the Kid*, the title role of which was well-played by Robert Taylor. In later years, part of the area was occasionally referred to as Mexican Street—which reflected the district's southwestern influence.

The familiar train chugging across this set was built in 1872.

Left: Ghost Town Street (1940).
Right: Billy the Kid Street in *Sea of Grass* (1947), starring Katharine Hepburn.

Purchased by the studio for *The Harvey Girls* (1946), the locomotive showed up in many Westerns. In 1949, it could be spotted carrying Esther Williams as K. C. Higgins, the new manager of a baseball team in *Take Me Out to the Ball Game.* In the '60s, it was even seen in an episode of *Combat!* (1962–1967). Shortly before it was sold in the 1970 studio auction, author and steam locomotive aficionado Gerald M. Best was allowed to inspect the then-nearly-hundred-year-old "prop." In his follow-up correspondence with the studio, he marveled at how the locomotive had "been around a lot longer than you or I will be. And I hope MGM appreciates what they have."

By the 1940s, as the studio's identification with more "highbrow" productions was diluted, any hesitation about traditional Westerns was forgotten. In 1948, John Wayne and director John Ford arrived to shoot *3 Godfathers* on this set. Not surprisingly, except when one considers the studio that made it, the film is a quintessential, al-

legorical, Western—one of the few in the studio's history to that time that could be called such.

Yet it was not Wayne, but the more introspective and urban Glenn Ford who became MGM's consummate Western hero in a series of films made here in the 1950s and 1960s. Billy the Kid Street was Oak Creek, and Ford was *The Fastest Gun Alive* in 1956. Two years later, he co-starred with Shirley MacLaine in the unexpectedly witty *The Sheepman* (1958). *Cimarron*, based on the Edna Ferber novel about the Oklahoma land rush, was supposed to be the studio's "big one" for 1960, but instead it was a bloated box office misfire. Ford returned in a better vehicle, a Civil War farce called *Advance to the Rear* in 1964, where he clowned on-set and on-camera with Stella Stevens and Melvyn Douglas. In 1965, he and Henry Fonda curtain called in the modern western *The Rounders.*

Among the most renowned Western television series shot here

was *Rawhide* (1959–1966), for which the set was redressed to play every settlement that series stars Eric Fleming and Clint Eastwood rode through between San Antonio, Texas, and Sedalia, Kansas —although the show itself would move to Republic Studios after 1962. During production of the series, guest stars like Julie Harris, Lon Chaney Jr., Peter Lorre, and Victor McLaglen brought some old-time glamour back to the lot.

The Western streets proved to be as vulnerable to the potent "Elvis Presley curse" as the rest of backlot was. When Elvis filmed *Charro!* here in 1969, it was close to the end for both the set and of that seminal rocker's film career. This particular picture, actually a potentially interesting break in the star's by-then aging formula of mindless rock and roll and comedy, was intended to be a gritty,

non-musical Western in the style of Sam Peckinpah, or the "spaghetti Westerns" then emerging out of Europe. The same recipe, after all, had worked well early in Presley's career with *Flaming Star* (1960) for Fox. Here, however, it was a clear, sad case of too little, too late. The grit that came so naturally to Europeans—who had to manufacture their sets, rather than walk across the street to where they stood prefabricated and ready for their cameras—could no longer be produced on a set that had participated in too much phony dramatics, and by a star who had indulged in more than a few of those dramatics himself. The stubble on Elvis's chin and the dirt painted onto the buildings only pointed out that for both the star and the set, being burned-out and tired doesn't necessarily make for realism—just tedium.

Left: St. Louis Street in 1946.
Right: St. Louis Street, again, in 1946. The numbers above the houses were used internally to identify the façades and correspond to the numbers on the studio map: The Smith House is on the left and the Bluett House is on the right.

52   ST. LOUIS STREET

Alongside Ghost Town Street and running parallel to it, east-west to the top of the lot, was the fabled St. Louis Street. This very long, very ornate, two-sided row of turn-of-the-last-century homes became a major source of contention between Cedric Gibbons and director Vincente Minnelli in 1944. Minnelli insisted that the studio build the street from scratch for his *Meet Me in St. Louis*, rather than redress the standing New England Street sets that already existed and that Gibbons felt would impart the same feeling onscreen (and at a fraction of the cost).

The friction between Minnelli and Gibbons had started even before that. Producer Arthur Freed had brought Minnelli, a noted theatrical designer, to the West Coast in 1940. Gibbons snorted in a studio memo that, "I absolutely refuse to work under any conditions with any man designing settings unless he is brought through to me as a member of my department." Ultimately, Mayer stepped in and sided with Minnelli, whom he perceived—and was proven to be correct—as a genuine wunderkind, a truly creative artist *and* technician. For the first time, Gibbons was forced to subvert his vision to that of a director. Today, it is impossible to conceive of it coming down any other way, but at the time—although no one involved could have know it—the victory of a filmmaker over his employers was perhaps the very first crack in the foundations of the studio system. Oddly, Minnelli would prove

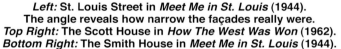

Left: St. Louis Street in *Meet Me in St. Louis* (1944).
The angle reveals how narrow the façades really were.
Top Right: The Scott House in *How The West Was Won* (1962).
Bottom Right: The Smith House in *Meet Me in St. Louis* (1944).

to be as much a company man as Gibbons or Mayer, surviving at the studio for 26 years.

Ultimately, what was assembled on Lot Three over Gibbons's objections cost nearly a quarter million dollars. The houses, and there were once eight of them, were each named, and had their own personality and character as dictated by Minnelli.

Gibbons, as usual, still took the credit for final project (with staffers Lemuel Ayers and John Martin Smith), but the project was a personal triumph for Minnelli and for his star Judy Garland, whom he married soon after the film was completed.

The set, too, was a triumph for the studio. In 1947 alone, it provided a home for Spencer Tracy and Lana Turner in *Cass Timberlane*;

appeared in the last of the long-running William Powell/Myrna Loy mystery series *Song of the Thin Man*; was a stop-off for a 1920s roadster full of all-star kids for *Good News*; and RKO brought Loretta Young here to work as a housemaid (and subsequently earn an Oscar for Best Actress) in *The Farmer's Daughter*.

Time ticked by. Garland returned here for *In The Good Old Summertime* (1949). A few years later, Minnelli also returned, perhaps for sentimental reasons. He used the Bluett House for *The Long, Long Trailer* in 1953 as the home of Lucille Ball's relatives. In the 1960s, Debbie Reynolds lived here twice, in *How The West Was Won* in 1962 (as San Francisco) and *The Unsinkable Molly Brown* in 1964 (as Denver).

In 1959, one of the most memorable episodes of Rod Serling's

Top Left: Director Vincente Minnelli, standing on the camera crane, films a scene for *Meet Me in St. Louis* (1944).
Top Right: Desi Arnaz and Lucille Ball try to maneuver their new trailer up the Bluett House driveway in *The Long, Long Trailer* (1954).
Bottom Photos: Left to Right: the first two photos are internal reference studies prepared for *Meet Me in St. Louis* (1944), and the third is for the much later film *All Fall Down* (1962).

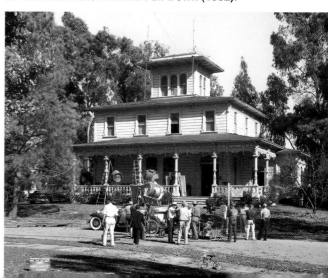

Left: Glenn Ford and Maria Schell in front of the Bluett House in *Cimarron* (1960).
Right: In *Bannerline* (1951), Keefe Brasselle reevaluates his parking skills with the Barkoff House in the background.

The Twilight Zone, entitled "Walking Distance" (1959), was filmed here with a tired Gig Young as a Madison Avenue executive who escapes into his own past. "Not long ago," Serling told the *New York Daily News* in 1959, "I was walking on a set at MGM when I was suddenly hit by the similarity of it to my hometown. Feeling an overwhelming sense of nostalgia, it struck me that all of us have a deep longing to go back—not to our home as it is today, but as we remember it. It was from this simple incident that I wrote the story 'Walking Distance.'"

Is it a stretch then, to imagine that the same sad longing to "go back" was possibly shared by Young himself? The actor would take his own life in 1978.

Producer George M. Lehr remembered working on St. Louis Street in the 1960s on *The Man from U.N.C.L.E.* TV series (1964–1968). "Each of the homes had names so we could tell them apart, since they were all built in the same style," he remembered. (For the record, the preserved names of the homes, going west down the street were: the Barkoff House, the Bluett House—although, the character played by Tom Drake, the boy next door who lived there in *Meet Me in St. Louis* was actually called "Truett"—the beloved Smith House, and the Scott Home.) In 2008, media writer Timothy Sexton named the Smith House one of the "Five Most Memorable Houses in American Film History," though the set had been destroyed in 1972.

Left: The studio-built rock formation façade seen here during the MGM auction in 1970. The vintage wagons were offered to the highest bidder, but the rocks were quickly broken up and bulldozed.
Right: A convicted James Stewart breaks up the rock pile in *Carbine Williams* (1952).

53 ROCK FORMATIONS

Vaguely parallel to St. Louis Street ran the wide but unimpressive Drumhead Road. Nearby to that, looking like a lopsided stone castle, and standing sentry over the entire district stood an enormous, artificial rock formation. In nature, something like this would be impressive, but not remarkable. This set, though, represents the deceptive hand of man, not nature, and so probably would merit a second look by studio visitors smart enough to realize this. The rocks were poured from cement (actually gunite) onsite, and were at the disposal of whatever production was shooting appropriate exterior sequences.

The boulders were featured throughout the 1950s in *The Bad and the Beautiful* (repainted to look like a fake studio set), *Invitation*, and *The Wild North* (all in 1952); *The Gypsy Colt* (a 1954 remake of *Lassie Come Home*—told with horses) and Esther Williams's *Jupiter's Darling* (1954); and bits of *The Time Machine* (1960) were shot here as well. In 1959, a single shot, a retake of Charlton Heston reacting to a divine revelation, was taken on the set for the studio's colossal, yet mostly Italian-made spectacle, *Ben-Hur*.

Above: An early view of the Lot Three Jungle and Lake already accessorized with artificial as well as imported, live trees.

54 LOT THREE JUNGLE AND LAKE

The Lot Three Jungle and Lake, like Lot Two's Cohn Park, were the result of the efforts of production head J.J.Cohn and the extraordinary success of Edgar Rice Burroughs' *Tarzan*.

The first three pictures in the series were a hodgepodge of Lot One, Two, location, sound stage work, and stock footage of Africa, as shot for *Trader Horn* (1931). The jungle was first utilized in *Tarzan Finds a Son* (1939), was revisited for *Tarzan's Secret Treasure* (1941), and was seen again for the series swansong *Tarzan's New York Adventure* (1942). Years later a remake of the first film would bring the Ape Man back, however.

When Cohn noticed how many times the company was going on location because the lakes on Lots One and Two were not big enough to accommodate Tarzan and his associates, he started suggesting that the company build an even bigger tropical area. A small jungle had existed on Lot Three from the beginning, but the set that Cohn had in mind was bigger than anything yet attempted in any studio. "Everyone thought I was insane. And so we built the lake and I said, 'Charge it to the picture, that's all.' It became fantastically valuable, because we bought trees whenever we could get them, and some of them we planted. We did all the elephant stuff in our own tank there. Made it about 300 feet. Gibbons designed it. I said, 'I want it designed so we could use it for various purposes.' Then we had a little inlet alongside of it, so we really utilized it. It paid for itself."

The lake, or "jungle river," as it was sometimes called, spanned 1,200 feet, included an island, and ranged from 4–10 feet deep. Some of the buildings and ships that were stored at Lot One's lake were moved here in the northwest corner of the lot where the seven-million-gallon river begins its winding route up into the jungle's heart of darkness.

The trees and plants growing along the lake and in the depths of the jungle were oft-times of families and varieties that were never

Left: The Lot Three Jungle and Lake set in *Malaya* (1950), starring James Stewart (in boat) and Spencer Tracy (on dock).
Right: Cast and crew prepare for the next scene to shoot for *Green Mansions* (1959) on the shore of the Lot Three Jungle and Lake.
Opposite: An artificial Tarzan tree along the shore of Lot Three's Jungle and Lake (1943).

meant to cohabitate in nature. Any sharp-eyed horticulturists in the audiences of pictures shot here must have been shaking their collective heads in amazement at the lush vegetation somehow coexisting in Culver City, of all places.

Employees of the studio's Greens Department did have their hands full tending to the problems inherent in getting foliage to grow in a desert climate, which L.A. basically has. Water was piped in, and sprinkler heads were honeycombed throughout the greenery and carefully hidden from the camera in order to keep everything green and alive.

It's surprising how well filled-in the jungle looked onscreen in even the earliest pictures shot there. The illusion held up even when exploring the physical set, which was eventually so cavernous and over-grown that it was literally possible to get lost in the tangles of foliage. Actor Richard Anderson remembered, "When I went out to the jungle I remembered seeing as a kid, it was exactly like I thought it would be when I saw the movies!" *Almost* exactly. According to studio rumors in the 1960s, unexplored corners of the jungle included gardens of secretly maintained marijuana.

The company continued to utilize its jungle property into the 1960s, although often in wildly ineffectual ways. In 1965, studio-head-of-the-moment Robert Weitman financed the construction of one last major set—a turn-of-the-century Seine laundry along the riverbanks—for *Lady L*, only to scrap the project and later produce the film almost entirely in Europe.

Left: The junction of Eucy Road and McCleary Lane in 1948.
Top Right: Eucy Road as it looked in 1950.
Bottom Right: Approximately the same section of Eucy Road as it looks today.

Numerous roads cut through the jungle and wound around Lot Three, including Drumhead Road, Ames Road, River Road, Island Road, McCleary Road, and Lady L Road. Eucy Road (again, as in "eucalyptus") was the largest of them all—not to be confused with Eucy Grove on Lot Two. "We had an extra piece of ground," recalled J. J. Cohn. "I said, 'Plant trees there. Make a country road out of it.'" The road became longer and longer and eventually included varying paved and unpaved sectors, several roadside buildings, and at least one gas

55 EUCY ROAD

station. It eventually rolled past the jungle and most of the way across the lot, and was used so often that it was sectioned off by facility bookkeepers for billing purposes as "Sector 17." George P. Erengis estimated that half of all MGM's pictures used this location one way or another.

A few hundred feet of Eucy Road survives today and can be seen along Freshman Drive at the edge of the West Los Angeles College campus. The eucalyptus trees are still there.

Left: An aerial view of the Salem Waterfront as it looked in the 1960s.
Right: The façades of the Salem Waterfront (1968).

At the very bottom of the Jungle Lake was a village known as the Salem Waterfront. The cobblestone street of colonial-style brick homes and storefronts, with a working dock and period port facing the water, was constructed in 1950 for *The Running of the Tide*, a vehicle proposed for Clark Gable, and later Howard Keel, that was never filmed.

The most notable aspect about the set, however, was not the façades themselves, but the odd collection of full-size watercraft that sat at anchor in its port, which itself was sometimes referred to as "Tortuga Bay."

For many years, there rested here a tugboat, first used aptly enough in the well-remembered picture *Tugboat Annie* (1933). The

ship was actually a refugee from the 1935 exodus out of Lot One when the backlot was removed. How the tug ended up out on Lot Three at all and how many other cinematic adventures she had there is open to speculation, although Wallace Beery, the star of *Tugboat Annie*, is thought to have skippered her again in *Barnacle Bill* (1941).

Also moored there was the largest prop ever constructed, at the time, for a motion picture—the *Cotton Blossom*, from the studio's remake of *Show Boat* (1951), as designed by Jack Martin Smith. Although her cotton-candy-colored paint eventually faded to gray, and grass sprung through the slats on her decks, it was hard not to draw an awe-inspired breath at the first sight of her. With her graceful lines and gingerbread detailing, she probably could not have functioned long as

Left: The *Cotton Blossom* prepares to dock, as recorded by the production staff on the left, for *Show Boat* (1951).
Right: Salem Waterfront in *Advance to the Rear* (1963).
Opposite: With the Lake drained of water, the finishing touches are applied to the *Cotton Blossom* for *Show Boat* (1951). Salem Waterfront can be seen in the background.

a real showboat. In fact, history and Edna Ferber, author of the source novel, tell us that actual Mississippi showboats were ugly barges that were towed from town to town up and down the river. Not so for this self-propelled (via two concealed diesel engines and underwater cables) grand lady.

MGMers who worked on the film remember her with awe. "They had it on that lake out in the backlot and you'd come in there in the morning in the fog and you'd swear to God you were on the Mississippi. It was gorgeous. It was just gorgeous!" actor Howard Keel remarked.

Indeed, the 171-foot-long confection—with a 34-foot beam, rising 57 feet to the top of her smoke stacks and with a 19.5-foot paddle wheel—was the studio's most expensive prop to date, when constructed, at a cost of $126,468. To the dismay of studio accountants back on Lot One, it would ultimately cost more. A fire during production almost burned the ship down when the tanks generating the black

smoke for the funnels set fire to the deck. Restoration and repair would cost the company an additional $66,000.

Flames of another kind nearly erupted at the very end of filming. Kathryn Grayson, one of the picture's stars, was dating billionaire Howard Hughes at the time. The jealous Hughes, convinced he was losing Grayson to co-star Howard Keel, proceeded to repeatedly dive-bomb the riverboat set in one of his noisy airplanes, ruining take after take on what was supposed to be a wedding scene between Keel and Grayson. Not surprisingly, according to Grayson, they never used that expensive sequence.

Because of its size and fame, the *Cotton Blossom* is easy to pick out in her later voyages. *Desperate Search* (1952) made scant use of her. *The Adventures of Huckleberry Finn* (1960) retitled her the "*Natchez Queen*." *Advance to the Rear* (1964) set some comic shenanigans on her decks, as did, oddly, the TV series *My Favorite Martian* (1963–1966), and Hank Williams Jr. posed for publicity photos on those decks to

Left: The *Mayflower* was built for the 1952 film *Plymouth Adventure,* starring Van Johnson.
Right: Salem Waterfront, and a repurposed *Mayflower*, in 1953's *All the Brothers Were Valiant.*

promote his acting debut in *A Time to Sing* (1968). In the late '60s, the studio even used her as a background prop to hawk a collection of high school prom dresses and to give an antebellum air to a charity reissue party for *Gone with the Wind*. During this era on the big screen, she was often relegated to being merely background, as in *How the West Was Won* (1962), where she can be viewed behind Gregory Peck in a single sequence. One of her last big screen appearances (excepting the inevitable Elvis vehicle) was in something called *Every Girl's Dream*, a promotional short for the American cotton industry featuring a tour of the backlot by Nancy Bernard, the "1966 Maid of Cotton." While walking gingerly in her high heels across those listing decks, a helpful narrator

reminded us this set was once "filled with the sounds of clicking dice, spinning wheels, and the memorable strains of 'Ol' Man River.'"

In the 1970 studio auctions, the *Cotton Blossom* would be sold for $15,000 to a theme park operator from Kansas City. After the auction, she was pulled up from the drained lake and shipped by truck across the country to the Worlds of Fun amusement park, where she was anchored alongside her former MGM alumni, the *Mayflower*. The vessel survived until about 1995, by which time she apparently had rotted away and sank. Visitors to the park have recalled that, until very recently, the foundation of the *Cotton Blossom* was visible on the bottom of the man-made lake that had long been her home.

Left: A crew boards the *Mayflower* in *Plymouth Adventure* (1952).
Top Right: The figurehead of the *Mayflower*, photographed during the MGM auctions of 1970.
Bottom Right: The boat piloted by *Tugboat Annie* (1933) in 1970.

The tallest ship anchored in this *Twilight Zone* port of call was a complete three-mast ship equipped with partial interiors, which was constructed in 1952 to portray the *Mayflower* for *Plymouth Adventure*. For that film, the studio built a wall around many of the standing Salem Waterfront façades because the architecture there didn't match that of the English seaport from which she sailed. The ship was also used in the rash of swashbucklers the studio produced in the 1950s, many to capitalize on its rising star, Stewart Granger, such as *Young Bess* (1953) and *All the Brothers Were Valiant* (1953). Follow-ups in which the ship can be seen include *The Scarlet Coat* (1955) and *The King's Thief* (1955). In fact *most* of the pictures shot on dry land out here included this ship

as part of the set, if not the plot.

"I was a kid and used to explore the whole lot with my sister," Todd Fisher remembered. "My mother [Debbie Reynolds] would let us have the run of the place. But I've got to say that the ship was my favorite thing there. As an 11-year-old boy, being able to swing from the yardarms and duel with imaginary mutinous pirates was a great way to grow up. Every kid sees these movies and wishes they could play in these places onscreen, but my sister Carrie and I really did so, every day. My frame of reference will always be a bit skewed, I suppose."

Left: The back of the Process Tank had elaborate reinforced scaffolding to support the "sky" backdrop; a set for *Raintree County* (1956) is in the foreground.
Right: The Process Tank was the set for a movie within a movie during *Two Weeks in Another Town* (1962).

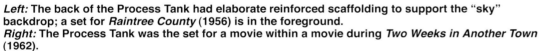

57   PROCESS TANK

A process tank is a controllable "ocean" upon which miniature or full-size aquatic sequences may be shot. A five-story-high cyclorama, upon which any part of the world may be painted, encircled the back of the set. Most of the Hollywood studios had variations on this idea at one time. As of this writing, Paramount and Universal still do, but none was ever as big as MGM's tank, which held more than *three million* gallons.

"The tank was 200 feet in width, but later we added another hundred feet and made it 300 by 300," Buddy Gillespie remembered. "It provided the best light in the world, because there's no electrician like the sun." So associated was Gillespie with this set, that on many

an in-studio memo or production report it was referred to officially as the "Gillespie tank." Everyone knew what that meant.

This set can be seen, if not specifically identified, as the home of the stormy seas in *Captains Courageous* (1937), one of the earliest uses of the new Lot Three property. It also appeared as the churning river waters of *Northwest Passage* (1940). The tank entered its most fruitful period after Pearl Harbor, when movies involving ships, boats, and submarines were understandably in vogue.

Thirty Seconds over Tokyo (1944) showed just how far the art of creating detailed miniatures—like all breeds of technology—had advanced from the prewar era just a couple years before by offering

Left: **One of several wind machines, actually converted airplanes, which provided the "waves" for the Process Tank (1970).**
Right: **The Process Tank in *Ice Station Zebra* (1968).**

viewers a banquet of meticulous and entirely convincing effects (even to modern eyes), recreating the 1942 Allied bombing of Tokyo. Technicians working here soon discovered that the key to creating successful miniatures was to make them paradoxically as large as possible and to photograph them using high-speed cameras and film; the ponderous result making "toy" boats (some of which were 20 feet across) look like city-block-long battle ships.

To quote Gillespie, "We had one ship that was 55 feet in length. The idea of a little boat in a bathtub makes a good cartoon, but it's not very realistic on film. The miniature carrier for *Thirty Seconds* was so large that it couldn't travel through the water very far; it would have run right into the painted backing. So we kept the ship stationary, and put

hydraulic rams on it for rock and tilt and pitch, and moved the ocean instead."

At times, no water was used to create magic in the tank. Most of *Quo Vadis* (1951) was shot overseas, but the splendid and spectacular burning of Rome sequence was shot on miniatures constructed on the three-foot-deep floor (on average) of the tank. In 1955, Frank Sinatra performed the title song for *The Tender Trap* out here, which ended up playing under the picture's stylized opening credits.

By the late 1950s, teenagers at nearby Culver City High School had discovered that by climbing a tree outside the fence facing Eucy Road, it was possible to jump inside the studio after dark and explore the property on the increasingly frequent evenings when no produc-

Top Left: The horizon line of the Process Tank and the tattered painted "sky" backdrop during the MGM Public Auction in 1970.
Bottom Left: Crews prepare the galley sequence for *Ben-Hur* (1959).
Right: Wading in the Process Tank, the film crew aligns the scale model miniatures for a scene in *Ben-Hur* (1959).

tion was happening and the entire lot was only patrolled by a couple of lonely security people. The experience became such a rite of passage for the locals that, eventually, students even distributed an underground lot map that was used for navigation by the interlopers. Award-winning illustrator and Culver City resident James C. Christensen has noted that those stolen evenings "were a big part of what formed me as an artist. . . . All that realistic illusion made a major impression on me." One of Christensen's most vivid memories was of "borrowing" a canoe and paddling around in the Jungle Lake and the big Process Tank. "One night, I was out there with a girl I was dating and the security guy drove up on his motorcycle. We only got away by crossing to the other side of the water where he couldn't follow and running away." Chris-

tensen looked back on his evenings at MGM with fondness. "It was better than Disneyland," he remembered. Similarly wistful memories were cherished by another "visitor," Reece Vogel, who could still recall "the smell of eucalyptus and wood and the sound of oil wells wheezing up on the hill" decades later.

By the time of *Ice Station Zebra* (1968), Hollywood had grown concerned that a generation, which had yet to be conceived during WWII, would no longer accept miniature boats floating in studio tanks. In addition, more and more of these sequences were shot on actual locations whenever possible. Today, such sequences are created using computers, aided by live footage shot in a studio tank. A studio tank which very much resembles the one conceived by Buddy Gillespie in 1937.

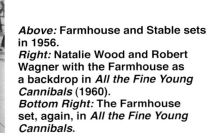

Above: Farmhouse and Stable sets in 1956.
Right: Natalie Wood and Robert Wagner with the Farmhouse as a backdrop in *All the Fine Young Cannibals* (1960).
Bottom Right: The Farmhouse set, again, in *All the Fine Young Cannibals.*

58 FARMHOUSE

Dating from about 1950, a large farmhouse set was completely equipped with all the accompanying barns, stables, and out-buildings that a real farmer would need to work real lands or raise horses. An entire second farm residence stood nearby for varia-tions, as well. The Red Skelton vehicle *Excuse My Dust* (1951), and *The Mating Game* (1959) with Debbie Reynolds and Tony Randall, are good representative titles for this set. The house and the surrounding barnyard were sometimes referred to as the "Las Vegas Stables" after *Meet Me in Las Vegas* (1956). Perhaps most unusually, "Elegy," a 1960 *Twilight Zone* episode, used this set as the site of a most unlikely alien planet as visited by American astronauts.

Left: The Kismet Staircase dressed for *An American in Paris* (1951).
Right: The Kismet Staircase is combined with an optical matte painting for the 1960 version of *The Time Machine*.
Opposite: The Kismet Staircase as part of the interior of a temple in *Kismet* (1944).

59 KISMET STAIRCASE

Behind the farmhouse was the backside of a staircase that rose up out of no place and went nowhere. This outdoor, poured-cement edifice could be used as the formal entrance to any public building and was nearly 100 feet across and 50 feet high. At the top of this staircase, however, there was no building.

The set dated back to the 1944 version of *Kismet*. Originally, the stairs were part of an elaborate Baghdad set built for that film. After this single picture, however, the studio decided to leave *Arabian Nights*-style adventures to smaller, less highbrow studios like Universal. Consequently, the set—with its white 40-foot-high walls and 80-foot onion domes—was little used. Although, amusingly, Bud Abbott and Lou Costello (on loan from Universal) romped through these façades in *Lost in a Harem* (1944) right after *Kismet* wrapped.

The coda to this story is that later, short-sighted studio executives insisted on demolishing the Baghdad set. It would have certainly come in handy by the time Elvis got around to *Harum Scarum* in 1965.

The staircase survived, however, and proved to be a most useful prop. From 1945's *Anchors Aweigh* on, the studio took to dropping any sort of building (via the magic of matte painting) at the top of the staircase they desired. A fine example of this trickery is the very end of *An American in Paris* (1951) where lovers Gene Kelly and Leslie Caron are reunited, and in which the staircase is made to seem even longer by trees and grassy lawns portioning off its two sections and clever matte work.

The set's 1960s ruined look proved popular for apocalyptic dramas like *The World, the Flesh and the Devil* (1959); *The Time Machine* (1960); *Atlantis, the Lost Continent* (1961); and the famous "Time Enough at Last" episode (1959) of *The Twilight Zone*—the one in which bookworm Burgess Meredith becomes the last man in the world, and consequently breaks his reading glasses.

In 1971, *Look* magazine paid to bus 52 shapely starlets out to the steps for a photoshoot about the struggles of young actresses in Hollywood. Among the then-unknowns draped across the stairway to nowhere could be found future superstar Farrah Fawcett, and a young actress named Skye Aubrey, whose father would very soon be instrumental in the studio's destruction.

Left: Easter Parade Street under construction.
Right: *Easter Parade* (1948) co-star Peter Lawford (left) visits the set.

At the end of Drumhead Road laid an empty, paved area that, in 1948, was the scene of another Judy Garland triumph. For her famous walk down Fifth Avenue with Fred Astaire in *Easter Parade*, studio art director Jack Martin Smith built a few feet of the actual street as it looked in New York in 1912, going about 10 feet up for almost two city blocks on one side of the street only. The other side of the street and the tops of the buildings on both sides were a matte painting created by Warren Newcombe, which was optically added in during post-production. Watching the film, it is close to impossible to figure out where the real street ends and the painted optic begins.

Once this scene was in the can, however, this virtual street—an early predecessor of today's virtual backlots—was completely removed, at least the sections that physically exited were, and shipped in pieces to Lot Two's New York Street.

Top Left: The Circus Grounds set in *Billy Rose's Jumbo* (1962).
Bottom Left: Doris Day and Stephen Boyd explore the Circus Grounds of *Billy Rose's Jumbo* in 1962.
Right: Here the Circus Grounds are decorated with a massive painted backdrop of Monument Valley, as created by the Scenic Arts Department, for *Annie Get Your Gun* (1950).

61 CIRCUS GROUNDS

Nearby was a nondescript six-acre open area known as the Circus Grounds. The earliest picture to so christen the space was apparently *O'shaughnessy's Boy* in 1935—before the property had even been purchased outright. For this film, and other subsequent circus pictures, the studio would always rent a big top as needed. It's very odd considering the company's policy of "buy it once, use it forever" that MGM apparently never thought to buy the equipment outright, although the circus came to town here with some regularity. In fact, the area was so busy in the 1950s that aerial shots of the lot reveal as many as six circus and sideshow tents standing out here at once.

Perhaps the most famous scenes haunting this set were created for *Annie Get Your Gun* (1950). All those spectacular musical rodeo numbers, including the "There's No Business Like Show Business" finale were shot here. That set, designed by art director Paul Groesse, included a 250-foot-long painted backdrop of Monument Valley, over 1,000 extras, and a $200,000 price tag.

When the circus was not in town, the set was often used as a baseball diamond with bleachers, or for any sequence in which an open field was required. *Take Me Out to the Ball Game* (1949) is an obvious example of this ballpark esthetic at work on-camera.

The set was surprisingly immune to the Elvis Presley Curse. The King shot three films here—the set's last three features—before the area was destroyed.

Above: A panoramic view of the Army Base set (1952).

Young actors playing recruits in all those war films made in the '40s were inevitably subjected to grueling basic training montages shot in the Army Base set. The base was visited not by signing up at an induction office, but by walking west from the circus grounds to the very bottom of the lot along Lot Three's western wall fronting Jefferson Boulevard. It consisted of long tin sheds, barracks, mess halls, Quonset huts, and training courses, and was built circa 1941 to service *The Bugle Sounds* (1942); *Pilot #5* and *Bataan* (both 1943); and other war films being force-fed into the MGM pipeline.

Gene Kelly led, and Mickey Rooney hosted, an all-star army camp show here in *Thousands Cheer* (1943). Robert Walker trained here in *See Here, Private Hargrove* (1944) and, due to considerable box office

62 ARMY BASE

grosses, returned for *What Next, Corporal Hargrove?* (1945). *Keep Your Powder Dry* (1945) told the "whipping raw recruits into seasoned soldiers" story with women like Lana Turner in the leads. Lassie did her part in *Son of Lassie* (1945) and *Courage of Lassie* (1946) too.

But after the war, as production of films with military backgrounds dwindled, there was notably less work for this set. Although television, including the Cold War cult series *The Outer Limits* (1963–1965) and *The Man from U.N.C.L.E.* (1964–1968), made occasional visits to the compound.

A much smaller, early version of this set—Quonset Village—once existed near Eucy Grove on Lot Two.

Left: A night shot of Dutch Street in *Seven Sweethearts* (1942).
Right: Dutch Street in *Desire Me* (1947).

Dutch Street laid somewhat southeast of the military barracks, and at the bottom of Ghost Town and Billy the Kid Street. Actually, the section was made up of three separate districts, identified as Melbury Street, Dutch Street, and Brooklyn Street, the last of which should not be confused with the large New York-style streets on Lot Two. This Brooklyn was an antiqued, turn-of-the-century variation on the theme, and often doubled for Europe.

Yet another large body of water, complete with cobblestone banks, dock, piers, and bridges fronted this 19th century European district. Although the six-foot-deep tank was empty, it was neighbor to a replica of the HMS *Bounty*, listing morosely near the bare floor

63	**DUTCH STREET**
64	**MELBURY STREET**
65	**BROOKLYN STREET**

of the lakebed.

MGM drew a great deal of publicity for its 1962 *Mutiny on the Bounty* remake for claiming to have constructed a full-scale, working replica of that ill-fated vessel. That they did. But the ship that was anchored alongside this set was most definitely not it. In fact, the Salem Waterfront vessel only played the ill-fated *Bounty* in the scenes where she is anchored in port.

Most of this district was constructed to play Denmark in 1942 for *Seven Sweethearts*, although it existed earlier in an embryonic stage. The set represented Scotland in *The Green Years* (1946) and was St. Pierre, Channel Islands, for *Green Dolphin Street* in 1947.

Left: Melbury Street in 1949.
Right: Brooklyn Street dressed for *Valley of Decision* (1945).
Opposite: Dutch Street in *Seven Sweethearts* (1942).

On television, the street and port was revisited in episodes of the ubiquitous *Combat!* (1962–1967), *Garrison's Gorillas* (1967–1968), and *The Man from U.N.C.L.E.* (1964–1968). In 1968, the filmmakers of *Ice Station Zebra* would break with local tradition by shooting their scenes there *after* the inevitable Elvis Presley vehicle *Double Trouble* (1967) had quit rocking.

Turning back to this street with its three contradictory names, a visitor to this set might have noticed that this particular neighborhood—at least when explored beyond the Dutch Street waterfront district—didn't really represent anything, or any place specifically at all. The hive of nondescript streets here could have played northern Europe, or New England, or a colonial island port, or an outpost in the American west.

This area may perhaps have actually been the perfect backlot. Not because of any remarkable or memorable qualities it possessed, but because of its bland anonymity.

Our wanderings across Hollywood's greatest backlot are at an end. At the gate, the same gate a visitor would have entered through a thousand movies before, traffic buzzes past. The fantasy is over. Reality takes hold.

PART FOUR:

BACKLOT BABYLON

"Hollywood's like Egypt," said David. "Full of crumbled pyramids. It'll never come back. It'll just keep crumbling until finally the wind blows the last studio prop across the sands."

—BEN HECHT,
A Child of the Century

"INSUBSTANTIAL PAGENTS"

Where the plaster and wood simulations of past time and different locales once stood, bulldozers, earthmovers, and pile drivers now hold sway. All that remains of these famous outdoor sets are some shadows on stripes of acetate.
But then, that's all they were ever meant to be.
—GEORGE P. ERENGIS

"The last great year of the studio was 1948," retired publicist Edward Lawrence said in 1974. "And from then on, the studio was like a patient with a chronic illness, kept alive by timely blood transfusions until the blood bank ran dry."

The watershed 12 months of 1948 marked the last over-confident grandstanding of the old studio system and signified the arrival of new rituals and rhythms by which the game would be played in the future. The klieg lights dimmed around the moguls and their empires so slowly that, at first, they probably didn't notice that anything had changed. But dim they did.

After the war, as box-office figures started to fall off, location shooting at MGM slowly started to increase. Many soldiers, returned from actual exotic locations in the armed forces, were suddenly perceived to be more interested in realism—or better able to recognize it—in their entertainment. And for the first time, lightweight equipment made this a viable possibility. MGM responded by reluctantly agreeing to shoot brief scenes of *On the Town* (1949) that year in New York.

By 1948, television was becoming widely available to Americans. The Emmys, the new industry's equivalent of the Oscars, were presented for the first time that year, heralding the arrival of this new hybrid of radio and motion pictures. *The Ed Wynn Show* (1949–1950) became the first network series to be broadcast out of Hollywood. The enemy was clearly no longer at the gate, but was actually *inside* it. And yet, the complacent studios and their aging moguls were unsure how to fix the problem.

Then, there was the trouble of an increasing number of freelancers floating about from studio to studio, choosing projects they wanted and taking a share of the profits. For example, over at Universal, former MGM contract star James Stewart negotiated a deal through his agent, Lew Wasserman, for a profit participation in *Winchester '73* in 1950—a move then virtually unheard of for actors. Important directors like Alfred Hitchcock (*North by Northwest* [1959]) and David Lean (*Dr. Zhivago* [1965], *Ryan's Daughter* [1970]) began turning to their old studios only for financing and distribution, a practice that continues to this day.

In Washington, D.C., the House Un-American Activities Committee commenced hearings in regard to supposed communist infiltration of American culture. Hollywood managed to repeatedly implicate its own, and generally represented itself very badly in front of the committee. "Those postwar years that seem so rosy in hindsight were really quite miserable politically," recalled Myrna Loy. "You could feel this cold wind blowing into Hollywood from the east, chopping the city into factions. There was a clash between the liberals and the conservatives. All you had to do was know someone of questionable political persuasion and you were labeled 'Commie.'"

1948 was also the year of the so-called "consent decrees." In May, the Supreme Court ruled that Hollywood studios' ironclad ownership of production, distribution, and exhibition constituted a monopoly. With one broad stroke, the empires that Arthur Loew and the other moguls had built their fortunes upon were effectively dismantled.

"It was the end of the golden goose," said Debbie Reynolds.

"I never understood this," said Mickey Rooney in his biogra-

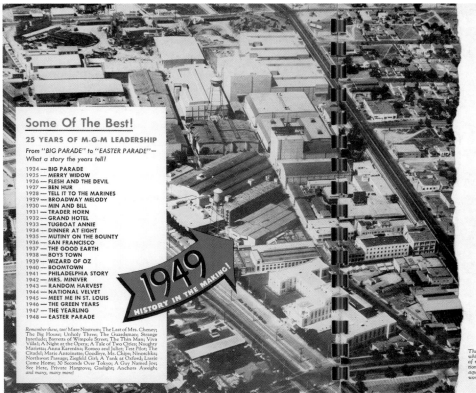

Some Of The Best!

25 YEARS OF M·G·M LEADERSHIP

From "BIG PARADE" to "EASTER PARADE"—
What a story the years tell!

1924 — BIG PARADE
1925 — MERRY WIDOW
1926 — FLESH AND THE DEVIL
1927 — BEN HUR
1928 — TELL IT TO THE MARINES
1929 — BROADWAY MELODY
1930 — MIN AND BILL
1931 — TRADER HORN
1932 — GRAND HOTEL
1933 — TUGBOAT ANNIE
1934 — DINNER AT EIGHT
1935 — MUTINY ON THE BOUNTY
1936 — SAN FRANCISCO
1937 — THE GOOD EARTH
1938 — BOYS TOWN
1939 — WIZARD OF OZ
1940 — BOOMTOWN
1941 — PHILADELPHIA STORY
1942 — MRS. MINIVER
1943 — RANDOM HARVEST
1944 — NATIONAL VELVET
1945 — MEET ME IN ST. LOUIS
1946 — THE GREEN YEARS
1947 — THE YEARLING
1948 — EASTER PARADE

1949
HISTORY IN THE MAKING!

*Remember them, too! Mare Nostrum; The Last of Mrs. Cheney;
The Big House; Unholy Three; The Guardsman; Strange
Interlude; Barretts of Wimpole Street; The Thin Man; Viva
Villa!; A Night at the Opera; A Tale of Two Cities; Naughty
Marietta; Anna Karenina; Romeo and Juliet; Test Pilot; The
Citadel; Marie Antoinette; Goodbye, Mr. Chips; Ninotchka;
Northwest Passage; Ziegfeld Girl; A Yank at Oxford; Lassie
Come Home; 30 Seconds Over Tokyo; A Guy Named Joe;
See Here, Private Hargrove; Gaslight; Anchors Aweigh;
and many, many more!*

We Face The Future Together

M-G-M is justifiably proud of the twenty-five years that occasion this year's Silver Anniversary celebration. Volumes that might be written about past achievements are instead condensed into the brief references on this and the facing page. The titles opposite, typical of M-G-M's preeminent product from 1924 to 1949, speak more eloquently than rhetoric of M-G-M's contribution to a great industry. M-G-M now looks ahead with optimism and confidence.

The balance of this brochure, therefore, is devoted to your future and M-G-M's future. You will find it an exciting prospect—and a source of satisfaction and reassurance in terms of theatre operation. The stars, the stories, the production values that have always characterized M-G-M product are assured in the years to come as in the past. Showmanship that comes with years of experience is brought to full fruition by a revitalized production organization that continues to be "the young blood of the industry."

With a sincere appreciation of the loyal support of its thousands of exhibitor customers, M-G-M on this occasion rededicates its entire personnel to the challenge of making our next twenty-five years even greater than the first. We can do this together.

★

The scene on this page is an aerial photo of the M-G-M Studios which cover 174 acres and include 30 vast sound stages, streets of many countries, jungles, water front harbors, railroad stations, homes, churches and a huge enclosed swimming pool for aquatic spectacles. 258 varieties of craftsmen totaling 3500 workers are employed.

Above: Although no one knew it at the time, and despite the optimistic tone of this promotional booklet, 1949 was actually the beginning of the end for the MGM empire.

phy. "Why was it wrong for MGM to show pictures in its own theatres if it was right for Ford and GM to sell cars in their own agencies or Kinney Shoes to manufacture shoes and sell them in its own stores?"

Hollywood had been turned upside down. One major studio, RKO, eventually ceased active production entirely. The companies on the bottom of the Hollywood food chain, Columbia and Universal—neither of which had ever depended on the profits from a significant number of theatres, anyway—now found themselves in a better position than their lordly competitors. Leaner and less encumbered by success, overhead, and real estate, they were already well equipped for the guerilla filmmaking tactics needed to economically produce television shows, which would become both Hollywood's damnation and salva-

tion in the coming decades.

A more abstract blow to the backlots came from Italy. Director Sidney Lumet recalled years later how "right after the war, the Italians just started creating a series of brilliant, brilliant, brilliant movies—all done on location. They had no stages, they had no choice. There were no studios. They couldn't afford the electricity, even. It was a very poor country. But it started—contributed—something to movies. . . ."

L. B. Mayer hated these so-called "neo-realist pictures." Sourly, he centered much of his frustration on MGM's new favored son, Dore Schary, a former RKO executive who was championing the production of a gritty, all-male film called *Battleground* (1949).

Mayer had initially liked Schary, who had written *Boys Town* (1938) and produced hits like *Journey for Margaret* (1942) and *Lassie Come Home* (1943). Schary's previous hit-making track record at RKO had only furthered the rumor among MGM employees that Mayer was grooming "another Thalberg."

But the paternal relationship between Mayer and Schary quickly cooled.

The initial *cause celebre* had been *Battleground*. The bleak realism of the picture was abhorrent to Mayer, but much embraced by critics and the public. Critics referred to it as a studio milestone much like Thalberg's *The Big Parade* (1925).

Yet Mayer never realized the dangerous position he put himself in when he agreed with Nicholas Schenck that MGM needed new executive blood. On August 19, 1948, Schary signed a long-term, 14-year contract to become vice president in charge of production at Metro Goldwyn Mayer.

Mayer had never been intimately involved in the day-to-day gears and sprockets of filmmaking. "His comments to producers were mostly criticisms limited to his long abhorrence of unkempt men and badly dressed women, dark photography and downbeat stories," Samuel Marx recalled. Although involved in a million managerial duties at the studio, Mayer's interests had turned elsewhere. He became more active politically (a role he had always enjoyed), fell in love, divorced, and remarried a vivacious widow named Lorena Danker.

Amidst the downswing in business, the witch hunts, the threat of television, and the looming split with Loew's, MGM—still perpetuating the illusion of prosperity—decided to hold its biggest party. On February 10, 1949, Mayer gathered an astonishing 58 of the biggest stars in history on the floor of the biggest soundstage in the world for a celebration of Metro Goldwyn Mayer's 25th anniversary. It was a mighty assemblage of talent, ballyhoo, and glamour that Hollywood has never seen since. For Louis B. Mayer (the old lion), sitting beside Dore Schary (the ambitious cub), it was a last chance to roar and defy the destructive forces attacking his studio.

Betty Comden and Adolph Green, Broadway playwrights who penned the screenplays and music for several memorable MGM musicals, had revealing recollections of the event. Green remembered Mayer introducing Schary to the group. "He gave this very involved talk, trying to rationalize why Dore was now there. I don't remember what he said, but whatever it was, none of us were convinced." Com-

Above: Louis B. Mayer and Dore Schary, Mayer's eventual replacement, side by side in happier times. The expression on Mayer's face foretells the coming great divide between the Mayer Camp and the Schary Camp.

den remembered, "It was a very hot day, and all the MGM stars and everybody else were sitting at these long tables. The chocolate lions melted to nothing before we could eat them. When I think about it now, it seems like such an obvious symbol of what ended up happening."

Two years later, Mayer was cast out from the company by Schenck. Since Schary appeared to be producing the pictures in touch with American taste, Schenck used this as his excuse to oust his nemesis. In a feeble attempt to minimize Mayer's link to the company, the studio tried to refer to itself simply as MGM, not Metro Goldwyn Mayer, and Mayer's chicken soup in the commissary became "MGM's Special Chicken Soup." Yet the past and its ghosts could not be so easily exorcised.

It soon became obvious in Hollywood—and increasingly apparent to moviegoers—that Metro Goldwyn *without* Mayer was not the golden profit machine it had been. Schary did not have the Thalberg touch, or even Mayer's talent for management or nurturing stars. The studio began to flounder badly when Schary pulled the plug on the women's pictures the company was renowned for, and instead concentrated on stark, gritty stories like *Take the High Ground!* (1953) and *Bad Day at Black Rock* (1955). Worse, for every hit like *King Solomon's Mines* (1950) and *Mogambo* (1953), Schary produced heavy handed "message pictures" like *The Next Voice You Hear…* (1950), *It's a Big Country* (1951), and *The Last Hunt* (1956).

Mayer must have been pleased to see that company troubles caused Schenck himself to be ousted in 1955, and Schary to relinquish Mayer's old throne the following year. Mayer would, in fact, attempt a comeback/takeover in 1957, but he was not successful.

Mayer's bitter fate was one Goldwyn and Ince had shared on

Above: Proof the MGM motto "More Stars Than There Are In Heaven" was no idle boast with this gathering of MGM contract stars and players in 1948. Within eight years, most of these performers would no longer be associated with the studio. From left to right, starting with the *Front Row:* Lionel Barrymore, June Allyson, Leon Ames, Fred Astaire, Edward Arnold, Mary Astor, Ethel Barrymore, Spring Byington, James Craig, Arlene Dahl, and Lassie. *Second Row:* Gloria DeHaven, Tom Drake, Jimmy Durante, Vera-Ellen, Errol Flynn, Clark Gable, Ava Gardner, Judy Garland, Betty Garrett, Edmund Gwenn, Kathryn Grayson, and Van Heflin. *Third Row:* Katharine Hepburn, John Hodiak, Claude Jarman Jr., Van Johnson, Jennifer Jones, Louis Jourdan, Howard Keel, Gene Kelly, Alf Kjellin, Angela Lansbury, Mario Lanza, and Janet Leigh. *Fourth Row:* Peter Lawford, Ann Miller, Ricardo Montaban, Jules Munshin, George Murphy, Reginald Owen, Walter Pidgeon, Jane Powell, Ginger Rogers, Frank Sinatra, and Red Skelton. *Top Row:* Alexis Smith, Ann Sothern, J. Carroll Naish, Dean Stockwell, Lewis Stone, Clinton Sundberg, Robert Taylor, Audrey Totter, Spencer Tracy, Esther Williams, and Keenan Wynn.

the same lot. But there was no pity, only enmity in Goldwyn's heart when he heard that the old lion was in exile. When Mayer attempted his studio comeback, Goldwyn bought a large block of shares in the company. "Here are 10,000 votes against him," Goldwyn declared. For many years the highest-paid man in America, Mayer spent his last days unemployed, seated alone in his booth at the Santa Anita racetrack, which the Hollywood crowd sarcastically referred to as "Lot Eight." Within a few years, the old man had made his exit from there as well. His last words on October 29, 1957, were, "Nothing matters. Nothing matters."

"He was a man of great stature," said David O. Selznick in his eulogy. "In the future, looking backwards, one will see his head and shoulders rising clearly above the misty memories of Hollywood's past."

Ava Gardner agreed, in her fashion. "MGM was a damned sight better when the old man was around. I never liked him much, but at least you knew where you stood."

"I can almost compare it to the loss of my late husband," said June Allyson. "You're suddenly standing on nothingness after being on solid ground for so long. . . . Mayer won in the end. When he died, I think he took the studio with him."

Cedric Gibbons must have had similar feelings, because his reign did not long survive Mayer's. Although his decades at MGM seemingly managed to bestow immortality to Gibbons's sets, the man himself proved ultimately as human and as vulnerable to time and politics and as his coworkers.

Gibbons must have realized his own days of empire building were waning because, like an increasingly large share of MGM pictures in the late '50s, there was a vague whiff of staleness about both his department and the studio. He suffered a heart attack in 1946, but refused to significantly cut back on his punishing, relentless workload. In 1950, the Society of Motion Pictures Art Directors presented the industry veteran with its first—and last—"Distinguished Achievement" award.

Gibbons's last picture was *The Rack*, with rising star Paul Newman, in 1956. He suffered a stroke the same year, thus rendering any prolonged return to his beloved studio a virtual impossibility. Essentially disappearing into his sleek modernist mansion, his only companion those last years was his wife, Hazel.

Gibbons survived Mayer by three years. When he died in 1960, it was in his unique, self-designed bedroom: the ersatz moon projected onto the wall casting shadows over his bed, the rain machine on the roof mimicking a gentle summer storm.

By the 1960s, the effervescence of the studio's in-house productions was largely gone. The films were no longer radiating that cheerful, ebullient wholesomeness, that confident lavishness that they had in the 1930s and the 1940s. Unlike then, the current audience wasn't buying what the studio was selling. The studio was, in fact, slowly being eaten away from the inside. Benjamin Thau had replaced Schary in 1956. Thau lasted two years and was usurped by Sol C. Siegel, who in turn was replaced by Robert Weitman in 1962, Clark Ramsey in 1967, Herbert F. Solow in 1969, and Daniel Melnick in 1973. The wheel continued to spin.

Things were changing outside the Thalberg Building, too, which was affecting the bottom line as well. In 1963, CBS Television, which was a major rental tenant on the lot, assumed control of the Republic Pictures facility in Studio City, and attempted to move all its productions to that property. CBS's *The Twilight Zone* (1959–1964) remained because creator Rod Serling disliked the cramped Republic backlot, but MGM still lost long-term, revenue generating series like *Rawhide* (1959–1966) and *Combat!* (1962–1967), and ended up attracting television commercials and independent productions instead. These smaller films would often schedule so that they could shoot what they needed at MGM in a single day, achieve a big budget "Hollywood look," and then get out before incurring any significant expenses. Independent cinema legend Roger Corman, for example, recalled renting the New York Street sets for *The St. Valentine's Day Massacre* in 1967 for a single (and very productive) day to recreate 1920s Chicago.

In 1967, the studio was purchased by investor Edgar Bronfman Sr. Bronfman's short, less-than-two-year reign set the studio on the path it would largely follow in coming decades: less money spent on fewer and smaller movies, the closing of or cutting back on departments and manpower, asset sales, and erratic, uncertain management.

On Lot One, morale was so low that employees took early retirement or allowed themselves to be laid off rather than deal with the uncertainties inherent in showing up for work. "For example, a fellow named Ray Klune was one of the great studio production managers," recalled Roger Mayer, who was MGM's vice president of administration at the time. "His career spanned the entire studio era. He started out working for D. W. Griffith. He did *Gone with the Wind* for Selznick. He worked for Zanuck at Fox, and was at MGM for years. Think of all he knew. All he could do. He retired rather than put up with it. Now, no one even remembers who he was." Elsewhere, departments like the casting office, which had operated since the Silent Era with the same employee base, were closed down. The staff was unceremoniously sent home, and their jobs farmed out to outside contractors.

"I was pretty glad I was near retirement," recalled George Gibson, head of the Scenic Arts Department, and a 35-year veteran of the studio. "It was a different world. We were gradually moving from one big unit making pictures to a series of people coming on the lot. We were getting independent companies coming on. There wasn't the intimacy that had existed."

The city council of Culver City did not want to be dragged down with the studio. Its relationship with MGM was decaying as quickly as the studio's facilities. Although the studio continued to spill around $750,000 a year in tax revenue into city coffers, local merchants were displeased with the miles of ratty chain-link fences surrounding increasingly blighted studio lots that made the business sector of Washington Boulevard look like a waterfront warehouse district. The city's opinion was proclaimed bluntly in a *Los Angeles Times* article headline in 1967: "Maximum [City] Improvement Can Be Attained Only If MGM Film Studio Moves." For their part—from the other side of those tall, white, peeling walls—MGM officials understandably declined comment.

Oddly that same year, the Beverly Hills chapter of the Native Daughters of the Golden West placed a plaque near the beleaguered studio's somewhat faded, but still majestic colonnade on Washington Boulevard, celebrating the site's "historic interest." Pete Smith, Ann Miller, and Chad Everett represented the Hollywood community at the dedication. Thomas Ince's widow was also in attendance.

In August of that year, Chairman of the Board Robert H.

Left: By the time *The Singing Nun* (1966) was released, it was becoming increasingly obvious in the industry, and even to audiences, that the sets on the MGM backlot were no longer being properly maintained, as is evident here.
Top Right: The 1967 Historic Landmark dedication to the studio, which was at the time falling apart as fast as the backlot sets. Within three years the kingdom would begin to vanish altogether.

M.G.M. STUDIO PLAN
ALBERT C. MARTIN AND ASSOCIATES
PLANNING | ARCHITECTURE | ENGINEERING

SITE PLAN

SCALE

O'Brien announced that he had purchased 1,849 acres of land in Thousand Oaks in the Conejo Valley with the intention of moving their studio operations there. Blueprints of the proposed complex imagined multiple soundstages, a film lab, acres of office and parking space and, interestingly enough according to the studio press release, a network of "exterior sets, which will recreate towns and cities of international character"—a.k.a. a backlot.

Hollywood was surprised that the company was willing to spend an enormous outlay of cash ($8.75 million) to purchase the land at a time when the studio could ill-afford it. But the plan, misguided though it was, did reflect continuing faith in the company as an ongoing concern. At one time, both Columbia and Fox were onboard as partners—before a squabble over a theatre chain in the Midwest caused them to pull out, leaving MGM alone in the endeavor. In the end, O'Brien spent a lot of money, conducted a lot of surveys, and finally used the undeveloped land for exteriors for a TV Western called *Hondo* (based on the 1953 John Wayne film of the same title). The property was quietly sold off.

In 1969, the studio was purchased by Kirk Kerkorian. Kerkorian was a Las Vegas-based airline and hotel financier, who as a teenager had once sweated on the backlot as a construction worker. He hired television executive James Aubrey to run the beleaguered empire. Aubrey was a cocksure, profane bulldozer of a man who famously was nicknamed the "Smiling Cobra" and did his best to live up to the reputation that title suggested.

Like Kerkorian, Aubrey's past was almost cosmically linked to the studio's. In 1946, as a magazine advertising salesman, he had been granted an audience with none other than Louis B. Mayer. "Mayer's desk was on a riser. He looked as if he were on a throne. There was a grand piano in one corner," he told reporter Martin Kasindorf in 1972.

Upon taking Mayer's old job, he moved into that very same office. He immediately tore out L. B.'s private elevator for fear of unauthorized access.

Aubrey then proceeded to do exactly the same thing, on a larger scale, to the rest of the studio. "I don't want to hear any more bullshit

Top Left: A drawing of the proposed new MGM Studio west of Thousand Oaks, California.
Bottom Left: Elaborate architectural plans for the new studio lot.

about the old MGM," he snapped. "The old MGM is gone." It was Aubrey who shifted the company's headquarters from New York to Culver City—reducing the payroll by $7.5 million.

Aubrey promptly installed many of the employees he brought out west in the Thalberg Building, which he renamed the Administration Building. He removed the commemorative plaque that had watched over the lobby for decades. "Aubrey felt that the company was old-fashioned," said Roger Mayer. "He felt that the old-fashionedness was hurting the company. I did not agree with that, but he therefore felt he needed to break the tradition and to change the attitudes. An example of his attitude was to take Thalberg's name off the Thalberg Building. . . . I put the plaque with the name on it in a drawer in my office and held on to it until they changed the name back a few years later."

Aubrey then turned his focus on the company's international assets: shuttering the British MGM studio, sending the employees home, and selling the real estate for $4.3 million. He closed the MGM Paris office and sold off a chain of theatres in South Africa, India, and Australia.

Aubrey closed down the Camera Department and sold off its assets to Panavision. He closed the studio firehouse. He leased out the studio's stock footage library, and directed the disposal of much of the equally valuable Music Department's library. On December 14, 1969, he announced that all but 20 acres of the studio's real estate would be next. "MGM used to be the Tiffany's of studios," mused producer Walter Seltzer, "by the 1970s, it wasn't even Woolworths."

Peter Bart, who was working at the studio at the time, recalled in his book *Fade Out* that a "studio officer" disastrously insisted on taking Aubrey and several of Kerkorian's people on a tour of the lot. While on the backlot, someone in Aubrey's party fatefully asked, "How often is this stuff used? It's just lying around all over the place."

In 1970, Aubrey made a deal with the David Weisz Company. For $1.5 million, the auction house was given its pick of the studio's

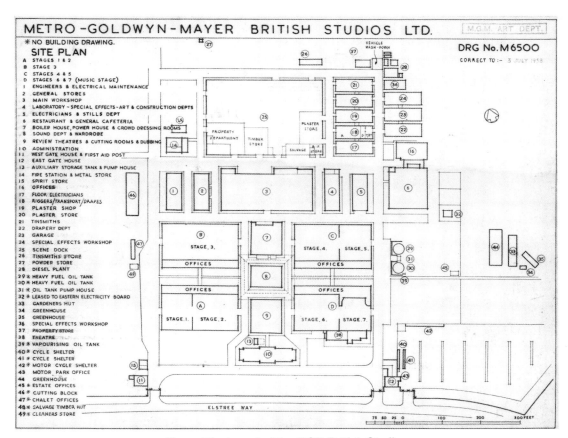

Above: The layout of the MGM British Studios.
Unfortunately, this facility shared the same fate as the backlots in Culver City—it was sold in 1969 and bulldozed for housing developments.

props and costumes to sell off to the highest bidder.

The resultant auction was dubbed by the *Hollywood Reporter* as "the greatest rummage sale in history." The *London Times* called the items on sale the "tatters of an empire," and eulogized that "once [MGM] sold shadows, and now they are selling the rags of shadows." Much later, aided by the benefit of perspective, Tom Walsh, current president of the Art Director's Guild, referred to this auction as "the defining moment when Rome was sacked and burned."

Producer Saul Chaplin was there. "I went to the MGM auction. As I walked in, I heard the album from *An American in Paris* playing on the PA, and I walked around and saw all those costumes from the bal-

EXHIBITION SESSIONS: SATURDAY, APRIL 25, THRU FRIDAY, MAY 1
FROM: 10:00 A.M. TO: 9:00 P.M.

AUCTION SCHEDULE

STAGE 27	STAGE 15	STAGE 30	LOT 2	LOTS 3 & 5	STAGE 27	AN UNDUPLICATED COLLECTION OF EXACT MODEL REPLICAS of Miniature Racing Cars, Ships, Planes, Locomotives, Trains and Tanks. CLASSIC ANTIQUE AUTOS dating back from 1894.
Antiques and Furniture	*Antiques and Furniture*	*Antiques and Furniture*	**12th DAY** Thursday, May 14 Starting 10:00 A.M.	**13th DAY 14th DAY** Friday, May 15, and Saturday, May 16 Starting 10:00 A.M.	**15th DAY** Sunday, May 17 Afternoon Session Starting 1:00 P.M. *A selected group of STAR WARDROBE*	
1st DAY Sunday, May 3 *Items #1 thru #753* Afternoon Session Starting 1:00 P.M. Evening Session Starting 7:00 P.M.	**4th DAY** Wednesday, May 6 *Items #5001 thru #5400* Evening Session Starting 7:00 P.M.	**8th DAY** Sunday, May 10 *Items #8001 thru #8902* Afternoon Session Starting 1:00 P.M. Evening Session Starting 7:00 P.M.	*150 trucks — Pickup to Dump Trucks, ½ Tracks, Sherman Tank, Automobiles, Trailers, Buses, Station Wagon, Roman Furniture and Objets D'Art, Statuary, Western and Wicker Furniture and Props, Gambling Equipment, Portable Dressing Rooms, Light Fixtures, Restaurant and Store Equipment, Antique Trunks. Complete authentic standard gauge STEAM LOCOMOTIVE COACHES FROM 1870*	*MAGNIFICENT PADDLE WHEEL STEAMER ("Cotton Blossom") featured in the motion picture "Show Boat," Harbor and Nautical Equipment, Wind and Wave Machines, Western and Church Furniture, Boats, Canoes, Movie Set Boats, Furnishings and Props used in the making of the picture "Kismet." 250 COACHES — English, Coronation, Stage, Hansom Cab, Surrey, Western Wagon, Fire Engine, Roman Chariots, Western Gear, etc.*	*(Separate catalogue provided for above)*	*(Separate catalogue provided for above)*
2nd DAY Monday, May 4 *Items #2001 thru #2676* Afternoon Session Starting 1:00 P.M. Evening Session Starting 7:00 P.M.	**5th DAY** Thursday, May 7 *Items #5401 thru #5975* Afternoon Session Starting 1:00 P.M. Evening Session Starting 7:00 P.M.	**9th DAY** Monday, May 11 *Items #9001 thru #9963* Afternoon Session Starting 1:00 P.M. Evening Session Starting 7:00 P.M.			**STAGES 7 AND 8**	**NURSERY**
3rd DAY Tuesday, May 5 *Items #3001 thru #3671* Afternoon Session Starting 1:00 P.M. Evening Session Starting 7:00 P.M.	**6th DAY** Friday, May 8 *Items #6001 thru #6940* Afternoon Session Starting 1:00 P.M. Evening Session Starting 7:00 P.M.	**10th DAY** Tuesday, May 12 *Items #10001 - #10842* Afternoon Session Starting 1:00 P.M. Evening Session Starting 7:00 P.M.	*(Separate catalogue provided for above)*		**16th DAY 17th DAY** Monday, May 18 Tuesday, May 19 Afternoon Session Starting 1:00 P.M. Evening Session Starting 7:00 P.M.	**18th DAY** Wednesday, May 20 Starting at 10 A.M. *Nursery — MGM's magnificent collection of Trees, Bushes, Plants, Flowers, etc.* AT RETAIL SALE to the PUBLIC. For direction follow signs from *OVERLAND GATE.*
4th DAY Wednesday, May 6 *Items #4001 thru #4286* Afternoon Session Starting 1:00 P.M.	**7th DAY** Saturday, May 9 *Items #7001 thru #7673* Afternoon Session Starting 1:00 P.M. (One session only)	**11th DAY** Wednesday, May 13 *Items #11001 - #11855* Afternoon Session Starting 1:00 P.M. Evening Session Starting 7:00 P.M.		*(Separate catalogue provided for above)*	*WEAPONRY — approx. 1,000 antique and modern RIFLES and HAND GUNS, Roman Armor, Swords, Spears, Bows and Arrows, Shields. Historic Military head gear.*	

II   III

Top Left: A "coronation coach" up for bid.
Second from Top Left: Dorothy's (Judy Garland) organdy blouse and blue and white gingham jumper from *The Wizard of Oz* (1939).
Third from Top Left: Massive scale model ship miniatures used in the Lot Three Process Tank.
Bottom Left: Period weaponry and scale model miniatures were some of the other items featured.
Top Right: The 1970 MGM Public Auction schedule.
Bottom Right: Curious participants enter Lot One's West Gate for the auction.

let that were going to be on sale. I couldn't stand it. It was so sad."

By the time the auctioneer's gavel had fallen, one of the storied steam locomotives had sold for $65,000. Producer George Pal's prop time machine went for $4,000. Mickey Rooney's Andy Hardy jalopy (actually a Ford Model A roadster) sold for $7,000. The shoes Elizabeth Taylor wore in *Father of the Bride* went for $200. Margaret Hamilton's witch hat sold for $450. Johnny Weissmuller's *Tarzan* loincloth sold for $600. Judy Garland's blue-and-white-checked gingham *Oz* dress went for $1,000, the wizard's suit for $650, and the Cowardly Lion's lion skin for $2,400. Clark Gable's trench coat sold for $1,250. Charles Laughton's hat from *Mutiny on the Bounty* sold for $300 and Fred Astaire's hobo hat from *Easter Parade* for $250. The most speculated about item however, was a young lady's shoes.

Ultimately, a pair of Judy Garland's ruby slippers from *The Wizard of Oz* sold for the then-astonishing amount of $15,000. Today, when movie memorabilia can fetch hundreds of thousands of dollars at auction, this amount seems downright trivial, but in 1970, movie

Above: A pair of Ruby Slippers from *The Wizard of Oz* (1939) were sold to the highest bidder for $15,000.

materials had no intrinsic value whatsoever. There was little feeling of nostalgia associated with the movies because much of Hollywood's history was still comparatively recent. Judy Garland, it's worth noting, had only died a few months before. So the majority of the items from the auction were ultimately purchased not as museum pieces to be displayed under glass, but as still-usable assets. For example, attorney Ronald Hughes, at the time preparing his defense of the Manson family, bought his suits at the auction with the intention of wearing them at trial (before he mysteriously vanished—a supposed victim of his clients).

Yet the auction became a public embarrassment to the studio when it was discovered just how grotesquely Aubrey's team had undersold the value of its past. The sale ultimately netted Weisz between $8 and $10 million—while MGM had to content itself with the $1.5 million it had paid the auctioneer to take the inventory off its hands. Subsequently, when the Prop Department needed to unload its final items nearly a decade later, employees were told to throw away or give away what was left, rather than hold another auction and potentially open the company up to public ridicule again.

On October 1, 1970, *Variety* finally broke the news that Aubrey had made good on his threat and had worked out a deal to sell Lot Three for $7.25 million to Levitt and Sons for the purpose of constructing a $60 million luxury apartment complex. Louis E. Fischer of Levitt and Sons—famous for their East Coast cookie-cutter communities for which the term "suburbia" had been coined—crowed, "It will be the first time we've built

Left: Andy Hardy fixes a flat on his Model A Roadster in *Judge Hardy and Son* (1939).
Right: Thirty-one years later, the same vehicle is up for bid.

MGM Parcel and Best Reuse	Gross Land Area (Acres)	Net Land Area (Acres)	Estimated Value Before Demolition	Per Sq.Ft.	Estimated Demolition Cost[1]	Estimated Value After Demolition	Per Sq.Ft.
Lot 1 – Area East of Overland Avenue Commercial and Commercial-Manufacturing	15.90	15.00[2]	$ 2,390,000	$3.66	$183,000[3]	$ 2,207,000	$3.38
Lot 2 – Area West of Overland Avenue Low-Rise Multiresidential	37.54	37.12	$ 4,851,000	$3.00	$100,000	$ 4,751,000	$2.94
Nine Miscellaneous Residential Lots North of Arizona Avenue Residential Property	1.21	1.21	$ 90,000	$1.71	–	$ 90,000	$1.71
Lot 3 – Southeast Corner of Jefferson Boulevard and Overland Avenue Industrial Park Development	65.57	58.20	$ 5,140,000	$2.03	$172,000	$ 4,968,000	$1.96
Lot 4 – Two Parcels on the North Side of Jefferson Boulevard Industrial Sites	5.40	5.34	$ 755,000	$3.25	–	$ 755,000	$3.25
Lot 5 – Southwest Corner of Jefferson Boulevard and Overland Avenue Multiresidential and Service Station Site	7.86	7.22	$ 1,078,000	$3.43	$ 20,000	$ 1,058,000	$3.36
Lot 6 – Northeast Corner of Jefferson Boulevard and Overland Avenue Industrial and Service Station Site	4.02	4.02	$ 737,000	$4.21	–	$ 737,000	$4.21
Total	137.50	128.11	$15,041,000		$475,000	$14,566,000	

(1) 1967 Estimate of Albert C. Martin and Associates as adjusted to reflect labor and other construction cost increases.

(2) Westerly portion of Lot 1 comprising approximately 15.0 acres of a total net acreage of 42.62 acres exclusive of property west of Ince Way.

(3) Allocation of the former and adjusted demolition cost estimate.

Source: Real Estate Research Corporation, January 1970.

homes on a site as full of nostalgia as this. We are cognizant of the memories associated with MGM's Lot Three." Ultimately, it turned out that the major holdup in finalizing the sale had been in convincing the city to revoke the property's studio zoning designation (Culver City having been the first city in the world to create such a denotation) so that the Levitt people could build their new community.

When these details were settled, Aubrey released a coldly ironic statement that the studio's backlots were "no longer a requisite for today's concept of movie-making with its emphasis on realism and truth, and these properties no longer contribute sufficiently or directly to profitability." Fischer, trying to put a more upbeat spin on what was to happen, emphasized that part of the Tarzan Lake would be retained in their designs as a setting for the townhouses he intended to build. He also mentioned that "50% of the lot's trees—pine, eucalyptus, oak, and olive that have matured, undisturbed for years—will be salvaged for the new community's landscaping." Ultimately, neither of these promises were carried out.

Levitt and Sons also contacted the City of Culver City, in the person of Syd Kroenethal, director of parks and recreation, to offer anything on the lot that the city would care to cart off. As it happened, a new park was being designed alongside the Marina-Slauson freeway entrance. Richard Bigler, described as a "prominent and off-beat landscape artist" by the *Los Angeles Times*, was selected to try to create playground equipment from whatever he could salvage from Lot Three. Bigler carefully walked the property and red-tagged the rusty hulk that had once been Fletcher Christian's *Bounty*. He also claimed part of the Army Base and cavalry fort set, an outcropping of fake boulders, a mini-forest of trees, the bridge that spanned the water in front of the Dutch Village, a bell tower steeple, and an entire train depot from Western Street that he intended to use as a children's birthday party facility.

Left: MGM's confidential internal demolition report showing the costs associated with implementing it.

Left: A brass bed from *The Unsinkable Molly Brown* (1964). The buyer told star Debbie Reynolds she could "come visit it any time."
Right: Prop vehicles line St. Louis Street at the time of the auction.

But these plans never came to fruition. The official explanation was that transportation costs, and maintenance and safety concerns, would be prohibitive. According to historian Julie Lugo Cerra, the same thing happened again when the Parks and Recreation Department accepted a backlot gazebo as a gift from the studio. "It was stored at the city yard for some time until the rain and elements finally got it and it was dumped," recalled Cerra. "So sad."

In August, the Levitt people held a party on St. Louis Street. Officials from the city and the two companies wandered around, poking their noses against dusty glass windows and playing "name that film" with the various façades. Paper streamers were attached to the buildings and drinks were served from long tables set up in the middle of Kensington Avenue. Music was piped in through portable speakers. Yet an unseasonable wind blew grit from the old sets into people's eyes and drinks, cutting the celebration short. As the partygoers filed out, they may well have passed workers at the nearby lake who were scrambling to rescue the thousands of soon-to-be homeless goldfish that were to be shipped to a Japanese village in Buena Park.

The writing was now clearly on the false walls when one MGM star developed her own plan for saving Lot Three. "It broke my heart to think that they were going to just get rid of everything," said Debbie Reynolds, who gathered friends, family, and Al Hart, head of City National Bank, together for a plan to buy back the lot. "My idea was to turn it into a Disneyland-type amusement park. Al Hart offered to raise five million dollars for the real estate. For some reason, the farsighted geniuses that were now running MGM couldn't see why anybody would want to tour a studio backlot.... They were only interested in selling the property for real estate development and they were *not* interested in preservation—only money.... They had to leave it to Lew Wasserman and Al Dorskind at Universal to show them." (The Universal Studios tour, as of this writing, hosts up to 35,000 people a day.)

Sadly, nothing came of these plans and, instead, in October of 1972, the caterpillars rolled onto Lot Three and the hundreds of matchless façades living there quickly tumbled like the fragile icons they were.

Walter Pidgeon, returning to the lot to make *Skyjacked* in 1972, was depressed by what he found. He told reporters: "Believe me, my homecoming was no sentimental affair. There's just not enough of the old gang around. Everybody's gone except for a few old-timers on the technical crews. My favorite lot—Lot Three—has been turned into a housing development."

About the same time, Peter Lawford also visited the studio and mentioned how "that old backlot number 2 hadn't been touched in years . . . it's completely overgrown with vines and bushes. I get moments of melancholia, middle-aged melancholia if you will."

James Stewart looked at it differently, finding his old studio inhabited by "ghosts, pleasant ghosts, happy ghosts, wishing me well."

With Lot Three's demolition an ongoing fact, there still seemed to be a chance for Lot Two. Aubrey's asking price was $6,892,000. This was not unreasonable, considering the real estate market at the time. And he undoubtedly could have gotten that amount, or close to it, with a little patience. However, the Levitt people, sensing blood, offered the mogul $5,000,000, which ironically was very close to the amount that Debbie Reynolds had been able to raise and that would have preserved the property for production. But so anxious was Aubrey at the time to

please Kerkorian in Las Vegas—which would of course be reflected in his own year-end bonus—that he hastily agreed. (In fact, a secret 1971 internal memo indicated that Aubrey would have been willing to reduce the price to $4,625,000 in exchange for a quick sale.)

At the about the same time, Aubrey worked out a deal to sell Lot Five for $900,000 and Lot Six for $600,000—also to the Levitt people. Lots Four and Seven were also liquidated at this time, Lot Seven going to an entity called "Discofair" and eventually becoming a shopping center. In total, an estimated $28,000,000 was generated from asset sales during this fiscal period.

The local and national media finally took notice. Eventually, even *60 Minutes* would run a story about what was happening in Hollywood. On November 26, 1972, an episode was aired for which reporter Mike Wallace was photographed on Lot Two. "I suppose that it's surprising that it has lasted this long," he mused while surveying Andy Hardy Street. At the end of the segment, the scene dissolved into an

Left: The final days of Cullem Street's hotel façade.
Right: The ruins of the New York Streets (1980).

exuberant musical number from *An American in Paris* as Wallace eulogized the "end of a Hollywood that disintegrates before the bulldozers coming down these now-deserted streets."

Around the country and in Europe, writers and journalists tried to find words to describe the company's apparent and very public death throes. More than one resorted to the same quote from Shakespeare's *The Tempest*—with throat catching aptness:

Our Revels now are ended. These our actors,
As I foretold you, were all spirits and
Are melded into air, into thin air:
And, like the baseless fabric of this vision,
The cloud-capp'd towers, the gorgeous palaces,
The solemn temples, the great globe itself,
Yea, all which it inherit, shall dissolve
And, like this insubstantial pageant faded,

Leave not a rack behind. We are such stuff
As dreams are made on, and our little life
Is rounded with a sleep.

At MGM itself, the same overworked studio PR men who had struggled to put a positive spin on the auctions and the layoffs, lacking Shakespeare's way with words, now tried to find an upbeat way of explaining what was happening across Overland Avenue. Consequently, *They Only Kill Their Masters* (1972), a suspense thriller starring James Garner, would be publicized as the last film to shoot on Lot Two, though it would ultimately turn out not to be the case. A nostalgia-rich cast was pulled in as part of the send-off. June Allyson, Peter Lawford, Harry Guardino, Tom Ewell, Edmond O'Brien, and Arthur O'Connell—all seasoned backlot veterans—joined Garner and Katharine Ross on Andy Hardy Street for a press event where the cameras, it was claimed, would turn for the last time.

Left: The west end of Fifth Avenue in 1980.
Right: A Hollywood "boulder" on Eastside Street.

An outside public relations firm—McFadden, Strauss and Irwin Incorporated—was hired by Aubrey to squeeze every drop of bitter irony available from the situation while taking care to still emphasize the upbeat, "new Hollywood" angle their client was insisting on. This proved tricky when members of the press gathered on the set to watch and to listen to director James Goldstone call "action" on the set. The street had decomposed so badly that, for the first time in its long life, the place looked like a cliché movie studio set. In the past, like an aging actress pulling it all together before the cameras rolled, there had always been 20 departments waiting in the wings to make the set "pop" for the cameras. Now, all of those departments had been broken up, their staffs sent home. The painters who had touched up the peeling flats, the greensmen who had dressed the yards, the plasterers who had replaced the oxidizing walls and shored up the crumbling fireplaces—all of them were now gone, victims of Aubrey's bottom-line politics. So director Goldstone was forced to shoot the set sans tricks, and the pitiful result was apparent on the set and on the screen—which perhaps intentionally only lent credence to new Hollywood's instance that film audiences would no longer accept backlot substitutes for real locations.

Co-star Ann Rutherford had graduated from Andy Hardy's girl-next-door to Beverly Hills hostess-next-door as the wife of Bill Dozier, producer of the *Batman* TV series. Like many MGM stars that visited the studio in later years, she was disappointed with her homecoming. "The day I reported for work, they flew a banner over the front gate that said, 'Welcome Home, Polly!' There's still a vestige of the old MGM showmanship left. The first thing I did was head for the commissary to have a bowl of Louis B. Mayer's famous chicken soup with matzoh balls. Well, they had never even heard of it. They even wanted to know who Mr. Mayer was. I was so devastated. I couldn't eat my lunch."

In spite of her wistful ambivalence, Rutherford was enlisted between takes to escort members of the press around the studio. As she led a reporter from *Midwest* magazine around Lot Two, she grew less nostal-

Below: **The deserted interior of the Cartoon Department (1979).**

gic and more outspoken, "It's sad, in a way, that they are tearing down all the backlots and selling them off, but it was necessary, I suppose, so you shouldn't get sentimental about it." The *Waco Tribune-Herald* caught her unguarded disbelief about how badly the place had aged. "Look at the weeds. It's like nobody has been here in years. Look over there, weeds even in the doorways." She concluded by adding, probably to the company's relief, that "the only thing this place is good for now is raising mushrooms."

Aubrey's quick sale of Lot Two, however, was not to be. In spite of the numerous print articles and the nationwide TV coverage regarding the Levitt deal, the actual sale, unreported until now, never took place.

On December 10, 1973, in a studio memorandum, Roger Mayer cited a ruinous recent newspaper article about Culver City's intention to place a moratorium on zone changes for multiple-unit housing. Additionally, Urbanetics—the builder Levitt was using to develop Lot Three—had recently been stalled by an untimely bankruptcy procedure. Consequently, in January, Levitt officially (but secretly) backtracked out of their agreement with Aubrey.

In order to save face after their recent and very public long goodbye to the property, Aubrey realized that another buyer—any buyer, suitable or not—would be needed, the only criteria being an ability to pay cash and accept the unresolved zoning issues. In February, such a buyer was presumably found in the persons of Mr. and Mrs. Ching C. Lin. The Lins were primarily scrap dealers who cannily realized that the electrical conduit wire that lay buried under the sets and snaked all the way over from the power plant on Lot One could be uprooted and sold as scrap copper.

The final deal, which would not be executed until April 11, 1978, would be complicated by nearly *four years* of missed payments, disputed interest amounts, mysterious offshore investment companies, frozen funds, and even claims by the already well-compensated Weisz auctioneering house regarding some of the items in storage on the property. The sale price, before legal fees, eventually amounted to $4,170,000, even less than Aubrey had secretly claimed to be willing to settle for.

After auctioning off props and costumes, having liquidated six of their seven properties (the plan to sell off half of Lot One to an automobile assembly company for $1,450,000 never materialized), and having sent the contents of innumerable studio filing cabinets into a pit as fill for the construction of the intersection of the San Diego and Golden State freeways, MGM had little left by the mid-1970s. Feature film production had been strangled to a trickle.

But the company was still one of the world's major suppliers of television, and the income stream from its rental business to outside producers had now been dialed down by the sale of Lots Two and Three. Yet the product still had to be made *somewhere.* Clearly something would need to be done if the pipeline, either internally or as a rental business, was going to continue support even a limited amount of production.

So reluctantly, Aubrey, perhaps realizing by now that his numerous management mistakes were too obvious to hide anymore, sent his representatives across the street to where the Lins were presumably excavating their precious copper wire. They discovered Lot Two pretty much at the same level of squalor as they had left it in. A phone call confirmed that, yes, the Lins would be happy to lease the land back to MGM for their immediate production needs in light of the continuing legal wrangling. The studio also subleased individual sets to independent producers. These producers recognized a deal, and took advantage of Lot Two's cheaper non-union status (a legal loophole arising from the property not being physically attached to Lot One). Although it quickly became an open secret in the industry that MGM no longer owned the property, the place continued to be known as the "MGM backlot."

The studio's filmic output in the 1970s is a bizarre collection, indeed, but a little hopefulness was bred

by films like *Kelly's Heroes* (1970), *Ryan's Daughter* (1970), *Skyjacked* (1972), *Soylent Green* (1973), and *Pat Garrett and Billy the Kid* (1973). Bringing novelist Michael Crichton on board at MGM was a temporary Band-Aid, with hits like *Westworld* (1973) and *Coma* (1978). But there were consistently more losers than hits, movies with unbelievable titles like *My Lover My Son* (1970), *Private Parts* (1972), *Lolly-Madonna XXX* (1973), *Nightmare Honeymoon* (1973), *Wicked, Wicked* (1973), and *Norman…Is That You?* (1976). Undeniably, the last vestiges of family values Louis B. Mayer had bred into the studio were gone.

A few film projects from this era are of interest today because of how the curious, forlorn atmosphere of pain, pride, and guilt that existed at the studio was reflected, tangibly, in their product. The first was *Hollywood: The Dream Factory* (1972), a one-hour television documentary produced by the studio in 1971 as a celebration of its incredible past. Hosted by Dick Cavett, the special questioned how MGM could squander its assets in such a public and undignified manner. Footage of the already infamous studio auctions was intercut with aerial views of the deteriorating backlots, presumably awaiting the wrecking ball. "At its worst, it was crass, vulgar, and spendthrift. But at its best, it offered a rich, romantic, compelling world of illusion," Cavett mused at the conclusion of the program. "Although no one can be certain, the world probably will not see anything quite like it again."

Even as the studio released its last financial statement as a major film distributor in 1973, more nostalgia was being prepared in the wings. MGM's 1974 compilation feature *That's Entertainment!* is primarily a celebration of the studio's musicals. Yet, it is also a eulogy to its physical past. There is, under the surface, something slightly ghoulish about the framing sequences involving vintage stars like James Stewart and Bing Crosby wandering about the deteriorating Lots One and Two, reminiscing about a bygone era. No longer was MGM showing us images of happy employees working together to bring a people's dreams to life as it had for decades.

Below: Fred Astaire and Gene Kelly pose in front of the Thalberg Building for publicity photos for *That's Entertainment! II* (1976).

Instead, we were given Fred Astaire walking through the forlorn, crumbling backlot train shed, pockmarked with age and graffiti; Donald O'Connor presiding over Esther Williams's drained swimming pool, now cracked and weed-infested; and Gene Kelly strolling down New York Street, his upbeat manner at odds with the dark, rotting interiors visible through the great smashed windows. At one point, Frank Sinatra surveys all that has been and muses, echoingly, "You can wait around and hope, but you'll never see the likes of this again."

Strangest of all these projects, and most telling, was a made-for-TV movie released the same year. *The Phantom of Hollywood* (1974) tells the story of a deranged actor who, upon learning that the backlot where he has lived for decades is about to be demolished, goes on a rampage of revenge. The film opens with a television film crew flying over the crumbling remnants of Lot Two, documenting its pending demolition for a news story. For the last time audiences were given a view of Mayer's old kingdom. "Got enough?" the pilot asks his cameraman. The cameraman pushes aside his viewfinder and looks past the studio into the sunset. "I could make a movie," he says.

"We intended it to be a feature film," the show's writer George W. Schenck recalled. "*That's Entertainment!* had just come out and they told us to find all the old stars we could. Later on they . . . reined us in and it became a television movie, but we still ended up with an amazing cast!" That cast included Jack Cassidy, Jackie Coogan, Brod-

Above: The Phantom of Hollywood (played by Jack Cassidy) is out for revenge (1974).

erick Crawford, John Ireland, Corinne Calvet, Billy Halop, Kent Taylor, John Lupton, Regis Toomey, Fredd Wayne, and Peter Lawford as the crass, Aubrey-like studio chief. The leading lady who plays Lawford's daughter is actress Skye Aubrey, who in the best tradition of Hollywood nepotism is actually the daughter of James Aubrey.

To paraphrase Rhett Butler, "It's easy to romanticize a lost cause after it's truly lost." But the fact that the company itself, that the executives making the decisions during those last days, seemed to know that they were destroying a cornerstone of our 20th-century culture—and that they let the wrecking ball swing anyway—is ironic, masochistic, and sadly indicative of what makes that culture tick.

The sum total of all of these projects was encapsulated by a much-quoted *Variety* review of *That's Entertainment!*: "While many may ponder the future of Metro-Goldwyn-Mayer, nobody can deny that it has one hell of a past!"

In 1974, MGM also produced an unusually ambiguous rate sheet aimed at independent producers interested in renting the facilities—this time at fire sale prices. At the time, the soundstages could be rented for $1,000 a day for the purpose of television production, or $1,250 for features. The "full service" package was slightly higher. No mention of any of the soundstages' specific sizes or amenities was given. Additionally, any standing sets on these soundstages, presumably once the client's check had cleared, could now be used at "no charge." The backlot sets on Lot Two were also included as an option ($1,100 a day for television and $1,250 for features), "if available."

In 1974, his job apparently completed to his satisfaction, James Aubrey vacated Mayer's big office. "I just don't want to do it anymore," he said, leaving lawyer Frank Rosenfelt, who had been with the company since 1955, Mayer's office and title. Aubrey had reportedly also been unhappy about the board's recent decision to dismember the film distribution arm of the company (during this era, UA would distribute MGM products) and this may also have led to his departure. He became an independent producer and his last project was a TV movie: *Dallas Cowboys Cheerleaders* (1979). He died in 1994.

Opposite: A slew of former MGM stars gather to celebrate the premiere of *That's Entertainment!* (1974), and the studio's 50th Anniversary. From left to right, starting with the *Front Row:* Craig Stevens, Gloria Swanson, James Stewart, Johnny Weissmuller, Russ Tamblyn, Audrey Totter, Elizabeth Taylor, Keenan, Wynn, Shirley MacLaine, Roddy McDowall, Lassie, and Jimmy Durante. *Second Row:* Gene Kelly, Phyllis Kirk, Janet Leigh, Myrna Loy, Marjorie Main, Tony Martin, Dennis Morgan, Fayard Nicholas, Harold Nicolas, Merle Oberon, Margaret O'Brien, Virginia O'Brien, Donald O'Connor, Donna Reed, Debbie Reynolds, Ginger Rogers, Ann Rutherford, and Alexis Smith. *Top Row:* Howard Keel, June Allyson, Adele Astaire, Fred Astaire, George Burns, Marge Champion, Cyd Charisse, Jackie Cooper, Dan Dailey, Vic Damone, Tom Drake, Buddy Ebson, Nanette Fabray, Glenn Ford, Eva Gabor, Zsa Zsa Gabor, Jack Haley, Ava Gardner, Charlton Heston, and George Hamilton.

Above: Filming the demolition of Lot Two façades for *The Phantom of Hollywood* (1974).

In 1975, two mysterious studio fires swept across part of Lot Two, the first in August, destroying the Girl's School set above Cohn Park and the Stable set that had been there since 1939, while the second, in November, leveled part of the venerable Andy Hardy Street. As they no longer had a personal interest in the property, the post-disaster, fire-damaged set, as tenant Metro saw it, wasn't *its* problem. So Mr. and Mrs. Lin were left to work out the details with the insurance company. The Lins, learning the lesson that playing slumlord for the "movies" could be financially risky—just as boarding house operators in turn-of-the-century Hollywood had—started dismantling the sets that were not being used in anticipation of a future sale.

In 1976, Paul D. Marks, an ambitious filmmaker with dreams of making a picture not on the streets like his contemporaries, but instead in the retro-style of old Hollywood, found himself at the ramshackle gates of Lot Two looking inside at the epicenter of that style. "The guard told me MGM didn't even *own* the place anymore," he remembered. "I asked who did and he pointed to a long black car that was pulling up behind me. The person inside was a very nice guy named Lin. I told him what I wanted to do. Eventually, we came to an agreement for me to shoot inside. That's how I got to make one of the very last pictures ever shot on the MGM backlot."

Marks remembered the shooting of his 16mm short *Show Biz* as being "hectic, filled with memories and ghosts. *King Kong* was shooting at about the same time. I still have a native torch. And I kept a brick (which my wife eventually threw away) because I used to imagine how Judy Garland might have danced on that very brick. For most of my cast, it was just another job, though. I think some of my actors were sneaking off and having sex in the façades." Marks eventually decided that the experience was "kind of an honor. Like I was a part of something historic. A final part of something good."

Even as the studio was dismantling its history, the company was being lauded for it. In 1977, 35,000 members of the American Film Institute voted *Gone with the Wind* (which was now breaking records for television viewership) the greatest of all American films. *The Wizard of Oz, Singin' in the Rain,* and *2001: A Space Odyssey* also landed in the top 10. Perhaps this explains the company's practice of naming studio buildings after famous alumni, which began the same year.

In 1978, Mr. and Mrs. Lin surrendered their dreams of buried copper and, shortly after the final payment was made to MGM, sold most of their interest in Lot Two and its problems to Goldrich and Kest Incorporated, which had already been developing the property for the Lins and announced plans to immediately build a housing complex—the zoning issues with Culver City having apparently been settled. "It's progress," said a representative of the company. Unlike the bemused Lin family, the Goldrich and Kest people were not interested in playing landlord for a storied, but impoverished film company—although they were not above exploiting that company and the cache that undoubtedly came with it in naming their streets. Their urban planners divided the area up into residential blocks named "Astaire Avenue," "Hepburn Circle," "Garland Drive," "Coogan Circle," "Lamarr Avenue," and "Skelton Circle." The development itself was called "Studio Estates."

So MGM was again chased back across the street, leaving Lot Two truly empty and relatively unguarded for the first time in its life. The imposing MGM "Keep Out" signs were still there, but some still wandered inside, and must have walked away with astonishingly vivid and perplexing memories. Vandals crept in at night and broke windows, pushed down statuary, and spray-painted graffiti on the Great Wall of China.

About the same time, Randy Knox, a local resident also armed with a camera, started walking in to explore and take pictures. On one

Above: The Lot Two housing development's street signs reflect the property's former glory (2008).

of these expeditions, he unexpectedly encountered a pair of Dobermans. "At sunrise, I had jumped the fence paralleling the railroad tracks along Culver Boulevard, took a few pictures and ran into the dogs. They were very well-trained animals that advanced on me as I retreated to the fence, but didn't attack so long as I left. Quite the incentive!"

Robert W. Nudelman, the late director of preservation for Hollywood Heritage Inc., was among these last visitors. Like many film fans since the release of *That's Entertainment!*, he had driven to Culver City to see what remained of this once-great studio. "By 1977, Lot Two looked even worse than it did in the film," recalled Nudelman. "Goldrich and Kest had already begun destroying the remaining sets, working from the western end of the lot east, parcel by parcel, for their housing development. I wondered why this destruction was taking place when Universal had saved and restored its lot, and it was now a major tourist draw."

With the thought of saving the lot for a theme park—and renting some of the sets to film companies—he began making calls and visiting MGM offices to enlist support in a last-ditch effort to save the lot. In the following weeks, Nudelman made almost a hundred calls. Many, he recalled, were supportive, like Vincente Minnelli, Altovise Davis

(Sammy Davis Jr.'s wife), and producer George Pal, who had some terrible experiences with the studio trying to make a sequel to *The Time Machine* (1960). He also made 11th-hour pleas to Mel Torme, Gene Kelly, and Fred Astaire; MGM stalwarts like William Tuttle, who was still working independently for the studio; and Gillespie, who had been at the studio since the Goldwyn days, also wanted to help. The studio's Art Department was particularly supportive, he remembered.

With the aid of the Art Department and other studio old-timers, Nudelman put together a persuasive package, documenting the historical importance of Lot Two and all its sets in voluminous detail with a budget, and sent it to Roger Mayer.

"Mayer was very nice when I spoke with him," said Nudelman. "But it was nonetheless clear that Kerkorian was liquidating the studio to build his hotels. Although he was supportive of the restoration effort, there was nothing Mayer could do."

In the meantime, the leveling continued. To raise awareness of Lot Two's predicament, Nudelman entreated local media to cover the story. Steve Harvey, a reporter for the *Los Angeles Times*, appeared on the lot one day and interviewed Nudelman and Wert Cunningham, the 53-year-old demolition engineer operating a Caterpillar bulldozer.

Below: Despite the supposed fragility of the sets, it took years to destroy Lot Two. Here, the very last of New York Street is demolished (1980).

"Cunningham had previously leveled portions of Lot Three and Lot Four and Fox's backlot," recalled Nudelman. "He was also the one in the tractor tearing down sets in *Phantom of Hollywood*. When the reporter said he needed a good photograph for the story, Cunningham horrified both of us by going behind the Southern Mansion and literally pushing it over for him. It was not scheduled for demolition yet."

Harvey asked Cunningham what he thought about when flattening such sets. "I wondered how many loads it would make. . . . It's just a job to me. . . . Sometimes I'm watching the late movie on TV and I see something I've destroyed—that's sort of a strange feeling. But I don't really feel sad."

"Some of the younger guys just plow through the sets on tractors," one worker told Harvey. "But Wert, he likes to set it up so it all falls down at once. A big splash." The article, published in February of 1978, stoked the fires of enmity between old-time studio employees, who were horrified, and studio management, which wanted to move on. "For example, the Art Department employees posted the article on

their bulletin board," said Nudelman. "Then studio management would order the Janitorial Department to take it down. The next morning, the article would be posted again, and again it would be taken down. There were literally battles going on like this internally at the studio,"

Other, no less passionate, battles were encapsulated by a *Los Angeles Times* letter to the editor published on March 8, 1978. Robert Downing Olson, who identified himself as the "president and chairman of the board of the Nob Hill Historical Restoration Society of San Francisco" had apparently been reading about what Cunningham and his tractor had been doing down south in Hollywood. "The demolition of Ashley Wilkes [*sic*] home in *Gone with the Wind*," he wrote, "was

Left: Lot Three after the demolition of Rawhide Street (foreground) and Dutch Street (background). The *Mutiny on the Bounty* ship façade (center) awaits the same fate.
Right: The final days of New York Street.
Opposite: After the demolition of Lot Two, hundreds of tons of wood, plaster, Cerlotex, and fiberglass had to be removed from the site. The process would take months.

probably one of the most tasteless and appalling acts of vandalism of this century. It might have been moved to another location so easily that this action almost seems like a crime against the national community."

Cunningham and his handlers apparently were not intimidated by the Nob Hill Historical Restoration Society of San Francisco because the destruction continued. With the hope that a last-minute investor would be found, Nudelman and his friends tried to clear remaining sets from the path of the bulldozers. He remembered being out there all night trying to pull sets out of the way. "I'd place them in the old storage racks out there, but the bulldozers went after those, too. We found a warehouse filled with all the neon signs ever used in MGM pictures. I recognized the ones used in the 'Broadway Melody' from *Singin' in the Rain*. But all that was plowed under, too."

Nudelman was shocked and appalled that thousands of actual antiques were destroyed as quickly as studio-made facsimiles. "I tried to sell the railroad cars, some of them actual European relics, to a collector, but that fell through, too. I realized at this point it was over."

Nudelman's last memory of the debacle was visiting Esther Williams's old swimming pool. "The developers were dumping garbage and mud into the pool, filling it up. I remember looking down into it, and seeing a bullfrog in there. I climbed down, removed him, and placed him in some nearby shrubbery—all that remained of the studio nursery. I can now say that I witnessed the last swimmer in Esther Williams's swimming pool!"

It took almost two years to flatten the dense, seemingly random tangles of walls and doors, and steeples and staircases. "Andy Hardy's street and a section of New York Street were the last to go," recalled Nudelman.

While the housing development was rising on one side of the lot, John Divola, an esteemed professional artist, was finding himself strangely drawn to the ruined cities on the other. He repeatedly picked up his camera and walked into the no-longer-gated, surviving acres of New York Street. "I went over there many times," he recalled. "I took so many photos of the place. No one else was ever there. No one bothered me." Divola remembered his visits as being "visually rich, not foreboding at all, both familiar and alien. . . ."

The last professional photographs ever taken of the world's most photographed location were taken in mid-July of 1980. By then, MGM was busy building a multi-story parking garage on its side of Overland Avenue (where the Lot One backlot had been). A photographer had been hired to chart the progress of the construction. Playfully at first, or perhaps out of boredom, this unnamed photographer would occasionally point his camera across the street, at the action and noise gong on over there. Then he would turn his camera back to the parking structure and finish the job he had been paid for. These photos document the Caterpillars tearing into the very last of New York Street, the last trace of which would finally be erased in 1981.

Edward Lawrence, a longtime studio publicist, was at a loss for words upon hearing that the backlot had finally been cleared. "Too bad . . . too bad," was all he could manage to say while shaking his head.

Years later, in the spring of 1984, Robert Nudelman met Roger Mayer again on another preservation effort. "Roger told me the studio realized its mistake almost immediately in selling and leveling Lot Two, but by then it was too late."

"Mayer had built MGM to last—it took 30 years of strip-mining to tear it down to bedrock," observed Louis B. Mayer biographer Scott Eyman.

In another twist of backlot irony, an MGM backlot tour was eventually instituted with great success in 1988—not in Culver City, however, but in far-away Orlando. That year, the studio licensed its logo to the Walt Disney Company for their Disney-MGM Studios theme park at Walt Disney World in Florida. A backlot tour ride was included, which rode past recreations of famous MGM sets ranging from *The Wizard of Oz* to *Singin' in the Rain*. MGM consumer product executives, desperate for the licensing fees, apparently were surprised by Kerkorian's fury when he found out that his company's logo had been leased to a rival studio. A seemingly endless siege of lawsuits between the two companies would eventually result in the park's name being formally changed to Disney's Hollywood Studios in 2008.

Above: The iconic Metro Goldwyn Mayer sign being replaced by the Lorimar sign symbolized, literally and figuratively, the end of an era.
Below: An aerial view of the newly christened "Lorimar Telepictures" studio. The cleared lot in the lower right corner was the former location of the Lot Two backlot.

With Aubrey gone, Kerkorian seemed to change his mind about MGM. He suddenly wanted to compete in the exploding global entertainment industry by producing more movies and more television shows. In 1981, he purchased United Artists, a prestigious, but floundering production/distribution company that had been distributing MGM products, for $380 million. The resultant company, now known as MGM/UA, enlarged the studio's library to 4,100 films (including the UA and pre-1948 Warner Bros. films and the lucrative James Bond and Pink Panther series).

Yet continuing success still eluded Kerkorian. Roger Mayer noted that "part of the problem is that it takes a long time to really understand the picture business. The MBAs Kerkorian kept hiring could never quite grasp that, unlike in any other industry. Every single movie had to be unique. A prototype."

By the mid-1980s, Kerkorian was ready to sell to the right buyer. In 1986, that buyer was media mogul Ted Turner, who purchased the studio for $1.5 billion. Turner also acquired $500 million of the company's debt, which forced him to go back to Kerkorian to sell back the United Artist portion of the company for a reported $480 million.

For the next 74 days, Turner owned MGM, lock, stock, and logo. Although he professed an interest in production when he made the decision to sell, it was the film library he chose to retain. The MGM name, studio, and logo—to everyone's surprise—went back to the wily Kerkorian for $300 million.

On October 17, 1986, Lorimar Telepictures purchased Lot One for $100 million dollars. Lorimar had been leasing much of the plant for production of their series like *Dallas* (1978–1991), *Knots Landing* (1979–1993), *Falcon Crest* (1981–1990), *Perfect Strangers* (1986–1993), and *Max Headroom* (1987–1988), as well as a modest number of feature films including *Being There* (1979), *The Morning After* (1986), and *Action Jackson* (1988) since 1979. The company, which had begun as a small production company on the Warner Bros. lot, had also captured

a unique foothold in the burgeoning home video industry with their *Jane Fonda Workout* series.

The last MGM picture to shoot at the studio under MGM's ownership was a Billy Crystal/Gregory Hines cop comedy ironically titled *Running Scared* (1986). Following a long studio tradition, a banner proclaiming the upcoming title had been hung on the gigantic Metro Goldwyn Mayer sign atop Stage 6. After the sale, Lorimar was informed that a permit was required to remove the old sign because it had "historic significance." After a flurry of hand-greasing, the appropriate permits were hastily obtained by the Lorimar lawyers and in November of 1986, sign and banner came down together.

MGM, now a corporate entity only, moved a few hundred feet across Madison Avenue to a 360,000-square-foot ziggurat-shaped building about which it has been reported (incorrectly) that Kerkorian had built with the intention of creating a Las Vegas-style destination resort. Uncomfortably, executives could see their old studio, and what they had lost, by merely looking out the windows of their new offices. Lorimar would own the lot until 1990.

Since 1972, Columbia Pictures had been co-habituating with Warner Bros. on their venerable Burbank lot. While the conventional wisdom of the '70s had been that the studios did not need soundstages or backlots in order to prosper in the "new Hollywood," by the late '80s, everyone had agreed that just maybe they had made a mistake.

If proof were needed that the day of the backlots was not entirely over, it could be found in popular culture. Outside the entertainment industry, it had long realized there was something wonderful and mysterious happening behind studio gates. In March of 2008, *Los Angeles* magazine even listed Hollywood's backlots as one of the "64 Great Things About L.A." Likewise, actual backlot usage has again been on the rise in recent decades, even as "virtual backlots"—sets created inside of a computer—have become practical. "Believe me, I'd dearly love to have that land back," Fox's Gary Erlich admitted in 1998, referring

Above: **The new Columbia Studios sign on the East Gate is modified once again, this time to read Sony Pictures (1992).**
Below: **The West Gate entrance to Sony Pictures Entertainment as seen today.**

to the loss of his studio's fabulous backlot that is now Century City. Director Ralph Senesky, who worked at most of the major studios backlots in the '60s, reflected that there was "definitely magic created on them—like walking into an old empty theatre with lingering ghosts." Senesky realized, like the studios themselves, after it was almost too late that "there are times when qualities other than the stark realism of a live location are called for."

By the 1980s, Warner Bros. executives were eager to reclaim ownership of their historic lot. To this end, the company purchased Lorimar and rolled it into its television division. Warner Bros. subsequently sold Lorimar's lot to Columbia in exchange for that company's 35% stake in Warner's Burbank plant. Columbia had recently been purchased by the Sony Corporation (in 1989), thus it was decided the old Culver City studios, although the home of Columbia Pictures, would bear the more synergetic name of

Sony Studios—the name that it retains today.

According to sources in Culver City at the time, Sony—the lot's fifth tenant—then began making discreet inquiries about buying back a portion of the real estate of Lots Two or Three. Negotiations progressed smoothly for a few days until word leaked out that the buyer was Sony. Greed kicked in, prices escalated, and the offers were quietly withdrawn. Ultimately, a few backlot-style façades were constructed on top of Lot One's existing studio buildings instead.

Across the street, it soon became apparent that the new MGM building was too small to house a corporation that had sprawled across Culver City for 68 years. But it wasn't until 1992—after Kerkorian had again sold the studio to Pathé Communications (whose CEO, Giancarlo Parretti, was eventually jailed on tax fraud charges, and after French bank Crédit Lyonnais had seized the company)—that the embattled and humiliated studio actually pulled up stakes and left Culver City for a comfortable suite of offices in Santa Monica.

A source at the studio who requested anonymity admitted later that the company was so strapped for cash during this period that the predominant bills owed were laid out on a conference room table where the few remaining executives had to decide which ones actually needed to be paid. Eventually, it was decided to pay the film lab because that was the only way to get MGM film prints to theatres where, hopefully, some income could be generated.

Salvation oddly came in 1996 when Kerkorian, backed this time by an Australian

Above: The Sony Studios "backlot" façades built over the fronts of existing buildings.
Below: An office tower in Century City houses the MGM "studios" today.

television network, again purchased the company. This time, his third go-round with the lion, the price tag was $1.3 billion.

Kerkorian continued his erratic, quixotic quest to revive the company. He built the studio's film library, once strip-mined into insignificance, back into one of the world's largest with the acquisition of the Samuel Goldwyn Company, Polygram, and Orion Pictures film libraries to supplement the existing United Artists catalog. (Warner Bros. ended up with the vintage MGM titles through their eventual purchase of the Turner Company.) He stabilized the management team, eventually settling on Alex Yemenidjian and Chris McGurk. He moved the company again, this time into a glass skyscraper in Century City, where Fox's backlot had once stood. The interiors of the new building were designed, not in the Art Deco-style of Hollywood, but to mimic one of Kerkorian's Nevada casinos.

What had pushed Kirk Kerkorian back under the klieg lights again is anyone's guess. Did the former studio handyman want to right past and perceived wrongs? Or did he just see a chance to strip the company down again? It did look to insiders that this time Kerkorian was intent on building up rather than ripping down.

The insiders were wrong. In 2004, Warner Bros. and Sony both announced they were negotiating with Kerkorian to buy the company. Sony was in possession of MGM's old lot, and Warner controlled the bulk of its library. On September 13, 2005, Warner pulled out of the competition and, for an estimated $5 billion, the Sony Corporation became perceived owners of its second Hollywood studio.

This announcement came just days before the Academy of Motion Picture Arts and Sciences hosted a special anniversary screening of *That's Entertainment!*, for which a few studio veterans made appearances. Metro Goldwyn Mayer was 80 years old. "This is a day which will live in irony," commented Roger Mayer, now Turner Entertainment company president and chief operating officer, at the beginning of the evening. After the movie, the survivors—Mickey Rooney, Debbie Reynolds, Cyd Charisse, Arlene Dahl, Nanette Fabray, Betty Garrett, Tony Martin, Dan Melnick, Julie Newmar, Margaret O'Brien, Janis Paige, and Russ Tamblyn—climbed to the stage to be photographed. A few of them had posed for another picture 55 years earlier on the occasion of the company's 25th anniversary. Most of them had gathered for a similar photo in 1974, for the studio's 50th anniversary at the Beverly Wilshire Hotel after the premiere of *That's Entertainment!* Robert Osborne summed it up poignantly days later in his column for the *Hollywood Reporter*: "Here in a stroke of timing that borders on the macabre, the very week it all happened, the announcement came that MGM—after 80 years—was no more, a company with a past, but no longer an active future."

Oddly, almost impossibly, it didn't work that way. In May of 2006, MGM—which has proven itself to be as resilient as it has been unlucky in recent decades—somehow ultimately surprised everyone, and against all odds and possibilities wrestled itself free of Sony and its billions of dollars.

It seems that Howard Stringer, head of Sony's United States division, had been forced by his bosses in Japan to place Sony at the head a consortium of investors organized to purchase MGM, rather than letting his company assume the debt involved in the purchase outright. This became his undoing when MGM's board voted to dismiss Sony Pictures Entertainment as distributor of their product. And Stringer, as a minority shareholder, found himself unable to do anything about it. "We screwed up," he was bluntly quoted as saying when asked about the deal.

MGM once again reorganized itself, this time under new CEO Harry Sloan as a marketing and distribution only company whose new goal was not to produce pictures, but to finance and acquire outside product for theatrical release (although the scarcity of viable independent product would soon push the company back into active production). In November of 2006, the United Artists brand name was reinstated by Tom Cruise and his partner Paula Wagner as a talent-friendly organization dedicated to producing four to five pictures a year for distribution by MGM. These terms echoed almost exactly the original intent of that company that had been created in 1919 by Charlie Chaplin, Mary Pickford, Douglas Fairbanks, and D. W. Griffith, a detail that Sloan took delight in pointing out by keeping the original UA founding agreement on hand in his office in Century City and showing it off to guests. Sloan would keep that office, and his job, until 2009. In November 2010, MGM was forced to file for bankruptcy protection.

Our ghostly wanderings behind the gates at MGM have now ended. Yet be warned that once visited, it is impossible to ever entirely leave MGM behind. The company itself continues today. The MGM library, thousands of titles strong, is the largest in the world and the logo is one of the most recognized corporate symbols in history. Perhaps no other type of business entity affects us as human beings on a personal level as a Hollywood studio does. Yet the memories that haunt us are not of the factory, but of the product, of course: Dorothy leaving Kansas for Oz and Oz for Kansas, Rhett leaving Scarlett, Lassie coming home, Ronald Colman rhapsodizing at the guillotine, Andy Hardy's heart-to-heart talks with his father, Tarzan's yodel, Sinatra's cool, Gene Kelly on that lamppost, Elvis showing the world how to rock and roll, W. C. Fields playing with an apple, San Francisco in ruins, and Mrs. Miniver keeping the home fires burning among many, many more.

And yet the movies themselves—which, after all, are only flitting shadows and tricks of light—tantalize us through their very unreality. The studio as a *place* was once upon a time both actual and solid, and could be found on any map. But that place has appropriately become just as ghostly and intangible as the product it created.

Through bad luck, poor decisions, corruption, and greed, MGM was ultimately destroyed by its history and its handlers. And yet, paradoxically enough because the place is gone, it is all the more remembered and revered. In Hollywood, the lost lands of MGM are a potent symbol of all that was and is no more: a 20th century Camelot, a Shangri-La to which we can visit only in our movies and in our imaginations. To allocate a phrase from one of the studio's best-remembered pictures, we can now look for this place "only in books, for it is no more than a dream remembered. . . . A civilization gone with the wind. . . ."

FILMS SHOT ON THE BACKLOT

Hollywood is a town that not only hides its past, but creates an alternate one.

—Louise Brooks

What follows is a comprehensive listing of MGM features, rental pictures for other companies, television productions, industrial films, music videos, and commercials shot on MGM's storied backlots. Surprisingly, nothing along these lines has ever been attempted before, not by historians, or internally by *any* of the major studios. The titles listed here are by no means complete. Attentive readers, or viewers, or surviving MGM alumni will no doubt be able to make further contributions as time passes, although a true accounting of how these busy sets contributed to our cinema and our popular culture will probably never again be possible.

The attentive reader will be rewarded by many an unexpected tidbit. Not the least interesting of which is how many famous pictures history has, until now, told us were shot on location, but oft-times staged major sequences on the backlot. The fact that this information has been largely a secret, until now, and that the origin of these sequences has never been unraveled by viewing the films themselves, proves, perhaps inadvertently (and sadly, decades after the fact), just how successful these backlots really were at mimicking life in the outer world.

Each set is listed in the same order and assigned the same number as the Lot maps in the main body of the text. The year listed after each film represents release dates, as opposed to production dates (which sometimes differ). If the project was made for television or for another studio this is also noted. Although TV projects for other studios or broadcast networks are not identified as such. Whenever possible, specific TV episodes from key series are listed, in quotation marks—although, every instance of that series using that set could not be accounted for. Notes involving the sets usage follow whenever possible. When these notes are in quotation marks it indicates that this is a quote taken from production records, which usually indicates which scenes, or where specifically a sequence for that film was shot. If these notations sometimes appear cryptic, please don't blame the authors, as the original records these notations came from, when they exist at all, are notoriously incomplete and idiosyncratic. Information sometimes seems contradictory. Some of the notes listed in the original production records possibly represent sequences later cut from the films under discussion. We have tried to clear up some of these mysteries by viewing a few thousand of the films themselves, which has immeasurably improved our book, if not our social lives.

LOT TWO

4) New York Dock and Ocean Liner
Student Tour (1934); assorted ports
A Night at the Opera (1935); shipboard and dock scenes
Whipsaw (1935); New York dock
Suzy (1936); European port
Exclusive Story (1936); dock scene
Parnell (1937); Clark Gable boards ship
Lord Jeff (1938); as the *RMS Queen Mary*
Honolulu (1939); Hawaii and New York
Arsène Lupin Returns (1938); France
Remember? (1939); assorted locations
I Love You Again (1940); ship arrives in New York
Third Finger, Left Hand (1940); unknown location
Susan and God (1940); return to America
Panama Hattie (1942); as the tropics
Ship Ahoy (1942); as the title vehicle
Nazi Agent (1942); as a New York dock
Three Hearts for Julia (1943); unspecified location
The White Cliffs of Dover (1944); as a British port
Till the Clouds Roll By (1946); the *RMS Lusitania*
Courage of Lassie (1946); the ship Lassie returns home on
The Green Years (1946); as a Scottish port
The Mighty McGurk (1947); as Bowery port
Luxury Liner (1948); as the title vehicle
Words and Music (1948); various locations
Intruder in the Dust (1949); unknown location
The Red Danube (1949); unknown location
Black Hand (1950); as New York dockyards
Please Believe Me (1950); as Southampton docks
Annie Get Your Gun (1950); as a New York pier and the deck of a cattle boat
King Solomon's Mines (1950); "departure"
The Outriders (1950); the prison camp near the boat dock
The Law and the Lady (1951); as New York for arrival
Callaway Went Thataway (1951); seen in montage
Royal Wedding (1951); as the European arrival
The Great Caruso (1951); assorted locations
Washington Story (1952); unspecified location
Woman of the North Country (1952, Republic); as the "boat dock"
Dangerous When Wet (1953); as London and New York docks

It's a Dog's Life (1955); as a pier
It Started with a Kiss (1959); car delivery scene
Billy Rose's Jumbo (1962); for the arrival in Europe
The Twilight Zone (television); "Passage on the Lady Anne" (1963)
One Step Beyond (television 1959–1961); "Night of April 14th" (1959), as the RMS *Titanic*.
The Americanization of Emily (1964); as Southampton Harbor
Double Trouble (1967); shots of "gangplank"
The Phantom of Hollywood (television 1974); seen during studio tour

5) Andy Hardy/New England Street
Ah, Wilderness! (1935); the New England town which the street was named after
Maytime (1937); American set scenes
A Family Affair (1937); as Carvel
The Last Gangster (1937); as Edward G. Robinson's family home
You're Only Young Once (1938); as Carvel
Judge Hardy's Children (1938); as Carvel
Love Finds Andy Hardy (1938); as Carvel
Out West with the Hardys (1938); as Carvel
The Story of Doctor Carver (short subject 1938); as a small town
Spring Madness (1938); as the college town
The Hardys Ride High (1939); as Carvel
Andy Hardy Gets Spring Fever (1939); as Carvel
The Adventures of Huckleberry Finn (1939); a Mississippi river town
Judge Hardy and Son (1939); as Carvel
On Borrowed Time (1939); "Nothrup home"
Babes in Arms (1939); title number shot here
The Secret of Dr. Kildare (1939); as the Kildare home
These Glamour Girls (1939); as the town of Kingsford
Dancing Co-Ed (1939); as an unnamed Midwestern town
Strike Up the Band (1940); as the town of Riverwood
Keeping Company (1940); "the Thomas home"
Third Finger, Left Hand (1940); "Merrick home"
Andy Hardy Meets Debutante (1940); as Carvel
Dr. Kildare Goes Home (1940); as the Kildare home
The Captain Is a Lady (1940); as Captain Peabody's home
Andy Hardy's Private Secretary (1941); as Carvel
Life Begins for Andy Hardy (1941); as Carvel
Dr. Kildare's Wedding Day (1941); as the Kildare home

Design for Scandal (1941); as a New England village
The Courtship of Andy Hardy (1942); as Carvel
Andy Hardy's Double Life (1942); as Carvel
The Vanishing Virginian (1942); as Lynchburg, Virginia
Keeper of the Flame (1942); as the "Forrest" family home town
Mokey (1942); as an unspecified southern town
Thousands Cheer (1943); unspecified locations
A Stranger in Town (1943); as "Crown Port"
Presenting Lily Mars (1943); as a town in Indiana
Air Raid Wardens (1943); as "Huxton"
Andy Hardy's Blonde Trouble (1944); as Carvel
Maisie Goes to Reno (1944); scenes before Maisie goes to Reno
The Thin Man Goes Home (1944); as Sycamore Springs
Thrill of a Romance (1945); unspecified locations
Love Laughs at Andy Hardy (1946); as Carvel
The Show-Off (1946); as the Fisher home
Up Goes Maisie (1946); as Maisie's neighborhood
Lady in the Lake (1947); as Little Fawn Lake
High Wall (1947); set used briefly
Cynthia (1947); "Bishop home"
The Unfaithful (1947); unspecified location
Merton of the Movies (1947); early scenes in Kansas
A Date with Judy (1948); as Jane Powell's family's home
Summer Holiday (1948); as Danville, Connecticut
The Stratton Story (1949); as James Stewarts's home
Father of the Bride (1950); Elizabeth Taylor's wedding
The Happy Years (1950); used the church at the end of the street
The Skipper Surprised His Wife (1950); as Robert Walker's home
Above and Beyond (1952); as Robert Taylor's home
Washington Story (1952); as suburban Washington D.C.
Lone Star (1952); used the "church"
Carbine Williams (1952); backgrounds only
The Bad and the Beautiful (1952); as Dick Powell's home town
Singin' in the Rain (1952); as Beverly Hills
You for Me (1952); "James Lee House"
The Belle of New York (1952); dressed for 1890s New York
The Affairs of Dobie Gillis (1953); as a Midwestern college town
All the Brothers Were Valiant (1953); as 1850s Massachusetts
Small Town Girl (1953); "Livingstone (Farley Granger) House"
Hit the Deck (1955); assorted locations
The Great American Pastime (1956); "Hallerton home"—although the backyard was on Lot Three
Tribute to a Bad Man (1956); street redressed slightly for a western look
Jailhouse Rock (1957); Elvis goes to party
Some Came Running (1958); as the town of Parkman, Indiana
Andy Hardy Comes Home (1958); as Carvel
High School Confidential! (1958); "Alice's" home—more likely the note means Arlene's home
The Big Operator (1959); Mel Torme is set afire on home's lawn here
The Twilight Zone (television); "The Monsters Are Due on Maple Street" (1960), "Nick of Time," (1960), "A Stop at Willoughby" (1960), "A World of Difference" (1960), "I Sing The Body Electric" (1962), "Mute" (1963), "Stopover in a Quiet Town" (1964), "Black Leather Jackets" (1964), and others
Sweet Bird of Youth (1962); houses and church

Period of Adjustment (1962); as small town in Florida
The Outer Limits (television); "The Galaxy Being" (1963)
A Ticklish Affair (1963); "Martin House," here and on Lot Three
Hootenanny Hoot (1963); "Henly (Pam Austin) home"
The Prize (1963); "church"
Night of the Iguana (1964); "St. James's Episcopal Church"
Your Cheatin' Heart (1964); as a town in Alabama
Clarence, the Cross-Eyed Lion (1965); unspecified location
Joy in the Morning (1965); marriage scene climax at church
See Here, Private Hargrove (television pilot 1964); unspecified location
Doctor, You've Got to Be Kidding (1967); "Halloran home"
The Impossible Years (1968); portions of motorcycle chase
Speedway (1968); Elvis Presley's last visit to street
The Traveling Executioner (1970); as a small town in 1918
They Only Kill Their Masters (1972); "Eden Landing"
That's Entertainment! (1974) Mickey Rooney returns to Carvel
The Phantom of Hollywood (television 1974); as Worldwide Pictures backlot
Show Biz (short subject 1976); unspecified location
Sgt. Pepper's Lonely Hearts Club Band (1978, Universal); as Heartland

6) Small Town Railroad Depot

Out West with the Hardys (1938); as Carvel rail station
Love Finds Andy Hardy (1938); as Carvel rail station
Dancing Co-Eds (1939); Midwestern rail station
Bad Little Angel (1939); seen behind Virginia Weidler
Fast and Furious (1939); "Seaside City"
These Glamour Girls (1939); "Kingsford"
Dr. Kildare Goes Home (1940); he comes here to come home
Edison, the Man (1940); assorted locations
Young Tom Edison (1940); as Port Huron station
Strike Up the Band (1940); "Riverwood Station"
Blossoms in the Dust (1941); a Texas rail station
Andy Hardy's Private Secretary (1941); as Carvel rail station
For Me and My Gal (1942); assorted rail stations
The Courtship of Andy Hardy (1942); as Carvel rail station
Andy Hardy's Double Life (1942); as Carvel rail station
Girl Crazy (1943); "out west"
Above Suspicion (1943); unspecified location
Best Foot Forward (1943); "Winsocki"
Air Raid Wardens (1943); as Huxton station
Meet Me in St. Louis (1944); seen during "Trolly Song" number
See Here, Private Hargrove (1944); Northern California
The Thin Man Goes Home (1944); as Sycamore Springs station
Keep Your Powder Dry (1945); as Chattanooga, Tennessee
Two Smart People (1946); assorted locations
The Harvey Girls (1946); set combined with Lot Three locations for a western look
The Secret Heart (1946); unspecified location
Love Laughs at Andy Hardy (1946); as Carvel rail station
Merton of the Movies (1947); early, Kansas-based departure
The Red Danube (1949); assorted European locations
The Great Sinner (1949); unspecified locations
The Stratton Story (1949); "Pasadena Railroad station"
The Happy Years (1950); as Eastchester Station

Annie Get Your Gun (1950); assorted locations
Too Young to Kiss (1951); assorted locations
The Tall Target (1951); assorted 1865 rail stations
Singin' in the Rain (1952); "Fit as a Fiddle" montage
Invitation (1952); unspecified location
Above and Beyond (1952); rare film to shoot scenes inside depot building
You for Me (1952); unnamed rural station
The Actress (1953); "Wollaston Station"
Scandal at Scourie (1953); as Scourie rail station
The Great American Pastime (1956); assorted locations
The Twilight Zone (television); "A Stop at Willoughby" (1960), "Of Late I Think of Cliffordsville" (1963), "Stopover in a Quiet Town" (1964), and others
Hello Dere (television pilot 1965); unspecified location
Joy in the Morning (1965); seen near campus setting
The Trouble with Girls (1969); a rail station in Iowa

7) Small Town Square

Fury (1936); an Illinois town
Night Must Fall (1937); seen briefly as an English village
A Family Affair (1937); as Carvel
You're Only Young Once (1938); as Carvel
Judge Hardy's Children (1938); as Carvel
Love Finds Andy Hardy (1938); as Carvel
Listen, Darling (1938); assorted small town locations
Judge Hardy and Son (1939); as Carvel
The Hardys Ride High (1939); as Carvel
Andy Hardy Gets Spring Fever (1939); as Carvel
Babes in Arms (1939); assorted locations
On Borrowed Time (1939); seen in background throughout film
Dancing Co-Ed (1939); as an unnamed Midwestern home
Bad Little Angel (1939); seen in background throughout film
Pride and Prejudice (1940); "Bennett home"
Strike Up the Band (1940); "Riverwood"
Edison, the Man (1940); assorted locations
Andy Hardy Meets Debutante (1940); as Carvel
The Philadelphia Story (1940); "library"
Dr. Kildare Goes Home (1940); as a small town
Northwest Passage (1940); dressed as a frontier-era, eastern town
Two Girls on Broadway (1940); unspecified location
Andy Hardy's Private Secretary (1941); as Carvel
Life Begins for Andy Hardy (1941); as Carvel
Honky Tonk (1941); as Yellow Creek
Maisie Was a Lady (1941); Maisie's town
The Courtship of Andy Hardy (1942); as Carvel
Andy Hardy's Double Life (1942); as Carvel
The Human Comedy (1943); as Ithaca, California
Presenting Lily Mars (1943); the town Lilly Mars comes from
Air Raid Wardens (1943); Laurel and Hardy visit the town of "Huxton"
Andy Hardy's Blonde Trouble (1944); as Carvel
The Thin Man Goes Home (1944); as Sycamore Springs
Maisie Goes to Reno (1944); Maisie's town
An American Romance (1944); graduation scene
The Valley of Decision (1945); as a Pennsylvania mill town
Love Laughs at Andy Hardy (1946); as Carvel

Two Smart People (1946); as Arizona
High Barbaree (1947); Van Johnson's home town
Good News (1947); as a college town
Cynthia (1947); assorted locations
Summer Holiday (1948); as Danville, Connecticut
Act of Violence (1948); unspecified locations
A Southern Yankee (1948); assorted locations
Take Me Out to the Ball Game (1949); assorted early 20th century towns
The Stratton Story (1949); assorted locations
In the Good Old Summertime (1949); period Chicago settings
Stars in My Crown (1950); as a western town
Two Weeks with Love (1950); as upstate New York
Too Young to Kiss (1951); unspecified location
Bannerline (1951); Lionel Barrymore's last visit to set
Above and Beyond (1952); Robert Taylor's home town
The Bad and the Beautiful (1952); Dick Powell's home town
Washington Story (1952); as Georgetown
Talk About a Stranger (1952); as a small California town
Pat and Mike (1952); unspecified location
Invitation (1952); as an unspecified small town
The Actress (1953); as the town of Wallacestone
All the Brothers Were Valiant (1952); as 1850s Massachusetts
Code Two (1953); assorted locations
Small Town Girl (1953); "street and courthouse"
The Affairs of Dobie Gillis (1953); a Midwestern college town
Dangerous When Wet (1953); as a Arkansas town
The Long, Long Trailer (1953); assorted locations
Those Wilder Years (1956); "Buffington"
Jailhouse Rock (1957); unspecified locations
Man on Fire (1957); "courthouse"
Raintree County (1957); Civil War battle of Chicamauga
Some Came Running (1958); as Parkman, Indiana
Andy Hardy Comes Home (1958); as Carvel
Handle with Care (1958); "small town college street"
The World, the Flesh and the Devil (1959); post-apocalypse, USA
The Twilight Zone (television); "Nick of Time" (1960), "A Stop at Willoughby" (1960), "I Sing the Body Electric" (1962), "Mute" (1963), "Of Late I Think of Cliffordsville" (1963), "Black Leather Jackets" (1964), "Stopover in a Quiet Town" (1964), and others
Gigi (1958); backgrounds for French carriage ride
Two Loves (1961); as New Zealand
Ada (1961); assorted locations
Period of Adjustment (1962); as a snow-covered southern town
Follow That Dream (1962); small town in Florida
Boys' Night Out (1962); James Garner and Tony Randall are the boys
The Wheeler Dealers (1963); the suburbs
Hootenanny Hoot (1963); "hotel"
Joy in the Morning (1965); as a college town
Clarence, the Cross-Eyed Lion (1965); unspecified location
Zebra in the Kitchen (1965); streets overrun with wild animals
Girl Happy (1965); as Fort Lauderdale, Florida
The Long, Hot Summer (television 1965–1966); in assorted episodes as Mississippi
Hot Rods to Hell (1967); "small town hospital"

The Trouble with Girls (1969) Elvis Presley's last visit to street
Every Little Crook and Nanny (1972); "grocery store"
They Only Kill Their Masters (1972); "Eden Landing"
The Phantom of Hollywood (television 1974); as Worldwide Pictures backlot
Sgt. Pepper's Lonely Hearts Club Band (1978, Universal); as the town of Heartland

8) Cemetery

The Mask of Fu Manchu (1932); seen briefly
Times Square Lady (1935); see also "Eucy Grove"
Night Must Fall (1937); headstones mostly removed
The Canterville Ghost (1944); seen near castle
Joan of Ark (1948, RKO); rented by production, but possibly never used
Stars in My Crown (1950); "Rehoebth Cemetery"
Glory Alley (1952); unspecified location
Tribute to a Bad Man (1956); "cemetery"
Sweet Bird of Youth (1962); southern cemetery
Combat! (television 1962; "Escape to Nowhere"(1962)
Twilight of Honor (1963); cemetery somewhere in the southwest
A Time to Sing (1968); unspecified location
Young Frankenstein (1974, Fox); sections of the grave robbing sequence
The Phantom of Hollywood (television 1974); explored by construction workers
Logan's Run (1976); outskirts of Washington D.C.

9) Lot Two (Tarzan) Lake and Lot Two Jungle

The Divorcee (1930); Norma Shearer seen with lake behind her
Trader Horn (1931); as Africa
Red Dust (1932); as Indochina
Kongo (1932); as Africa
Tarzan the Ape Man (1932); as Africa
Treasure Island (1934); as the title character
Tarzan and His Mate (1934); as Africa, and used for the crocodile fight
Tarzan Escapes (1936); as Africa
Tarzan Finds a Son (1939); as Africa
Cass Timberaine (1947); outskirts of town
Little Women (1949); assorted locations
Stars in My Crown (1950); "Uncle Famous Prill's" cabin near water
The Outriders (1950); as the prison camp
Scaramouche (1952); "boat dock near meadow"
Callaway Went Thataway (1952); assorted locations
Sky Full of Moon (1952); wood in Nevada
Everything I Have Is Yours (1952); unspecified location
Desperate Search (1952); water near plane crash site
Code Two (1953); unspecified location
Many Rivers to Cross (1955); as Kentucky
The Opposite Sex (1956); "Central Park lake"
Lust for Life (1956); "Paris woods and lake"
Santiago (1956, Warner Bros.); "Ext: Vicksburg"
Gigi (1958); as Paris
Tarzan the Ape Man (1959); as Africa
Home from the Hill (1960); unspecified location in Texas
Atlantis, the Lost Continent (1961); near Atlantis

All Fall Down (1962); "Ohio"
Hootenanny Hoot (1963); "swimming hole"
Joy in the Morning (1965); near campus
The Spy with My Face (1965); The Man from U.N.C.L.E. feature
The Trouble with Girls (1969); unspecified location
The Phantom of Hollywood (television 1974); "trap door"

10) Waterloo Bridge

The Clock (1945); a bridge in Central Park
The Green Years (1946); a bridge in Scotland
Desire Me (1947); a bridge in Brittany, France
Till the Clouds Roll By (1946); unspecified location
If Winter Comes (1947); a bridge in "Penny Green," England
The Three Musketeers (1948); a bridge in France
Command Decision (1948); unspecified location
Hills of Home (1948); a bridge in Scotland
Rich, Young and Pretty (1951); a bridge in Paris
Challenge to Lassie (1949); a bridge in Scotland
Stars in My Crown (1950); unspecified location
Royal Wedding (1951); Jane Powell sings "Too Late Now" here
Rich, Young and Pretty (1951); a bridge in France
Scaramouche (1952); "Bridge de Maynes Castle"
Scandal at Scourie (1952); unspecified location
Young Bess (1953); "Chelsea Bridge"
Bright Road (1953); a bridge in Alabama
The Affairs of Dobie Gillis (1953); Bobby Van hitchhikes here
The Student Prince (1954); as Heidelberg Bridge
It's a Dog's Life (1955); unspecified location
The Opposite Sex (1956); unspecified location
The Wings of Eagles (1957); seen in B&W newsreel behind John Wayne
Until They Sail (1957); a bridge in New Zealand
Merry Andrew (1958); unspecified location
Gigi (1958); a bridge in France
The Miracle (1959, Warner Bros.); a bridge in Spain
The World, the Flesh and the Devil (1959); unspecified location
The Twilight Zone (television); "Elegy "(1960)
Combat! (television); "The Cossack" (1965) and others
Hootenanny Hoot (1963); somewhere in Missouri
36 Hours (1965); James Garner and Eva Marie Saint picnic near bridge
The Extraordinary Seaman; (1969); unspecified location
Young Frankenstein (1974, Fox); monster chased across bridge by angry villagers
That's Entertainment! (1974); Bing Crosby's salute to the backlot
The Phantom of Hollywood (television 1974); as the Worldwide Pictures backlot

11) French Courtyard

Camille (1936); "horse auction" scene
The Emperor's Candlesticks (1937); used the house at the top of the street
The Great Waltz (1938); used the house at the top of the street
Marie Antoinette (1938); chateau
Bitter Sweet (1940); used the house at the top of the street
The Cross of Lorraine (1943); as France
Joan of Ark (1948, RKO); "Beaudricourts" and "Le Ruyers"

The Three Musketeers (1948); used with Three Musketeers Court
Battleground (1949); World War II Europe
The Red Danube (1949); as Post War Vienna
Go for Broke! (1951); World War II Europe
An American in Paris (1951); as Paris
The Story of Three Loves (1953); unspecified location
Atlantis, the Lost Continent (1961); assorted locations
Combat! (television); "Dateline" (1965) and others
The Venetian Affair (1967); "Sidewalk café"

12) Three Musketeers Court
The Three Musketeers (1948)
Scaramouche (1952); 1700s France
The Prisoner of Zenda (1952); unspecified European locations
Young Bess (1953); as Elizabethan England
Moonfleet (1955); as 18th century England
Diane (1956); as 16th century France
36 Hours (1965); as the Nazi command center
Atlantis, the Lost Continent (1961); assorted locations
The Wonderful World of the Brothers Grimm (1962); "The Singing Bone" segment used as the "Hotel Treville"
The Phantom of Hollywood (television 1974); as Worldwide Pictures backlot

13) Copperfield Street
David Copperfield (1935); assorted locations
The Great Waltz (1938); as Vienna
A Christmas Carol (1938); as London
Comrade X (1940); unspecified location
Pride and Prejudice (1940); as England
Smilin' Through (1941); assorted locations
Journey for Margaret (1942); as World War II London
The Seventh Cross (1944); assorted European locations
Julia Misbehaves (1948); unspecified location
That Forsyte Woman (1949); as England
Royal Wedding (1951); as England
The Merry Widow (1952); "Mariskova"
Million Dollar Mermaid (1952); assorted locations
Rhapsody (1954); as Zurich, Switzerland
The Student Prince (1954); as Heidelberg
The Last Time I Saw Paris (1954); unspecified location
The Glass Slipper (1954); assorted French locations
The King's Thief (1955); as 1600s England
Combat! (television 1962–1967); assorted locations
The Time Machine (1960); London over several centuries
The Singing Nun (1966); as Belgium

14) Quality Street
Quality Street (1927); the street's namesake
Marianne (1929); as a French village
The Secret of Madame Blanche (1933); dressed for the early 20th century
Queen Christina (1933); dressed for the 17th century
Escapade (1935); as 19th century Vienna
Mark of the Vampire (1935); as village outside Prague
Marie Antoinette (1938); assorted French locations
Three Comrades (1938); unspecified location
The Great Waltz (1938); assorted Viennese locations

The Emperor's Candlesticks (1937); assorted locations, possibly Russian
Bitter Sweet (1940); assorted Viennese locations
Pride and Prejudice (1940); unspecified location
Escape (1940); as a Bavarian village
Random Harvest (1942); as a British village
Above Suspicion (1943); unspecified European locations
The Cross of Lorraine (1943); assorted locations
Lassie Come Home (1943); Lassie jumps from window
National Velvet (1944); English village
Green Dolphin Street (1947); pieces of the title street
The Three Musketeers (1948); assorted locations
Battleground (1949); unspecified location
Scene of the Crime (1949); used for a modern setting
That Forsyte Woman (1949); assorted Victorian era settings
Royal Wedding (1951); as London
Go for Broke! (1951); WWII era Europe
An American in Paris (1951); assorted French side streets
Scaramouche (1952); as 1700s France
The Last Time I Saw Paris (1954); house at top of street
Rhapsody (1954); as Zurich, Switzerland
Deep in My Heart (1954); assorted European locations
Interrupted Melody (1955); Paris sidewalk café
Gaby (1956); as London
Diane (1956); as France
Les Girls (1957); unspecified location
Combat! (television 1962–1967); assorted locations
The Wonderful World of the Brothers Grimm (1962); assorted locations
36 Hours (1965); assorted WWII locations
The Singing Nun (1966); as Belgium
The Spy in the Green Hat (1966); *The Man from U.N.C.L.E.* feature, as "large house"
Young Frankenstein (1974, Fox); a Transylvanian village
The Phantom of Hollywood (television 1974); as Worldwide Pictures backlot
Show Biz (short subject 1976); unspecified location
Stayin' Alive (Bee Gees music video 1977); house at the top of the street
Sgt. Pepper's Lonely Hearts Club Band (1978, Universal); the village of "Fleu de Coup"
Directors Guild Documentary (1980); interview with director King Vidor (filmed in 1978)
The Stunt Man (1980, Fox); Steve Railsback is chased through the street by a tank

15) Railroad Terminal #2
Smilin' Through (1932); unspecified location
Sequoia (1934); as a northern California rail station
Anna Karenina (1935); Anna meets her lover in the snow
Our Vines Have Tender Grapes (1945); Margaret O'Brien visits an elephant
If Winter Comes (1947); as an English rail station
Three Little Words (1950); "Buffalo Railroad Station"
Singin' in the Rain (1952); seen in montage
The Red Danube (1949); a station somewhere in Vienna
Interrupted Melody (1955); "Australian rail station"
Lust for Life (1956); "Dutch rail station"

Raintree County (1957); Atlanta Railroad yards
The Student Prince (1954); Heidelberg railroad station
The Brothers Karamazov (1958); as Russia

16) Grand Central Station
Going Hollywood (1933); part of title musical number
Broadway to Hollywood (1933); unspecified location, possibly Broadway or Hollywood
Anna Karenina (1935); Greta Garbo throws herself under train tracks
The Public Hero #1 (1935); an unspecified rail station
Rendezvous (1935); unspecified location
Broadway Melody of 1936 (1935); New York's Grand Central Station
Fury (1936); unspecified location
Suzy (1936); Paris rail station
Love on the Run (1936); assorted locations
The Emperor's Candlesticks (1937)
Saratoga (1937); unspecified location
Spring Madness (1938); assorted locations
Ninotchka (1939); Paris rail station
Idiot's Delight (1939); unspecified European depot
The Mortal Storm (1940); unspecified European depot
Waterloo Bridge (1940); WWII era London station
Random Harvest (1942); WWII era London station
Journey for Margaret (1942); WWII era rail station
Music for Millions (1944); unspecified location
Song of Russia (1944); a Soviet rail station
The White Cliffs of Dover (1944); an English rail yard
The Clock (1945); New York's Grand Central Station
Desire Me (1947); unspecified location
The Hucksters (1947); "Clayport Station"
If Winter Comes (1947); an English rail yard
Julia Misbehaves (1948); unspecified European location
B.F.'s Daughter (1948); "Union Station" and "Fulton Airport"
The Barkleys of Broadway (1949); New York's Grand Central Station
Crisis (1950); an unspecified European terminal
Mrs. O'Malley and Mr. Malone (1950); "Penn Station" and "Union Station"
Strictly Dishonorable (1951); "Penn Station"
The Tall Target (1951); as various 1860s rail stations
Rich, Young and Pretty (1951); as a Paris railroad station
Skirts Ahoy! (1952); unspecified location
Above and Beyond (1952); as "Washington Railroad terminal"
Washington Story (1952); as Newchester Railroad Station
Everything I Have Is Yours (1952); as New York's Grand Central Station
The Band Wagon (1953); Fred Astaire performs "By Myself"
The Story of Three Loves (1953); unspecified location
Confidentially Connie (1953); a rail stations somewhere in New England
The Student Prince (1954); unspecified location
Interrupted Melody (1955); unspecified location
Gaby (1956); as an unnamed British terminal
Silk Stockings (1957); a Paris rail station
North by Northwest (1959); a Chicago station
Some Like It Hot (1959, UA); a Chicago station

The Wonderful World of the Brothers Grimm (1962); last scene
  was shot inside the terminal
It Happened at the World's Fair (1963); as Seattle "monorail
  station"
The Outrage (1964); 1800s setting
Combat! (television); "What are the Bugles Blowin' For?"
  (1964) and "A Child's Game" (1966)
36 Hours (1965); "Lisbon airport gate"
The Rat Patrol (television); "The Trial by Fire Raid" (1967)
Garrison's Gorillas (television); "The Grab"(1967)
Young Frankenstein (1974, Fox); Gene wilder says goodbye to
  Madeline Kahn
The Phantom of Hollywood (television 1974); set seen in
  comparison to its former self
That's Entertainment! (1974); Fred Astaire toasts Gene Kelly
Stayin' Alive (Bee Gees music video 1977); used the ruins of
  the set

17) Chinese Street
China Seas (1935); prototype of set constructed
The Good Earth (1937); assorted Chinese locations
They Met in Bombay (1941); as the titled city
Dragon Seed (1944); assorted Chinese locations
Thirty Seconds Over Tokyo (1944); as Japan
This Man's Navy (1945); as southeast Asia
The Pirate (1948); as the Caribbean
Malaya (1949); as the titled city
Green Dolphin Street (1947); as China
Rogue's March (1953); as Bombay
Valley of the Kings (1954); as Cairo
Jupiter's Darling (1955); as ancient Rome
The Prodigal (1955); as Egypt
The Seventh Sin (1957); "Me-Tan-Fu Street"
Never So Few (1959); as Burma
Flower Drum Song (1961, Universal); as China
The Islanders (television); "La Costa Vendetta" (1961), as
  Singapore
Atlantis, the Lost Continent (1961); as Atlantis
The Hook (1963); as Korea
The Man from U.N.C.L.E. (television); "The Cherry Blossom
  Affair" (1965)
Harum Scarum (1965); "Street of Jackals"

18) Joppa Square and Castle Finckenstein
The Good Earth (1937); as China
Conquest (1937); as Prussia, gave Castle Finckenstein its name
Maytime (1937); 1850s France
They Met in Bombay (1941); the title city
The Three Musketeers (1948); as a French castle
Crisis (1950); unspecified location
The Prisoner of Zenda (1952); "Zenda"
Scaramouche (1952); French Revolution era
Plymouth Adventure (1952); early scenes in Europe
Athena (1954); "Joppa market"
The Student Prince (1954); as Heidelberg
The Prodigal (1955); ancient Damascus and "Joppa Square"
The Glass Slipper (1955); "palace gates"
Moonfleet (1955); castle in 18th century England

Diane (1956); "palace courtyard"
Atlantis, the Lost Continent (1961); "temple courtyard"
Harum Scarum (1965); "exterior parapet"
Schlitz beer commercial (television 1967); "Joppa Square"
The Phantom of Hollywood (television 1974); Castle
  Finckenstein destroyed on-camera

19) Verona Square
Romeo and Juliet (1936); as Verona
The Firefly (1937); as Spain
The Girl of the Golden West (1938); as Monterey, California
The Bad Man (1941); as Spanish California
Panama Hattie (1942); South America
Gaslight (1944); as Italy
Yolanda and the Thief (1945); "Patria"
The Kissing Bandit (1948); as old California
The Pirate (1948); a Caribbean village
The Bribe (1949); a seedy South American town
A Lady Without Passport (1950); as Havana
Crisis (1950); as South America
The Great Caruso (1951); as Europe
Go for Broke! (1951); as WWII Europe
The Merry Widow (1952); "To the Inn We're Marching" number
Latin Lovers (1953); as Brazil
The Student Prince (1954); as Heidelberg
Diane (1955); 16th century France
Go Naked in the World (1961); a Mexican Street
Combat! (television); "Finest Hour" (1965)
36 Hours (1965); unspecified location
Harum Scarum (1965); as the middle east
The Spy in the Green Hat (1966); *The Man from U.N.C.L.E.*
  feature
3M commercial (television 1966)
One Spy Too Many (1966); *The Man from U.N.C.L.E.* feature
Kool cigarette commercial (television 1966); "winter vacation"
The Venetian Affair (1967); "Venice hotel"
The Scorpio Letters (television 1967); unspecified European
  location
Garrison's Gorillas (television); "Friendly Enemies"(1967)
Kool cigarette commercial (television 1970)
That's Entertainment! (1974); Liza Minnelli's tribute to Judy
  Garland
The Phantom of Hollywood (television 1974); destroyed by
  teenage vandals
Winter Kills (1979, AVCO Embassy); a Mexican Village

20) Spanish Street
Susan Lenox (*Her Fall and Rise*) (1931); unspecified location
The Cuban Love Song (1931); as Cuba
The Kid from Spain (1932, Goldwyn)
As You Desire Me (1932); as Greece
Letty Lynton (1932); as South America
Faithless (1932); unspecified location
Storm at Daybreak (1933); as Sarajevo
The White Sister (1933); unspecified location, possibly Italy
Viva Villa! (1934); as Mexico
The Barretts of Wimpole Street (1934); as England
The Merry Widow (1934); "Marshovia"

I Live My Life (1935); as Greece
Romeo and Juliet (1936); Juliet's Funeral procession through
  Vienna
Anna Karenina (1935); as Venice
Student Tour (1934); as Venice
The Firefly (1937); as Spain
The Girl of the Golden West (1938); as California
The Bad Man (1941); as somewhere in the southwest
Yolanda and the Thief (1945); "Patria"
Fiesta (1947); as Mexico
The Kissing Bandit (1948); as old California
Callaway Went Thataway (1951); as old California
The Merry Widow (1952); "Marshovia"
Holiday for Sinners (1952); as New Orleans
Glory Alley (1952); as New Orleans
The Red Danube (1949); as Vienna
Jeopardy (1953); as Tijuana
Sombrero (1953); a Mexican village
The Student Prince (1954); as Heidelberg
The Prodigal (1955); as Damascus
It Started with a Kiss (1959); as Spain
Go Naked in the World (1961); "Mexican Jail and Street"
Combat! (television 1962–1967); assorted locations
Harum Scarum (1965); the middle east

21) English Home
Five and Ten (1931); the Rarick home
Arsène Lupin (1932); as Paris home
Smilin' Through (1932); "Grantham College"
Lovers Courageous (1932); the Blayne house
Downstairs (1932); the Von Burgan house
Red-Headed Woman (1932); the Legendre home
Letty Lynton (1932); the snow covered "Darrow house"
Peg o' My Heart (1933); "Chichester house"
Turn Back the Clock (1933); "Evans home"
The Painted Veil (1934); "polo club terrace"
Mutiny on the Bounty (1935); Franchot Tone toast
Reckless (1935); "Harrison (Francot Tone) home"
Mark of the Vampire (1935); house haunted by Bela Lugosi
Ah, Wilderness (1935); unspecified location
David Copperfield (1935); unspecified location
A Tale of Two Cities (1936); Lucie's home
A Christmas Carol (1938); assorted locations
Rage in Heaven (1941); unspecified location
Maisie Was a Lady (1941); Maisie works here as a maid
Whistling in the Dark (1941); unspecified location
Mrs. Miniver (1942); unspecified location
Random Harvest (1942); Ronald Coleman's estate
Mrs. Parkington (1944); a New York house
The White Cliffs of Dover (1944); British house
The Canterville Ghost (1944); unspecified location
The Big Hangover (1950); unspecified location
Royal Wedding (1951); as the home admired by Fred Astaire
The Bad and the Beautiful (1952); unspecified location
Please Don't Eat the Daisies (1960); Doris Day and David
  Niven's house
The Singing Nun (1966); unspecified location

22) Eucy Grove

Trader Horn (1931); as Africa
Red Dust (1932); as Indochina
Kongo (1932); as Africa
Freaks (1932); grove where the freaks frolicked
The White Sister (1933); Italian woods
Tarzan and His Mate (1934); as Africa
Mutiny on the Bounty (1935); the South Seas
Last of the Pagans (1935); the South Seas
Times Square Lady (1935); a cemetery
Moonlight Murder (1936); a concession stand adjacent to the
　　Hollywood Bowl
Love on the Run (1936); unspecified location
Tarzan Finds a Son (1939); as Africa
The Canterville Ghost (1944); British woods
King Solomon's Mines (1950); insets of Africa
Summer Stock (1950); farmlands
The Red Badge of Courage (1951); "woods"
Soldiers Three (1951); "village"
Desperate Search (1952); "woods"
Code Two (1953); "woods"
Bright Road (1953); "school playground"
Night of the Quarter Moon (1959); "tree-lined road by bay end
　　estate"
The Twilight Zone (television); "Still Valley" (1961)
Platinum High School (1960); "Crip's tree"
All Fall Down (1962); as Ohio
Combat! (television 1962–1967); assorted locations
The Hawaiians (1970); unspecified location
King Kong (1976, Paramount); a native village and Shea
　　stadium
Show Biz (short subject, 1976); assorted locations
New York, New York (1977, UA); "hitchhiking" scenes

23) Camille Cottage

Camille (1936); as the title character's cottage
Love on the Run (1936); a French country home
Aresène Lupin Returns (1938); an estate in France
The Kid from Texas (1939); seen in the background
Till the Clouds Roll By (1946); Jerome Kern's home
The Prisoner of Zenda (1952); Ruritanian home
The Legend of Lylah Clare (1968); "Zarken's estate"

24) Formal Garden and Cohn Park

The White Sister (1933); an Italian villa
Stage Mother (1933); grounds of Boston estate
The Painted Veil (1934); unspecified location
A Tale of Two Cities (1935); "Manette Gardens"
Anna Karenina (1935); Russian lawns
Camille (1936); "the duel"
Love on the Run; (1936); assorted locations
Marie Antoinette (1938); a garden at Versailles
Gone with the Wind (1939); the Atlanta home and grounds
Forty Little Mothers (1940); the school grounds
Pride and Prejudice (1940); British lawns
Strike Up the Band (1940); unspecified location
H.M. Pulham, Esq. (1941); the Boston estate grounds
Eyes in the Night (1941); unspecified location

Random Harvest (1942); the Rainier estate grounds
Lassie Come Home (1943); Nigel Bruce's estate grounds
The Secret Heart (1946); unspecified location
Journey for Margaret (1942); unspecified English location
The White Cliffs of Dover (1944); British lawns
The Canterville Ghost (1944); the castle grounds
Nothing But Trouble (1944); Laurel and Hardy at a garden party
Son of Lassie (1945); unspecified location
The Great Sinner (1949); unspecified Monte Carlo location
The Reformer and the Redhead (1950); unspecified location
King Solomon's Mines (1950); unspecified location
The Happy Years (1950); prep-school grounds
Father's Little Dividend (1951); unspecified location
Singin' in the Rain (1952); unspecified location
Invitation (1952); unspecified location
Pat and Mike (1952); production records cited "Cohn Park" as
　　an unspecified location
The Bad and the Beautiful (1952); unspecified location
Scaramouche (1952); "Gavrillac Rose Garden"
Young Bess (1953); "terrace and lawn"
I Love Melvin (1953); unspecified location, possibly Central
　　Park
Dream Wife (1953); unspecified location
It's a Dog's Life (1955); outdoor festival scenes
Tea and Sympathy (1956); school grounds
High Society (1956); estate grounds
The Wings of Eagles (1957); garden party scene
The Twilight Zone (television); "The Jungle"(1961) and "The
　　Fugitive" (1962)
National Velvet (television); "The Fall" (1961)
Cain's Hundred (television); "Blue Water, White Beach" (1961)
Boys' Night Out (1962); "City Park"
All Fall Down (1962); "park"
Two Weeks in Another Town (1962); as Italian lawn, seen in
　　dailies
A Ticklish Affair (1963); production records cited "Cohn Park"
Hootenanny Hoot (1963); "interiors of tent"
The Man from U.N.C.L.E. (television 1964–1968); assorted
　　locations
A Patch of Blue (1965)
Hold On! (1966); "Page estate"
Mister Buddwing (1966); "Washington Square"
A Fine Madness (1966, Warner Bros.); "Para Park" in New York
　　City
Don't Make Waves (1967); "playground"
Double Trouble (1967); "garden party"
The Legend of Lylah Clare (1968); "Zarken's grounds"
The Courtship of Eddie's Father (television 1969–1972); single
　　episode in 1969
The Trouble with Girls (1969); unspecified location
Zigzag (1970); "golf course"
Shell gasoline commercial (television 1970); "Formal Garden"
Hearts of the West (1975); open area within the garden

25) Esther Williams Pool

Everybody Sing (1938); "Bellaire pool"
Love Finds Andy Hardy (1938); where Mickey Rooney meets
　　Lana Turner

Another Thin Man (1939); unspecified location
The Philadelphia Story (1940); the Lord family pool
Forty Little Mothers (1940); unspecified location
Maisie Was a Lady (1941); the Rawlston pool
Love Crazy (1941); unspecified location
Andy Hardy's Double Life (1942); Esther Williams's first dive in
Three Hearts for Julia (1943); unspecified location
Bathing Beauty (1944); school pool
Thrill of a Romance (1945); Esther Williams
Up Goes Maisie (1946); unspecified location
Living in a Big Way (1947); the Morgan pool
This Time for Keeps (1947); Esther Williams again
Merton of the Movies (1947); unspecified location
The Hucksters (1947); as Los Angeles pool
This Time for Keeps (1947); Esther Williams
Invitation (1952); seen in background
Fearless Fagan (1952); unspecified location
The Bad and the Beautiful (1952); a pool in Los Angeles
Dangerous When Wet (1953); "Lanet pool"
The Girl Who Had Everything (1953); "Bascomb pool"
Easy to Love (1953); mostly filmed in Florida
Deep in My Heart (1954); a pool in Beverly Hills
The Wings of Eagles (1957); the lawn party pool
Jailhouse Rock (1957); pool party
High School Confidential! (1958); "Joan Staples pool"
The World, the Flesh and the Devil (1959); unspecified location
The Twilight Zone (television); "The Trouble with Templeton"
　　(1960), "The Bewitchin' Pool" (1964), and "Queen of the
　　Nile" (1964)
Sweet Bird of Youth (1962); as hotel pool
Two Weeks in Another Town (1962); Kirk Douglas tosses
　　someone in
Honeymoon Hotel (1964); as hotel pool
Hold On! (1966); "Hotel Pool"
Spinout (1966); "the Ranley pool"
Penelope (1966); unspecified location
The Venetian Affair (1967); unspecified location
The Scorpio Letters (television 1967); unspecified location
How to Steal the World (1968); *The Man from U.N.C.L.E.*
　　feature
The Phantom of Hollywood (television 1974); seen on
　　Worldwide Pictures studio tour
That's Entertainment! (1974); Donald O'Conner's tribute to
　　Esther Williams

26) Southern Mansion

The Toy Wife (1938); the Vallaire plantation
Man-Proof (1938); unspecified location
Love Finds Andy Hardy (1938); the country club
Dancing Co-Ed (1939); unspecified location
Babes in Arms (1939); unspecified location
The Kid from Texas (1939); the country club
Sporting Blood (1940); unspecified location
New Moon (1940); "Wainwright"
Blossoms in the Dust (1941); unspecified location, possibly the
　　foundlings' home
The Vanishing Virginian (1942); dressed for a 1920s setting
Whistling in Dixie (1942); as plantation

Kid Glove Killer (1942); the Chatsburg home
The Human Comedy (1943); as Ithaca home
Love Laughs at Andy Hardy (1946); unspecified location
Undercurrent (1946); Washington D.C. home
Good News (1947); part of Tate University campus
Cass Timberlane (1947); unspecified location
Killer McCoy (1947); unspecified location
On an Island with You (1948); unspecified location
B. F.'s Daughter (1948); the Fulton home
A Southern Yankee (1948); "Twelve Oaks"
In the Good Old Summertime (1949); the house is blocked from view
The Great Sinner (1949); house is covered by bandstand
You for Me (1952); unspecified location, possibly Peter Lawford's home
Skirts Ahoy! (1952); unspecified location
Invitation (1952); unspecified location
The Affairs of Dobie Gillis (1953); Bobby Van sings "I'm through With Love" on steps
Her Twelve Men (1954); as the Boarding school
High Society (1956); part of the Lord home
The Wings of Eagles (1957); garden party scene
Raintree Country (1957); "plantation"
Some Came Running (1958); "the old Carmichael place"
High School Confidential! (1958); house is seen in background
Handle with Care (1958); unspecified location
The Twilight Zone (television); "Spur of the Moment" (1964)
The World, the Flesh and the Devil (1959); unspecified location
Ada (1961); Tennessee plantation
Sweet Bird of Youth (1962); "Boss Finley's home"
All Fall Down (1962); unspecified location, possibly the Willart home
Hootenanny Hoot (1963); as "Norburg College"
The Outer Limits (television); "The Invisibles" (1964)
Advance to the Rear (1964); as "Confederate Headquarters"
Your Cheatin' Heart (1964); southern home
Ford Reception commercial; (television 1964)
Joy in the Morning (1965); campus building
The Long, Hot Summer (television 1965–1966); Varner plantation
The Man from U.N.C.L.E. (television); "The Her Master's Voice Affair" (1966), "The Take Me to Your Leader Affair" (1966), and others
Hold On! (1966); seen behind party
The Spy with My Face (1965); *The Man from U.N.C.LE.* feature

27) Vinegar Tree House

Rich Man, Poor Girl (1938); Harrison house
National Velvet (1944); the Brown home
The Prisoner of Zenda (1952); British home
Please Don't Eat the Daisies (1960); the back of the Mackay house
Joy in the Morning (1965); the back of this set was a campus home
The Karate Killers (1967); *The Man from U.N.C.LE.* feature, an unspecified location
How to Steal the World (1968); *The Man from U.N.C.LE.* feature
A Time to Sing (1968); unspecified location

The Phantom of Hollywood (television 1974); "bushes near house"
Jeep commercial (television 1966); "Holy Toledo"

28) Stable

Stand Up and Fight (1939); 1840s stable
The Women (1939); country club stable
The Philadelphia Story (1940); the Lord family stable
Lassie Come Home (1943); seen in background
National Velvet (1944); stable at racetrack
Son of Lassie (1945); as the Carraclough stable
Undercurrent (1946); as the Hamilton stable
My Brother Talks to Horses (1947); as a stable in Maryland
Cass Timberlane (1947); unspecified location
A Southern Yankee (1948); as the Weathearby stable
Neptune's Daughter (1949); unspecified location
It's a Dog's Life (1955); unspecified location
National Velvet (television 1960–1962); assorted locations
One of Our Spies is Missing (1966); *The Man from U.N.C.L.E.* feature

29) Girl's School

The Captain Is a Lady (1940); part of retirement home
Waterloo Bridge (1940); unspecified location
Andy Hardy Meets Debutante (1940); "orphanage"
Love Crazy (1941); "rest home"
The Feminine Touch (1941); Digby College
Best Foot Forward (1943); the Winsock Military Institute
Broadway Rhythm (1944); unspecified location
A Letter for Evie (1946); as a military hospital
Love Laughs at Andy Hardy (1946); as Wainwright College
Good News (1947); as Tate University
Cynthia (1947); "Napoleon High School"
Killer McCoy (1947); unspecified location
The Sea of Grass (1947); unspecified location
Three Darling Daughters (1948); "Miss Drake's School for Girls"
Summer Holiday (1948); Danville, Connecticut
The Happy Years (1950); as Lawrenceville Prep School
Kim (1950); "school"
Bannerline (1951); as Carravia High School
The Affairs of Dobie Gillis (1953); "Grainbelt University"
Her Twelve Men (1954); Oaks Boarding School
The Glass Slipper (1955); unspecified location
The Cobweb (1955); as a sanitarium
It's a Dog's Life (1955); unspecified location
Tea and Sympathy (1956); school set, also tennis court near lawn
The Wings of Eagles (1957); as a military academy
Merry Andrew (1958); Danny Kaye's school
Handle with Care (1958); as the law school
High School Confidential! (1958); Jerry Lee Lewis sings "High School Hop" in front of the set
Night of the Quarter Moon (1959); "Cloverdale Sanitarium"
Where the Boys Are (1960); the snowy campus the girls flee from to Ft. Lauderdale
Mutiny on the Bounty (1962); Captain Bligh's inquest site
The Wheeler Dealers (1963); "Cotton Mather Inn"

Hootenanny Hoot (1963); "Norburg College"
Get Yourself a College Girl (1964); as Wyndham college
Joy in the Morning (1965); as a campus
A Patch of Blue (1965); unspecified location
When the Boys Meet the Girls (1965); "college"
How to Steal the World (1968); *The Man from U.N.C.L.E.* feature
The Trouble with Girls (1969); unspecified location
Mame (1974, Warner Bros.); "Ransom University" and "Boniface Academy"
That's Entertainment! (1974); Peter Lawford hosts in front of "Tate University"
The Phantom of Hollywood (television 1974); as Worldwide pictures backlot
Logan's Run (1976); as outskirts of ruined Washington D.C.

30) Old Mill House

When Ladies Met (1941); they meet here
Mrs. Miniver (1942); as an English country home
The Three Musketeers (1948); "Inn of the Flowers"
Little Women (1949); June Allyson is wooed by Peter Lawford here
Too Young to Kiss (1951); remodeled for a "modern" look
Invitation (1952); house is used without the water wheel
The Time Machine (1960); mostly hidden
Signpost to Murder (1964); unspecified location
The Spy with My Face (1965); *The Man from U.N.C.L.E.* feature
The Phantom of Hollywood (television 1974); as Worldwide Pictures backlot
Sgt. Pepper's Lonely Hearts Club Band (1978, Universal); "A Day in the Life" number

31) Lord Home

The Philadelphia Story (1940); as the Lord home
Dr. Kildare's Wedding Day (1941); unspecified location
The Hoodlum Saint (1946); unspecified location
The Hidden Eye (1945); unspecified location
Three Wise Fools (1946); the title character's home
Killer McCoy (1947); unspecified location
The Sun Comes Up (1949); a southern home
Athena (1954); the Mulvain home
The Last Time I saw Paris (1954); as post-WWII Paris home
Love Me or Leave Me (1955); as Doris Day's home
High Society (1956); used the "lawn and door"
The Twilight Zone (television); "A World of Difference" (1960), "Long Live Walter Jameson" (1960), and "Mute" (1963)
The Eleventh Hour (television 1962–1964); assorted locations
The Americanization of Emily (1964); as an English home
Miller beer commercial (television 1966); "Bar-B-Q"

32) Prison

The Big House (1930); Wallace Berry in prison
Pardon Us (1931); Laurel and Hardy in prison
Hold Your Man (1933); Jean Harlow in prison
The Public Hero #1 (1935); Chester Morris in prison
Exclusive Story (1936); unspecified location
David Copperfield (1935); the debtor's prison
A Tale of Two Cities (1935); walls of the Bastille

33) Copperfield Court

David Copperfield (1935); assorted London locations
Love on the Run (1936); assorted European locations
Waterloo Bridge (1940); assorted British locations
Journey for Margaret (1942); as England
The Seventh Cross (1944); as Zurich, Switzerland
Julia Misbehaves (1948); assorted French locations
Challenge to Lassie (1949); fire scenes
Royal Wedding (1951); assorted British locations
The Prisoner of Zenda (1952); coronation parade
Million Dollar Mermaid (1952); unspecified location
The Student Prince (1954); as Heidelberg
Rhapsody (1954); as Zurich, Switzerland
The Last Time I Saw Paris (1954); unspecified location
The Time Machine (1960); London over several centuries
The Singing Nun (1966); unspecified location
Double Trouble (1967); seen on Elvis Presley's "European" tour

34) Wimpole Street

The Barretts of Wimpole Street (1934); as a 19th century street
Kind Lady (1935); as London
Waterloo Bridge (1940); as World War I London
Dr. Jekyll and Mr. Hyde (1941); as 19th century London
That Forsyte Woman (1949); the townhouse
Gaslight (1944); as 19th century London
Mrs. Parkington (1944); assorted 1870s locations
The White Cliffs of Dover (1944); as England
The Picture of Dorian Gray (1945); as 19th century London
Without Love (1945); as 1940s Washington D.C.
My Brother Talks to Horses (1947); as Baltimore
The Hucksters (1947); as New York
That Forsyte Woman (1949); as old London
The Man with a Cloak (1951); as 19th century New York
The Law and the Lady (1951); assorted locations
Kind Lady (1951); remake of the 1935 film
The Belle of New York (1952); as 1890s New York
Hit the Deck (1955); assorted locations
The Power and the Prize (1956); the London scenes
Combat! (television, 1962–1967); as assorted European locations
The 4 Horsemen of the Apocalypse (1962); as 1940s Europe
Two Weeks in Another Town (1962); sidewalk café
The Man from U.N.C.L.E. (television); "The Test Tube Killer Affair" (1967)
The Venetian Affair (1967); as "Italian Hotel"
Garrison's Gorillas (television 1967–1968); "The Grab," as "Esson Street"
The Maltese Bippy (1969); unspecified location

35) Waterfront Street

The Barretts of Wimpole Street (1934); as a 19th century street
A Tale of Two Cities (1935); as London
Kind Lady (1935); as Victorian London
Too Hot to Handle (1938); unspecified location
They Met in Bombay (1941); the set's very edge is visable, leading to "Eastside Street"
Random Harvest (1942); site of Ronald Coleman's walk after regaining his memory

A Yank at Eton (1942); unspecified British location
Above Suspicion (1943); unspecified European location
The Seventh Cross (1944); unspecified European location
The Thin Man Goes Home (1944); unspecified location
Gaslight (1944); as Victorian London
Two Smart People (1946); as New Orleans
Easter Parade (1948); as New York
Madame Bovary (1949); as Normandy, the "Mardi Gras scene"
Challenge to Lassie (1949); as Edinburgh
Scene of the Crime (1949); as an American city
That Forsyte Woman (1949); as Victorian England
An American in Paris (1951); as Paris
Go for Broke! (1951); as WWII Europe
Rich, Young and Pretty (1951); "Momarte Street" and "Marie's Apartment"
The Man with a Cloak (1951); as New York City in 1848
The Prisoner of Zenda (1952); unspecified location
Kind Lady (1951); as Victorian London
Lovely to Look At (1952); as Paris
The Story of Three Loves (1953); unspecified location
Take the High Ground! (1953); unspecified location
The Last Time I Saw Paris (1954); as Paris
The Student Prince (1954); as Heidelberg
Rhapsody (1954); as Zurich, Switzerland
Interrupted Melody (1955); unspecified European location
It's a Dog's Life (1955); unspecified location
It's Always Fair Weather (1955); as an "Italian Village"
The King's Thief (1955); "underpass"
The Power and the Prize (1956); as "Bond Street"
Les Girls (1957); unspecified European location
Combat! (television 1962–1967); assorted locations
The 4 Horsemen of the Apocalypse (1962); as 1940s Paris
The Prize (1963); as Stockholm
One of Our Spies is Missing (1966); *The Man from U.N.C.L.E.* feature, as "Antwerp"
The Singing Nun (1966); unspecified European location
Double Trouble (1967); unspecified European location

New York Streets

*Original New York Street set as salvaged from Lot One (1928–1935)

The Cameraman (1928); also Lot One
The Lady of Scandal (1930); as England
Son of India (1931); as Bombay
Politics (1931); as an American city
Possessed (1931); as an American city
Hell Divers (1931); scenes set on dry land
Skyscraper Souls (1932); as New York
The Passionate Plumber (1932); as Paris
Prosperity (1932); "Warren Bank"
Red-Headed Woman (1932); as an unidentified American city
The Wet Parade (1932); assorted locations
Turn Back the Clock (1933); as New York
Hold Your Man (1933); Pawn shop sequence
Gabriel Over the White House (1933); assorted sequences
Looking Forward (1933); as London
The Woman in His Life (1933); "Spot Club" exteriors
Made on Broadway (1933); as New York

The White Sister (1933); unspecified location
Midnight Mary (1933); assorted sequences
Broadway to Hollywood (1933); "Pontiac Hotel"
Another Language (1933); "toy shop"
The Woman in His Life (1933); unspecified location
The Gay Bride (1934); as New York
Stamboul Quest (1934); "Hotel Excelsior"
Fugitive Lovers (1934); bus depot(s) scenes
The Cat and the Fiddle (1934); as Brussels
Hide-Out (1934); early scenes in New York
Manhattan Melodrama (1934); as New York
Sadie McKee (1934); as New York
A Wicked Woman (1934); "Madame LaRue's Hat Shop"
Whipsaw (1935); unspecified location
The Casino Murder Case (1935); unspecified location
Reckless (1935); "Vaudeville house" and "newspaper stand" scenes
Times Square Lady (1935); as New York
Public Hero #1 (1935); on theatre marquee: "Vincent and his trained Monkeys"
It's in the Air (1935); assorted locations
O'shaughnessy's Boy (1935); circus parade
The Murder Man (1935); "Regent Apartment"
A Night at the Opera (1935); opera house
Reckless (1935); "Eastside Street" (not to be confused with a later set of the same name)
Rendezvous (1935); as WWI era New York
Exclusive Story (1936); unspecified location
Absolute Quiet (1936); opening city scenes

37) Brownstone Street

The Devil is a Sissy (1936); as New York
Young Dr. Kildare (1938); as New York
Rich Man, Poor Girl (1938); unspecified location
Man-Proof (1938); as New York
Calling Dr. Kildare (1939); as New York
These Glamour Girls (1939); unspecified location
The Secret of Dr. Kildare (1939); as New York
Another Thin Man (1939); as New York
Dr. Kildare's Strange Case (1940); as New York
Dr. Kildare Goes Home (1940); as New York
Dr. Kildare's Crisis (1940); as New York
The People vs. Dr. Kildare (1941); as New York
Dr. Kildare's Wedding Day (1941); as New York
Eyes in the Night (1941); unspecified location
Life Begins for Andy Hardy (1941); Andy goes to New York City
Dr. Kildare's Victory (1942); as New York
Calling Dr. Gillespie (1942); as New York
Dr. Gillespie's New Assistant (1942); as New York
Dr. Gillespie's Criminal Case (1943); as New York
3 Men in White (1944); as New York
Music for Millions (1944); unspecified location
Her Highness and the Bellboy (1945); as New York
The Hidden Eye (1945); unspecified location
Between Two Women (1945); unspecified location, possibly New York
The Picture of Dorian Gray (1945); as London

The Clock (1945); Judy Garland and Robert Walker deliver milk in New York
Dark Delusion (1947); as New York
High Wall (1947); unidentified big city
Take Me Out to the Ball Game (1949); assorted locations
In the Good Old Summertime (1949); turn of the century Chicago
On The Town (1949); as New York
The Yellow Cab Man (1950); as Los Angeles
The Big Hangover (1950); unspecified location
Three Little Words (1950); as New York
Dial 1119 (1950); as New York
The People Against O'Hara (1951); as New York
Strictly Dishonorable (1951); as 1920s New York
Invitation (1952); unspecified location
Give a Girl a Break (1953); as New York
Latin Lovers (1953); assorted locations
The Clown (1953); assorted locations
Remains to Be Seen (1953); "Valeska's (Angela Lansbury's) New York apartment"
Rouge Cop (1954); as New York
It's Always Fair Weather (1955); as New York
Gaby (1956); dressed for London blitz
Somebody Up There Likes Me (1956); as New York
This Could Be the Night (1957); as New York
Designing Women (1957); as New York
The Thin Man (television); "Housewarming" (1958) and others
It Started with a Kiss (1959); assorted locations
The Twilight Zone (television); "Mr. Bevis" (1960) and "The Big Tall Wish" (1960)
Ask Any Girl (1959); "apartment house"
Bells Are Ringing (1960); as New York
Dr. Kildare (television); "Johnny Temple" (1961) and others
The Asphalt Jungle (television); "The Professor" (1961)
The Eleventh Hour (television 1962–1964); assorted locations
Sunday in New York (1963); "Adam's apartment"
The Man from U.N.C.L.E. (television 1964–1968); "Del Floria's Tailor Shop" (U.N.C.L.E. headquarters)
The Spy with My Face (1965); *The Man from U.N.C.L.E.* feature
Every Girl's Dream (short subject 1966); seen on studio tour
One Spy Too Many (1966); *The Man from U.N.C.L.E.* feature
Mister Buddwing (1966); "crosstown liquor store"
The Fugitive (television); "The Walls of Night" (1967)
Medical Center (television 1969–1976); assorted locations
Show Biz (short subject 1976); assorted locations
CHiPs (television); "Supercycle" (1978)
Buck Rogers in the 25th Century (1979, Universal); Chicago

38) Eastside Street
Wife vs. Secretary (1936); as New York
San Francisco (1937); as San Francisco
They Met in Bombay (1941); as Bombay
Journey for Margaret (1942); as London
Tarzan's New York Adventure (1942); as New York
Nazi Agent (1942); as New York
Whistling in Brooklyn (1943); assorted locations
Her Highness and the Bellboy (1945); as New York
The Unfinished Dance (1947); unspecified location

High Wall (1947); "106 Maple Street"
Tenth Avenue Angel (1948); as New York
Words and Music (1948); as New York
Scene of the Crime (1949); as New York
East Side, West Side (1949); as New York
The Asphalt Jungle (1950); "Donatos"
The Yellow Cab Man (1950); as Los Angeles
The Big Hangover (1950); as New York
Dial 1119 (1950); as New York
Side Street (1950); as New York
Singin' in the Rain (1952); as Hollywood—title number
I Love Melvin (1953); as alley and street
The Actress (1953); unspecified location
A Slight Case of Larceny (1953); unspecified location
The Clown (1953); "Aladdin Café"
Deep in My Heart (1954); assorted locations
Somebody Up There Likes Me (1956); as New York
The Asphalt Jungle (television); unidentified 1961 episode
Cain's Hundred (television); "Cain's Final Judgment" (1961)
How the West Was Won (1962); as a St. Louis music hall
The Eleventh Hour (television 1962–1964); "My Problems Have Problems" (unidentified episode, working title) and as "Eastside Street Café"
Sunday in New York (1963); as New York
Honeymoon Hotel (1964); unspecified location
A Patch of Blue (1965); as New York
Dr. Goldfoot and the Bikini Machine (1965, AIP); as a big city
Joy in the Morning (1965); assorted locations
The Money Trap (1965); candy store, bar, and Rosalie's apartment
The Spy in the Green Hat (1966); *The Man From U.N.C.L.E.* feature
The Phantom of Hollywood (television 1974); for "backlot party" scenes
The Ultimate Warrior (1975, Warner Bros.); as "city slums"

39) Warehouse Alley
Lassie Come home (1943); as England and Lassie's escape
The Band Wagon (1953); "alleyway"
Torch Song (1953); "alley"
Kiss Me Kate (1953); as New York and "alley"
The Opposite Sex (1956); "backstage alley"
Designing Women (1957); theatre alley
This Could Be The Night (1957); an alley
Hot Summer Night (1957); "back alley"
Party Girl (1958); "Southside club and alley"
The World, the Flesh and the Devil (1959); "alleys and fire escapes"
The Gazebo (1959); "stage door and alley, hardware store"
The Subterraneans (1960); as San Francisco
The Twilight Zone (television); "Five Characters in Search of an Exit" (1961)
Your Cheatin' Heart (1964); "Alley entrance"
The Fugitive (television); "Landscape With Running Figures" (1965), and "Alley and Tenement Street"
The Ultimate Warrior (1975, Warner Bros.); a destroyed futuristic city

40) Church Street
High Wall (1947); unspecified location
Big City (1948); assorted locations
A Lady Without Passport (1950); "street near convent"
Scaramouche (1952); unspecified location
Small Town Girl (1953); unspecified location
It's Always Fair Weather (1955); as New York
Until they Sail (1957); as New Zealand
The World, the Flesh and the Devil (1959); Harry Belafonte walks through the street
Quick Before It Melts (1964); unspecified location
Joy in the Morning (1965); opening scenes

41) Fifth Avenue
Wife vs. Secretary (1936); as New York
Suzy (1936); Fifth Avenue shrouded in fog
Rose-Marie (1936); the opera house set
After the Thin Man (1936); assorted locations
San Francisco (1936); as San Francisco
The Great Ziegfeld (1936); assorted locations
The Last Gangster (1937); as New York
Double Wedding (1937); as Los Angeles
The Shopworn Angel (1938); as New York
Test Pilot (1938); assorted locations
Four Girls in White (1939); assorted locations
Another Thin Man (1939); as New York
Ninotchka (1939); as Moscow
Little Nellie Kelly (1940); Saint Patrick's Day parade sequence
Two Girls on Broadway (1940); as New York
Broadway Melody of 1940 (1940); as New York
Comrade X (1940); as Russia
I Take This Woman (1940); unspecified location
Babes on Broadway (1941); assorted locations
Shadow of the Thin Man (1941); as New York
The Big Store (1941); New York department store exteriors
Dr. Kildare's Wedding Day (1941); as New York
Design for Scandal (1941); unspecified location
Married Bachelor (1941); unspecified locations
H.M. Pulham, Esq. (1941); assorted locations
Nazi Agent (1942); as New York
Journey for Margaret (1942); as London
Fingers at the Window (1942); New York show opened at theatre
Pride of the Yankees (1942, Goldwyn); unspecified locations
Girl Crazy (1943); as New York
Lost Angel (1943); unspecified locations
The Human Comedy (1943); as California, *Mrs. Miniver* is playing at the theatre
Slightly Dangerous (1943); as New York
Music for Millions (1944); as New York
The Thin Man Goes Home (1944); unspecified locations
The Seventh Cross (1944); as Nazi Germany
Maisie Goes to Reno (1944); unspecified locations, possibly Reno
Week-End at the Waldorf (1945); as New York
Her Highness and the Bellboy (1945); as New York
Yolanda and the Thief (1945); as Red Square
Abbott and Costello in Hollywood (1945); as Los Angeles
The Clock (1945); assorted locations

Up Goes Maisie (1946); assorted locations
Song of the Thin Man (1947); as New York
The Mighty McGurk (1947); unspecified location
Three Darling Daughters (1948); Fifth Avenue
Words and Music (1948); Mickey Rooney's death scene
Big City (1948); as New York
Act of Violence (1948); unspecified locations
Easter Parade (1948); title number staged here (refer to Lot Three)
In the Good Old Summertime (1949); as Chicago
The Red Danube (1949); as a bank façade used as army headquarters
The Secret Garden (1949); interior of façade used as a shed
The Yellow Cab Man (1950); as Los Angeles
Shadow on the Wall (1950); as New York
The Asphalt Jungle (1950); the jewelry store robbery was staged here
Three Little Words (1950); as New York
Dial 1119 (1950); as New York
A Lady Without Passport (1950); "Broadway and 42nd Street"
Two Tickets to Broadway (1951); as New York
Callaway Went Thataway (1951); as the hotel
Royal Wedding (1951); as London
An American in Paris (1951); as a Parisian street
Too Young To Kiss (1951); unspecified locations
No Questions Asked (1951); "Chancellor Hotel"
Lone Star (1952); "Bowery set"
Above and Beyond (1952); unspecified location
Singin' in the Rain (1952); as Hollywood
The People Against O'Hara (1952); "Knuckles Fish Market"
Lovely To Look At (1952); as Paris
Skirts Ahoy! (1952); unspecified location
Just This Once (1952); unspecified location
The Belle of New York (1952); Fred Astaire dances on the top of a streetcar
Everything I Have Is Yours (1952); as New York
Holiday for Sinners (1952); as New Orleans
Easy to Love (1953); unspecified location
Give a Girl a Break (1953); "Regal Theater"
The Girl Who Had Everything (1953); as New York
Jeopardy (1953); "burlesque theatre"
I Love Melvin (1953); as New York
Dream Wife (1953); unspecified location
The Band Wagon (1953); "Plaza Hotel, Times Square," etc.
Executive Suite (1954); office building
Rogue Cop (1954); as New York
Athena (1954); "health food store"
The Blackboard Jungle (1955); "North Manual High School"
It's Always Fair Weather (1955); Gene Kelly dances on roller-skates
Love Me or Leave Me (1955); "Marty's Nightclub"
The Tender Trap (1955); "Bergie's Restaurant"
I'll Cry Tomorrow (1955); "Fifth Ave., 8th Ave., and 10th Ave."
Ransom! (1956); bank façade on Fifth Avenue, also TV station
The Power and the Prize (1956); "refugee office"
Silk Stockings (1957); as Moscow
Tip on a Dead Jockey (1957); "Reno Street"
The Thin Man (television 1957–1959); assorted locations

Man on Fire (1957); unspecified location
Designing Women (1957); "Lori's apartment"
Party Girl (1958); "criminal courts building"
North by Northwest (1959); New York auction house exteriors
Never So Few (1959); as Burma
The World, the Flesh and the Devil (1959); as New York
The Mating Game (1959); courthouse played "IRS Building"
The Big Operator (1959); unspecified location
The Big Circus (1959, Allied Artists); unspecified location
Ask Any Girl (1959); "Albemarle Hotel"
The Twilight Zone (television); "One For the Angels" (1959), "I Dream of Genie" (1963), "Cavender is Coming" (1962), "The Incredible World of Horace Ford" (1963), and others
All the Fine Young Cannibals (1960); "Fifth Ave. church"
Cimarron (1960); "Wyatt University"
Bells are Ringing (1960); "subway and office building entrances"
The Subterraneans (1960); "San Francisco and bookstore"
Dr. Kildare (television 1961–1966); assorted hospital locations
Period of Adjustment (1962); unspecified location
Combat! (television 1962–1967); assorted locations
Boys' Night Out (1962); Greenwich Village
All Fall Down (1962); Fifth Avenue decorated for Christmas
The Courtship of Eddie's Father (1963); "penny arcade and theatre lobby"
The Richard Boone Show (television 1693–1964); assorted locations
The Wheeler Dealers (1963); as New York
The Man from U.N.C.L.E. (television 1964–1968); "The Never-Never Affair" (working title for unknown episode) and others
The Trials of O'Brien (television 1965–1966); location for courthouse
Mister Buddwing (1966); "exterior 3rd street"
The Girl from U.N.C.L.E. (television); "The Garden of Evil Affair" (1966)
The St. Valentine's Day Massacre (1967, Fox); assorted Chicago locations
Where Were You When the Lights Went Out? (1968); as New York
The Maltese Bippy (1969); as Queens, New York
Soylent Green (1973); as futuristic New York
That's Entertainment! (1974); Gene Kelly's tribute to Fred Astaire
The Ultimate Warrior (1975, Warner Bros.); as a futuristic city
ABC *Afterschool Specials* (television); "Gaucho" (1978)

42) Cullem Street
That Forsyte Woman (1949); as Victorian London and "large building at end of Cullem Street"
Made in Paris (1966); probably Cullem Street
The Venetian Affair (1967); "corner of Cullem Street"

43) Park Avenue
San Francisco (1936); as the title city
It's Always Fair Weather (1955); Gene Kelly roller-skates by
In the Good Old Summertime (1949); as Chicago
Third Finger, Left Hand (1940); as Park Avenue
It's Always Fair Weather (1955); assorted locations

The World, the Flesh and the Devil (1959); assorted locations
Dr. Kildare (television 1961–1966); assorted hospital exteriors
The Wheeler Dealers (1963); as New York

LOT THREE

45) Monterey Street
Strange Cargo (1940); as Devil's Island
Tarzan's New York Adventure (1942); outpost outside jungle
Carbine Williams (1952); unspecified location, probably prison sequences
Escape from Fort Bravo (1953); part of fort
Rawhide (television 1959–1966); assorted locations
The Twilight Zone (television); "Deaths-Head Revisited" (1961), as Dachau concentration camp
The Gunslinger (television 1961); an army outpost
A Thunder of Drums (1961); "Fort Canby"
Combat! (television); "Gideon's Army" (1963) and a Nazi concentration camp
Advance to the Rear (1964); "Fort Hoolar"
Dirty Dingus Magee (1970); an unnamed fort

46) Western Street
Out West With the Hardy's (1938); as the West
Stand Up and Fight (1939); unspecified location
Go West (1940); as Dead Man's Gulch
Barbary Coast Gent (1944); as 1880s San Francisco
Our Vines Have Tender Grapes (1945); as Wisconsin
The Harvey Girls (1946); as Sandrock
High Barbaree (1947); unspecified locations
The Sea of Grass (1947); as Salt Pork, New Mexico
A Southern Yankee (1948); as a southern town
Summer Holliday (1948) as Danville, Connecticut
Stars in My Crown (1950); as an 1860s frontier town
Annie Get Your Gun (1950); assorted locations
The Return of Jesse James (1950, Lippert); unspecified location
Excuse My Dust (1951); unspecified location
Show Boat (1951); assorted locations
The Law and the Lady (1951); assorted locations
Westward the Women (1951); as a California Western town
Ride, Vaquero! (1953); unspecified location
Scandal at Scourie (1953); as a Canadian town
Battle Circus (1953); "railroad spur" in Korea
Seven Brides for Seven Brothers (1954); as 1850s Oregon
Bad Day at Black Rock (1955); some exteriors shot here
Raintree County (1957); assorted locations
Union Pacific (television 1958–1959); records indicate space was rented in 1957 for an unidentified episode
The Law and Jake Wade (1958); as New Mexico
The Horse Soldiers (1959, UA); assorted Civil War locations
Rawhide (television 1959–1966); assorted locations
Philip Marlowe (television 1959–1960); "Railroad depot" and "Oaks house" used for an unidentified episode
Cimarron (1960); rail station and other sections
Sergeant Rutledge (1960, Warner Bros.); assorted locations
All the Fine Young Cannibals (1960); as Pine Alley, Texas
The Twilight Zone (television); "Dust" (1961), "The Grave"

(1961), "Showdown with Rance McGrew" (1962), and "Valley of the Shadow" (1963)
The Gunslinger (television 1961); assorted locations
Pabst Blue Ribbon beer commercial (television 1962)
Billy Rose's Jumbo (1962); the circus parade
How the West Was Won (1962); "blacksmith's shop, livery stable, etc."
Marx toys commercial (television 1963)
The Travels of Jamie McPheeters (television 1963–1964); assorted episodes
Your Cheatin' Heart (1964); a railroad station
The 7 Faces of Dr. Lao (1964); "Willow Falls"
The Unsinkable Molly Brown (1964); "Leadville Street"
A Man Called Shenandoah (television 1965–1966); assorted locations
The Rounders (television 1966–1967); assorted locations
Hondo (television 1967); assorted locations
The Fastest Guitar Alive (1967); assorted locations, possibly San Francisco
Support Your Local Sheriff (1969, UA); a Western boom town
The Traveling Executioner (1970); unspecified location
Wild Rovers (1971); unspecified location

47) Cloudy Street
Anna Karenina (1935); allegedly as Russia
Rosalie (1937); European village
The Girl of the Golden West (1938); as northern California
Balalaika (1939); a Russian village
Song of Russia (1944); a Russian village
The Wild North (1952); a Canadian village
Rose-Marie (1954); a Canadian village
The Brothers Karamazov (1958); Russian village

48) Fort Canby
A Thunder of Drums (1960); "Fort Canby"
Rawhide (television 1959–1966); assorted locations
Advance to the Rear (1964); "Fort Hoolar"

49) Fort Scott
Carbine Williams (1952); as a prison
Escape from Fort Bravo (1953); as Fort Bravo
Rawhide (television 1959–1966); assorted locations
Advance to the Rear (1964); "Fort Hoolar"
Dirty Dingus Magee (1970); as a Cavalry fort

50) Billy the Kid Street
Billy the Kid (1941); assorted New Mexico locations
Girl Crazy (1943); a small town near campus
The Green Years (1946); apparently used as a Scottish Village
The Harvey Girls (1946); used for scenes not involving the railroad
The Sea of Grass (1947); "Daggett Livery Stable"
High Barbaree (1947); unspecified location
Annie Get Your Gun (1950); assorted locations
Callaway Went Thataway (1951); rural locations
Excuse My Dust (1951); 1895 small town settings
Lone Star (1952); as 1840s Texas
Apache War Smoke (1952); "hacienda"

Escape from Fort Bravo (1953); as Mescal Street
The Fastest Gun Alive (1956); "Oak Creek'
The Hired Gun (1957); as Texas and New Mexico
The Sheepman (1958); assorted locations
The Law and Jake Wade (1958); a New Mexico frontier town
Rawhide (television 1959–1966); assorted locations
Cimarron (1960); an Oklahoma boom town
The Fastest Guitar Alive (1967); unspecified location
Sol Madrid (1968); "Cantina" in Mexico
Charro! (1969, National General); somewhere near Mexico
Dirty Dingus Magee (1970); unspecified location

51) Ghost Town Street
Boom Town (1940); as the title street
Go West (1940); as parts of the town
Mrs. Parkington (1944); "Ghost Town Street"
Bad Bascomb (1946); Wallace Beery robs the bank
Duel in the Sun (1947, Selznick); as Paradise Flats, Texas
Three Godfathers (1948); as New Jerusalem, Arizona
Annie Get Your Gun (1950); assorted locations
Devil's Doorway (1950); "Medicine Bow"
Vengeance Valley (1951); as Colorado
The Wild North (1952); as Canada
Westward the Women (1952); "California Street"
Scandal at Scourie (1953); as Canada
Gypsy Colt (1954); assorted locations
Rose-Marie (1954); as Canada
Seven Brides for Seven Brothers (1954); as 1850s Oregon
The Last Hunt (1956); unspecified location
The Hired Gun (1957); unspecified location
Northwest Passage (television 1958–1959); assorted locations
The Twilight Zone (television); "Mr. Denton on Doomsday" (1959), "Still Valley" (1961), and "Once Upon a Time" (1961)
Rawhide (television 1959–1966); assorted locations
The Gunslinger (television 1961); assorted locations
The Outer Limits (television); "The Zanti Misfits" (1963)
Advance to the Rear (1964); assorted locations
The Unsinkable Molly Brown (1964); as Colorado town(s)
Mail Order Bride (1964); as the town Buddy Ebsen lives by
Tickle Me (1965); "modern" Western town
The Man Called Shenandoah (television 1965–1966); assorted locations
The Rounders (television 1966–1967); a "modern" Western town
Hondo (television 1967); assorted locations
The Man from U.N.C.L.E. (television); "The Maze Affair" (1967)
Return of the Gunfighter (television 1967); Robert Taylor rides into town
Charro! (1969, National General); as a Mexican border town
Dirty Dingus Magee (1970); "Yerkey's Hole"
The Hired Hand (1973, Universal); the old set is well used by Peter Fonda

52) St. Louis Street
Meet Me in St. Louis (1944); "Kensington Avenue"
Valley of Decision (1945); as Pittsburgh
Till the Clouds Roll By (1946); the set is seen briefly

My Brother Talks to Horses (1947); a Baltimore neighborhood
Cass Timberlane (1947); the family home is here
Song of the Thin Man (1947); visited during investigation
The Sea of Grass (1947); as St. Louis
Cynthia (1947); Elizabeth Taylor's neighborhood
Good News (1947); neighborhood visited by Tate University students
The Farmer's Daughter (1947, RKO); as the neighborhood Loretta Young works in
In the Good Old Summertime (1949); used in the scene that featured Liza Minnelli
Cheaper by the Dozen (1950, Fox); as the Gilbreth home
The Happy Years (1950); as 1896 New York
Show Boat (1951); apparently, used briefly
Bannerline (1951); as a modern-day (1950s) neighborhood
Excuse My Dust (1951); as a late-19th century neighborhood
Scandal at Scourie (1953); as Canada
The Long, Long Trailer (1953); Lucy and Desi visit relatives here
The Cobweb (1955); Richard Widmark's neighborhood
It's Always Fair Weather (1955); "farmhouse"
The Twilight Zone (television); "Walking Distance" (1959), "Elegy" (1960), and "The Shelter" (1961)
Meet Me in St. Louis (television 1959); "Kensington Avenue"
Cimarron (1960); as a neighborhood in Oklahoma
Please Don't Eat the Daisies (1960); apparently used as background
Summer and Smoke (1961, Paramount); as Mississippi
A Thunder of Drums (1961); dressed for the 19th century
Ada (1961); as a southern neighborhood
Go Naked in the World (1961); "Stratton Home"
All Fall Down (1962); "Cleveland"
The Eleventh Hour (television 1962–1964); assorted episodes
How the West Was Won (1962); Debbie Reynolds' San Francisco home
Twilight of Honor (1963); "the Harper home"
The Unsinkable Molly Brown (1964); Debbie Reynolds' Denver home
Please Don't Eat The Daisies (television 1965–1967); assorted episodes
The Man from U.N.C.L.E. (television 1964–1968); assorted episodes
Meet Me in St. Louis (television 1966); "Kensington Avenue"
The Helicopter Spies (1967); *The Man from U.N.C.L.E.* feature
The Maltese Bippy (1969); as Flushing, New York
The Reivers (1969, Cinema Center Films); a street in 1900s Mississippi
Night Gallery (television); "Deliveries in the Rear" (1972)

53) Rock Formations
Tarzan's Secret Treasure (1941); encountered during Tarzan's journey
Du Barry Was a Lady (1943); seen along European road
Thirty Seconds Over Tokyo (1944); used for World War II battles
The Bad and the Beautiful (1952); a studio location on a backlot
Invitation (1952); as rustic areas
Carbine Williams (1952); "rock quarry"
The Wild North (1952); "Spain"

Gypsy Colt (1954); encountered out west
Rose-Marie (1954); somewhere up north
Jupiter's Darling (1955); the rocks are seen in ancient times
Tribute to a Bad Man (1956); as a Western location
The Last Hunt (1956); seen during the Buffalo hunt
Gun Glory (1957); used for "rocks and explosion"
Ben-Hur (1959); single shot taken here in rock crevice
The World, the Flesh and the Devil (1959); "mine and pit head"
Tarzan the Ape Man (1959); as Africa
Green Mansions (1959); as South America
The Time Machine (1960); location for unknown inserts
Atlantis, the Lost Continent (1961); "crater"
The Twilight Zone (television); "A Quality of Mercy" (1961)
Combat! (television); "The Old Men" (1965)
The Fastest Guitar Alive (1967); chase sequences
How to Steal the World (1968); *The Man from U.N.C.L.E.* feature

54) Lot Three Jungle and Lake
Too Hot to Handle (1938); as Brazil
The Adventures of Huckleberry Finn (1939); "Jackson's Island"
Lady of the Tropics (1939); as French-Indochina
Congo Maisie (1940); as a lake
Strange Cargo (1940); as New Guinea
Barnacle Bill (1941); as a lake
Tarzan's Secret Treasure (1941); jungle
White Cargo (1942); outskirts of African plantation
Cairo (1942); "jungle"
Tarzan's New York Adventure (1942); African, pre-New York sequences
Mrs. Miniver (1942); the lake
Cry Havoc (1943); as Bataan
The Human Comedy (1943); the lake
See Here, Private Hargrove (1944); unspecified sequences
Thirty Seconds Over Tokyo (1944); the return to Allied territory
Keep Your Powder Dry (1945); unspecified location
A Southern Yankee (1948); "battle-scarred woods"
On an Island with You (1948); "native village"
Little Women (1949); the woods outside of town
The Hills of Home (1948); as Scotland
Big Jack (1949); "cabin in woods"
Malaya (1949); used in *White Cargo* dock set
The Toast of New Orleans (1950); as the old south
The Outriders (1950); as the Arkansas River embankment
Duchess of Idaho (1950); used for "boat on river"
Stars in My Crown (1950); a Western-era location
A Lady Without Passport (1950); "everglades"
The Reformer and the Redhead (1950); "jungle trees and boat dock"
Two Weeks with Love (1950); upstate New York
Mystery Street (1950); "car dumped into pond" scenes
Watch the Birdie (1950); unspecified location
Kim (1950); "the road to Kaneboh"
Show Boat (1951); the Mississippi River
Soldiers Three (1951); Kipling's 19th century India
Bannerline (1951); "lookout point"
Texas Carnival (1951); "riverbank"
Go for Broke! (1951); World War II European setting

The Bad and the Beautiful (1952); unspecified location
Invitation (1952); rural settings
The Wild North (1952); as Canada
Carbine Williams (1952); assorted locations
Washington Story (1952); unspecified location
Just This Once (1952); unspecified location
Scaramouche (1952); French countryside
The Prisoner of Zenda (1952); Ruritanian countryside
Million Dollar Mermaid (1952); "river and inlet"
Westward the Women (1952); "river"
Sombrero (1953); "river and falls"
Scandal at Scourie (1953); "park and pond" and "Quebec Countryside"
Latin Lovers (1953); "river"
Battle Circus (1953); as Korea
Dangerous When Wet (1953); the Higgins' swimming hole
All the Brothers Were Valiant (1953); "Worthen's dock"
Cry of the Hunted (1953); "swamplands"
Bright Road (1953); "countryside near caterpillar tree"
Gypsy Colt (1954); assorted locations
Green Fire (1954); the coffee plantation and house built in the jungle
Rose-Marie (1954); scene of the "Mounties marching song"
Valley of the Kings (1954); "Turaeg Camp"
Tennessee Champ (1954); "pier and river"
Prisoner of War (1954); Robert Horton tortured by Korean soldiers here
Jupiter's Darling (1955); an ancient rural setting
Many Rivers to Cross (1955); as the Kentucky frontier
Hit the Deck (1955); assorted locations
The Glass Slipper (1955); forest glade
Oklahoma! (1955, RKO/Fox); exteriors near lake
Jupiter's Darling (1955); unspecified location
The Scarlet Coat (1955); river and dock
I'll Cry Tomorrow (1955); unspecified location
The Cobweb (1955); woods outside of town
It's a Dog's Life (1955); "woods and stream"
Tribute to a Bad Man (1956); western settings
The Last Hunt (1956); some of the title hunt set here
The Opposite Sex (1956); scenes involving the "canoe on lake"
Raintree County (1957); "river bayou" and "Paradise Lake"
Don't Go Near the Water (1957); a site outside of a Navy Base
The Seventh Sin (1957); "exterior peninsula land"
House of Numbers (1957); outside of prison
Something of Value (1957); "mountain bluffs and camp"
Gun Glory (1957); used for "rocks and explosion"
The Badlanders (1958); unspecified location
Merry Andrew (1958); "English Countryside"
Ben-Hur (1959); pick-up shots
The World, the Flesh and the Devil (1959); assorted locations
Never So Few (1959); as World War II China
Green Mansions (1959); "South American Runi village," "river," etc.
The Beat Generation (1959); "lovers lane"
Watusi (1959); "assorted jungle locations"
Tarzan the Ape Man (1959); jungle, also used bean field (outside of studio, now West Los Angeles College)

Night of the Quarter Moon (1959); "old ruins at river trail, boat and jetty"
The Twilight Zone (television); "The Purple Testament" (1960) and "The Hunt" (1962)
The Time Machine (1960); "lake"
The Adventures of Huckleberry Finn (1960); Mississippi River backgrounds
Home from the Hill (1960); "pond" scenes
Two Loves (1961); "Maori village"
The Islanders (television); "The Pearls of Ratu" (1961)
Cain's Hundred (television 1961–1962); assorted episodes
Atlantis, the Lost Continent (1961); "slave camp" and "crater"
Billy Rose's Jumbo (1962); outside of town
The Horizontal Lieutenant (1962); "country road"
Sweet Bird of Youth (1962); as St. Cloud, Florida
Drums of Africa (1963); assorted locations
The Lieutenant (television 1963–1964); "rainforest-stream" for unidentified episode
Combat! (television); "Survival" (1963), "The First Day" (1965), and others
Advance to the Rear (1964); "Sioux Landing"
Your Cheatin' Heart (1964); unspecified location
Signpost to Murder (1964); as Great Britain
The Americanization of Emily (1964); as Great Britain
The Unsinkable Molly Brown (1964); unspecified location
Harum Scarum (1965); unspecified middle eastern location
The Singing Nun (1966); "Jungle Island"
The Spy in the Green Hat (1966); *The Man from U.N.C.L.E.* feature
Daktari (television 1966–1969); most exteriors shot at "Africa USA" in Redwood Shores, California
Hot Rods to Hell (1967); somewhere in the western U.S.
Double Trouble (1967); "African village"
The Scorpio Letters (1967); "river, pier"
Chevrolet Camero commercial (television 1967)
The Helicopter Spies (1967); *The Man from U.N.C.L.E.* feature, as "jungle island"
The Fastest Guitar Alive (1967); assorted locations
How to Steal the World (1968); *The Man from U.N.C.L.E.* feature
Marlowe (1969); "ext: boat and shrubbery"
Support Your Local Sheriff (1969, UA); unspecified location
The Courtship of Eddie's Father (television 1969–1972); used lake for unspecified episode
Burger King commercial (television 1970); "jungle cave"
Kool cigarette commercial (television 1970); "swamps & lake"

55) Eucy Road
Moonlight Murder (1936); road to the Hollywood Bowl
Pride and Prejudice (1940); English road
Notorious (1946, RKO); Ingrid Bergman's drunken Florida drive
High Wall (1947); unspecified location
The Barkleys of Broadway (1949); unspecified location
Any Number Can Play (1949); "gas station"
Stars in My Crown (1950); "country road"
The Law and the Lady (1951); as a country road
The Strip (1951); a road in Los Angeles

Go for Broke! (1951); "muddy road"
Excuse My Dust (1951); "crash road"
Soldiers Three (1951); "jungle River Road"
Carbine Williams (1952); chain gang scenes
Scaramouche (1952); "meadow road"
Pat and Mike (1952); unspecified location
Fearless Fagan (1952); "road near camp"
Scandal at Scourie (1952); as Canadian woods
You for Me (1953); unspecified location
Battle Circus (1953); Korean "road with refugees" and "highway"
The Affairs of Dobie Gillis (1953); road into town
Dangerous When Wet (1953); "road to Higgins' Farm"
A Slight Case of Larceny (1953); road and gas station
Athena (1954); "lonely road"
Deep in My Heart (1954); travel scenes
The Student Prince (1954); "road for king's coach"
Rose-Marie (1954); wilderness and road
Executive Suite (1954); "road and lake"
Tennessee Champ (1954); "motel and road"
The Scarlet Coat (1955); the highwayman road
The Glass Slipper (1955); "forest road"
Those Wilder Years (1956); "country road"
The Great American Pastime (1956); "road with cop"
House of Numbers (1957); "highway near woods"
Merry Andrew (1958); "McCleary Road"
Cat on a Hot Tin Roof (1958); "road to estate"
High School Confidential! (1958); "drag trip"
North by Northwest (1959); Cary Grant's car accident "near dump pile & tree lane"
The Mating Game (1959); "hillside road"
The Twilight Zone (television); "Walking Distance" (1959), "The Hitch-Hiker" (1960), "Still Valley" (1961), and others
Where the Boys Are (1960); "highway"
National Velvet (television 1960–1962); "McCleary Road"
All the Fine Young Cannibals (1960); "country road"
Atlantis, the Lost Continent (1961); "tree-lined road"
Two Loves (1961); unspecified New Zealand location
Period of Adjustment (1962); the road to Florida
The Horizontal Lieutenant (1962); "hill and fence road"
Billy Rose's Jumbo (1962); circus caravan road
Combat! (television); "Lost Sheep, Lost Shepherd" (1962), "Operation Fly Trap" (1964), "The First Day" (1965), "Ask Me No Questions" (1966), and others
The Outer Limits (television); "The Man with the Power" (1963), "Specimen: Unknown" (1964), "The Forms of Things Unknown" (1964), and others
My Favorite Martian (television 1963–1966); assorted episodes
The Unsinkable Molly Brown (1964); "road to the Brown cabin"
The Man from U.N.C.L.E. (television); "The Gurnius Affair" (1967) and others
The Fugitive (television); "Landscape With Running Figures" (1965), as "narrow road and gas station phone booth"
Girl Happy (1965); Elvis' "Doing the Clam" number
The Man Called Shenandoah (television 1965–1966); assorted locations
The Scorpio Letters (television 1967); "ditch and road"

Garrison's Gorillas (television); "Now I Lay Me Down to Die" (1967) and others
Double Trouble (1967); "country lane"
Then Came Bronson (television 1969–1970); road scenes were shot here in 1968
The Moonshine War (1970); as assorted back roads

56) Salem Waterfront
Show Boat (1951); "*Cotton Blossom*"
The Strip (1951); "*Cotton Blossom*"
Plymouth Adventure (1952); "*Mayflower*" launch
The Light Touch (1952); "Carthage Harbor"
My Man and I (1952); "asparagus field (boat dock)"
Washington Story (1952); a boat dock at Newchester
Young Bess (1953); British port
Desperate Search (1953); "*Cotton Blossom*"
All the Brothers Were Valiant (1953); used the "*Mayflower*" and waterfront
The Scarlet Coat (1955); an American Revolution setting
I'll Cry Tomorrow (1955); unspecified location
The King's Thief (1955); as a British port
The Adventures of Huckleberry Finn (1960); "*Cotton Blossom*"
Ada (1961); unspecified location
How the West Was Won (1962); dock and "*Cotton Blossom*"
Advance to the Rear (1964); "*Cotton Blossom*"
The Man from U.N.C.L.E. (television); "The Finny Foot Affair" (1964)
My Favorite Martian (television); "Go West, Young Martian" (1965), used the "*Cotton Blossom*"
Every Girl's Dream (short subject 1966); "*Cotton Blossom*" and "dock, port"
Frankie and Johnny (1966, UA); Elvis Presley sings "Down by the Riverside"
Garrison's Gorillas (television 1967–1968); "The Prison Break Story" (working title for unknown episode)
Carlton cigarettes commercial (television 1967)
Double Trouble (1967); "Hotel"

57) Process Tank
Captains Courageous (1937); storms at sea
I Take This Woman (1940); unspecified location
Northwest Passage (1940); the forging of the river
Strange Cargo (1940); the boat at sea
New Moon (1940); unspecified location
Stand by for Action (1942); World War II Naval battles
Cairo (1942); torpedo attack and lifeboat scenes
Tarzan's New York Adventure (1942); Tarzan's jump off of the Brooklyn Bridge
Nazi Agent (1942); unspecified locations
Tortilla Flat (1942); unspecified locations
Mrs. Miniver (1942); bombing sequences
A Guy Named Joe (1943); sea battle on coast of New Guinea
Pilot #5 (1943); bombing sequences
Bataan (1943); battle miniatures
Thirty Seconds Over Tokyo (1944); the bombing of Tokyo
The White Cliffs of Dover (1944); miniatures
They Where Expendable (1945); sea battles
This Man's Navy (1945); assorted naval sequences

Green Dolphin Street (1947); ships at sea
Homecoming (1948); unspecified location
Luxury Liner (1948); miniatures of title vessel
Three Darling Daughters (1948); possibly used for Cuban cruise sequences
Malaya (1949); unspecified aquatic locations
Annie Get Your Gun (1950); the trip to Europe
Kim (1950); unspecified location
Royal Wedding (1951); the trip to Europe
Inside Straight (1951); "mine shots"
Rich, Young and Pretty (1951); unspecified location
Quo Vadis (1951); miniatures of burning Rome
Plymouth Adventure (1952); "*Mayflower*" miniatures at sea
The Light Touch (1952); "sinking lifeboat inserts"
All the Brothers Were Valiant (1953); scenes with ships at sea
Rogue's March (1953); unspecified locations
Easy to Love (1953); "big sky backing"
Young Bess (1953); "Thames River process plates"
Valley of the Kings (1954); "sandstorm" special effects
The Tender Trap (1955); seen during performance of the title song
Kismet (1955); miniatures and full size sets as well
Around the World in 80 Days (1956, UA); miniature boats for effects shots
Tip on a Dead Jockey (1957); "flare effects shots'
Torpedo Run (1958); "Tokyo harbor"
Never So Few (1959); used for "blues screen shots"
Ben-Hur (1959); the battle at sea
The *Wreck of the Mary Deare* (1959); the title sequence
The World, the Flesh and the Devil (1959); unspecified location
Atlantis, the Lost Continent (1961); "Atlantis sinking into the sea"
Mutiny on the Bounty (1962); the "*Bounty*" at sea
Two Weeks in Another Town (1962); a studio tank supposedly at Rome's Cinecitta Studios
The Hook (1963); Korean War sea battles
Hidden Magic commercial (television 1965); "swamp boat"
Double Trouble (1967); inserts of debris at sea
Ice Station Zebra (1968); miniatures and frozen landscapes
The Extraordinary Seaman (1969); unspecified location

58) Farmhouse
The Devil's Doorway (1950); "Livery Stable"
Excuse My Dust (1951); "Joe's Barn"
Rich, Young and Pretty (1951); "Jim's ranch"
Lone Star (1952); "barn"
Fearless Fagan (1952); "Ardley Farm"
Gypsy Colt (1953); "corral"
Dangerous When Wet (1953); Higgins's Farm
Take the High Ground! (1953); unspecified location
Arena (1953); the stables
Latin Lovers (1953); "stables"
Her Twelve Men (1954); "stables"
Meet Me in Las Vegas (1956); "ranch house"
The Opposite Sex (1956); "ranch and gates"
The Last Hunt (1956); "stable"
Those Wilder Years (1956); unspecified location
The Hired Gun (1957); "Indian Springs barn"

The Sheepman (1958); barnyard
Handle with Care (1958); as a farmhouse
The Mating Game (1959); "Larkin farm"
The Twilight Zone (television); "Elegy" (1960), "It's a Good
  Life" (1961), "The Last Rites of Jeff Myrtebank" (1962),
  "Jess-Belle" (1963), and others
Rawhide (television 1959–1966); assorted episodes
All the Fine Young Cannibals (1960); "Davis Farm"
The Adventures of Huckleberry Finn (1960); the farmhouse
  visited by Huck
All Fall Down (1962); farmhouse
How the West Was Won (1962); George Peppard and Lee J.
  Cobb's confrontation in livery stable
Billy Rose's Jumbo (1962); farmhouse
A Ticklish Affair (1963); "Amy's barn"
The Rounders (1965); the ranch house
The Rat Patrol (television 1966–1968); flashbacks for "The
  Final Roundup Raid" (working title for unknown
  episode)
A Time to Sing (1968); "Dodd Farm"

59) Kismet Staircase
Kismet (1944); as temple
Lost in a Harem (1944); as Arabian palace
Anchors Away (1945); as New York location
Crisis (1950); "palace steps"
An American in Paris (1951); as Paris steps—last scene in movie
The Unkown Man (1951); as steps to city building
The Prisoner of Zenda (1952); as castle steps
Latin Lovers (1953); unspecified location
Harum Scarum (1965); Arabian staircase
The Prodigal (1955); Damascus palace steps
The World, the Flesh and the Devil (1959); as a New York
  location
All the Fine Young Cannibals (1960); a city building's steps
The Time Machine (1960); staircase into futuristic temple
The Twilight Zone (television); "Time Enough To Last" (1959),
  "A Nice Place to Visit" (1960), "Two Loves" (1961), and
  city steps in New Zealand
Atlantis, the Lost Continent (1961); as a staircase in Atlantis
The Girl from U.N.C.L.E. (television 1966–1967); unidentified
  episode

60) Easter Parade Street
Easter Parade (1948); as 1912 New York

61) Circus Grounds
O'shaughnessy's Boy (1935); as a circus setting
Rosalie (1937); Eleanor Powell's kingdom is built near here
At the Circus (1938); as a circus setting
Maisie (1939); unspecified location
Tarzan's New York Adventure (1942); as a circus setting
Thousands Cheer (1943); location for Army shows
Hills of Home (1948); "Kildrumie fair"
Take Me Out To the Ball Game (1949); as a ballpark
The Stratton Story (1949); as a ballpark
Annie Get Your Gun (1950); Wild West show location
Texas Carnival (1951); as the title event

Fearless Fagan (1952); Fagan's show
Million Dollar Mermaid (1952); "Greenwich Carnival"
Jupiter's Darling (1955); "elephant compound"
The Great American Pastime (1956); as a ballpark
Merry Andrew (1958); circus setting
The Big Circus (1959, Allied Artists); circus setting
It Started with A Kiss (1959); as Madrid Air Force Base
Billy Rose's Jumbo (1962); circus setting
Boys' Night Out (1962); a ballpark
The Horizontal Lieutenant (1962); Honolulu baseball game
The Courtship of Eddie's Father (1963); a ballpark
The 7 Faces of Dr. Lao (1964); a circus setting
Roustabout (1964); a carnival setting
Tickle Me (1965); "Rodeo" scenes
The Trouble with Girls (1969); unspecified location

62) Army Base
Escape (1940); as somewhere in Germany
The Bugle Sounds (1942); as an Army base
Thousands Cheer (1943); as an Army camp
Pilot #5 (1943); as an Army base
Bataan (1943); as an Army base
See Here, Private Hargrove (1944); Fort Bragg Army base
Thirty Seconds Over Tokyo (1944); as military base
Keep your Powder Dry (1945); the Woman's Army Core base
Son of Lassie (1945); a prison compound
What Next, Corporal Hargrove? (1945); as an Army base
Courage of Lassie (1946); unspecified location
The Red Danube (1949); as the Army camp
Callaway Went Thataway (1951); as a training camp
Fearless Fagan (1952); as Army headquarters
Above and Beyond (1952); as an Air Core base
Carbine Williams (1952); as a prison
Take the High Ground (1953); as an Army camp
The Last Hunt (1956); "Army headquarters"
Somebody Up There Likes Me (1956); "Fort Dix"
Raintree County (1957); "streets only"
Imitation General (1958); U.S. Army base in France
High School Confidential! (1958); "drag race" scene
It Started with a Kiss (1959); European U.S. Army base
The Horizontal Lieutenant (1962); "barracks"
The Outer Limits (television 1963–1965); assorted episodes
The Man from U.N.C.L.E. (television 1964–1968); assorted
  episodes
See Here, Private Hargrove (television pilot 1964); assorted
  locations
One Spy Too Many (1966); *The Man from U.N.C.L.E.* feature

63) Dutch Street
Pride and Prejudice (1940); used early version of district
Seven Sweethearts (1942); "Dutch Street" constructed for film
The Three Musketeers (1948); dockside village and waterfront
The Green Years (1946); as Scotland
Green Dolphin Street (1947); assorted locations
Desire Me (1947); as a Brittany village
The Three Musketeers (1948); as France
Madame Bovary (1949); as a 19th century French town
The Toast of New Orleans (1950)

Scaramouche (1952); as 18th century France
Lili (1953); as a French village
Young Bess (1953); as 1500s England
Rogue's March (1953); as 19th century Afghanistan
The King's Thief (1955); as 17th century England
Merry Andrew (1958); unspecified location
The *Wreck of the Mary Deare* (1959); as a British port
All the Fine Young Cannibals (1960); unspecified location
Mutiny on the Bounty (1962); as a 1789 British sea port
Combat! (television); "Glory Among Men" (1964) and others
The Man from U.N.C.L.E. (television); "The Finny Foot Affair"
  (1964)
Hawaii (1966, UA); as a New England village port
Ice Station Zebra (1968); early scenes presumably shot here
The Wreck of the Mary Deare (1960); village on the English
  Channel
Signpost to Murder (1964); as an unidentified English city
Garrison's Gorillas (television 1967–1968); assorted episodes
Double Trouble (1967); assorted European locations

64) Melbury Street
The Man from U.N.C.L.E. (television); "The Survival School
  Affair" (1967)
The Man with a Cloak (1951); 19th century New York
Kind Lady (1951); unspecified location
36 Hours (1964); as World War II Europe

65) Brooklyn Street
The Pride of the Yankees (1942, Goldwyn); as New York
Whistling in Brooklyn (1943); as New York
Valley of Decision (1945); as Pennsylvania
The Mighty McGurk (1947); unspecified location
It Happened in Brooklyn (1947); as New York
Homecoming (1948); Clark Gable and Lana Turner return here
The Magnificent Yankee (1950); as turn of the century New York
The Man with a Cloak (1951); 19th century New York
The Law and the Lady (1951); assorted locations
Kind Lady (1951); assorted Locations
All the Fine Young Cannibals (1960); unspecified location
The Twilight Zone (television); "The Incredible World of
  Horace Ford," (1963), as "Randolph Street"
The Girl from U.N.C.L.E. (television); "The Danish Blue
  Affair" (1966), as "warehouse"

PHOTO CREDITS

All photographs, except where noted below, are Copyright © TURNER ENTERAINMENT COMPANY used courtesy of Warner Bros. Entertainment Inc.

Other photos courtesy of:

Authors' collection: 21 (right), 31 (right), 37 (inset), 39 (inset), 41 (right), 45 (right), 47 (right), 48 (right), 51 (right), 63 (bottom right), 64 (bottom left), 72 (right), 78 (right), 82, 86 (right), 148 (bottom left), 155 (bottom left), 168, 170 (right), 172 (left), 185 (top), 198, 200 (right), 202 (left, top right), 203, 218 (top), 244 (right), 269 (top right), 283 (left), 287 (right), 288

The Bison Archives, Marc Wanamaker: 7, 17, 23, 26, 28 (bottom right), 29 (right), 38, 39, 41 (left), 49 (left), 56 (center), 58, 60 (right), 62 (right), 65, 73, 74 (right), 76 (left), 77 (left), 79 (top left), 80 (left), 86 (left), 87 (top left), 91 (right), 92, 95 (top left, bottom right), 97 (top right), 98 (right), 99 (right), 103 (center), 112, 114, 115, 119 (left), 120, 123 (top left), 124, 126, 127 (bottom left), 129, 130 (left), 131, 133 (bottom right), 138, 139, 144, 145, 156, 157, 159 (left), 162 (left), 163, 174, 175 (left), 178 (top, bottom center, bottom right), 183 (top left), 194 (right), 196 (left), 209 (left), 212, 234, 229 (right), 231 (left), 233, 234 (left), 235 (left), 237 (left), 238 (bottom right), 247 (right), 248 (right), 250 (left), 251 (right), 261, 262, 263, 283 (right), 286, 287 (center)

Julie Lugo Cerra: 175 (top right)

Ben Cowitt: 69 (left)

John Divola: 217 (bottom center), 276, 277, 278, 284 (right)

The Gillespie family: 84 (left), 85, 252 (bottom left, right)

Randy Knox: 148 (right), 231 (top right)

Paul D. Marks: 189 (right)

Brainard Miller: 164 (inset), 228, 230 (bottom left), 240 (left), 249 (top right, bottom right), 252 (top left), 272 (left, bottom right), 273 (center, right), 275, 284 (left)

David L. Snyder: 113

USC Cinematic Arts Library, Ned Comstock: 236 (right), 238 (bottom left, bottom center)

Lou Valentino: 165 (bottom left)

INDEX

BIBLIOGRAPHY

Hundreds of invaluable books, articles, records, archives and movies were consulted in preparation of this book. Below are just a few of the works which were directly utilized in the preparation of the text. A complete bibliography will be posted on our website at http://www.mgmbacklot.info

BOOKS

Allyson, June. *June Allyson*. Berkeley: Berkeley Press, 1983.

Barbara, Joseph. *Joe Barbara: My Life in Pictures*. Atlanta: Turner Publishing, 1994.

Bart, Peter. *Fade Out*. New York: Harper Collins, 1990.

Berg, A. Scott. *Goldwyn: A Biography*. New York: Riverhead Books, 1998.

Bergman, Ingrid. *Ingrid Bergman: My Story*. New York: Warner Books, 1995.

Boller, Paul F. Jr., and Ronald Davis. *Hollywood Anecdotes*. New York: Ballantine Books, 1987.

Bradbury, Ray. *The Golden Apples of the Sun*. New York: Avon Books, 1990.

Cerra, Julie Lugo. *Culver City, The Heart of Screenland*. 2nd ed. Culver City, CA: Culver City Chamber of Commerce, 2000.

———————. *Images of America, Culver City*, Charleston, SC: Arcadia Publishing, 2004.

Davies, Marion. *The Times We Had: Life with William Randolph Hearst*. New York: Ballantine Books, 1985.

Day, Beth. *This Was Hollywood: An Affectionate History of Filmland's Golden Years*. London: Sidgwick and Jackson, 1960.

Eames, John Douglas. *The MGM Story*. New York: Portland House, 1990.

Eyman, Scott. *Lion of Hollywood: The Life and Legend of Louis B. Mayer*. New York: Simon & Schuster, 2005.

Fitzgerald, F. Scott. *The Love of the Last Tycoon*. New York: Charles Scribner's Sons, 1941.

Floherty, John J. *Moviemakers*. New York: Doubleday, Doran, 1935.

Fordin, Hugh. *The World of Entertainment! Hollywood's Greatest Musicals*. New York: Doubleday and Company, 1975.

Friedrich, Otto. *City of Nets*. New York: Harper & Row, 1986.

Gordon, Lester. *Let's Go to the Movies!* Santa Monica, CA: Santa Monica Press, 1992.

Grams, Martin Jr. *The Twilight Zone: Unlocking the Door to a Television Classic*. Churchville, MD: OTR Publishing, 2008.

Harmetz, Aljean. *The Making of the Wizard of Oz: Movie Magic and Studio Power in the Prime of MGM*. New York: Hyperion, 1998.

Hay, Peter. *MGM: When the Lion Roars*. Atlanta, GA: Turner Publishing Company, 1991.

Hecht, Ben. *A Child of the Century*. New York: Simon & Schuster, 1954.

Hepburn, Katharine. *Me: Stories of My Life*. New York: Alfred A. Knopf, 1992.

Isherwood, Christopher. *Prater Violet*. New York: Farrar, Straus and Giroux, 1945.

Knox, Donald. *The Magic Factory: How MGM Made An American in Paris*. New York: Praeger Publishers, 1973.

Kotsilibas-Davis, James. *Myrna Loy: Being and Becoming*. New York: Donald L. Fine, 1998.

Lamarr, Hedy. *Ecstasy and Me: My Life as a Woman*. New York: Fawcett Publications, 1967.

Lamparski, Richard. *Whatever Became of…? Fourth Series*. New York: Bantam Books 1975

Leigh, Janet. *There Really Was a Hollywood*. New York: Doubleday, 1984.

Maltin, Leonard. *Leonard Maltin's Movie & Video Guide*. New York: Signet Press, 2010.

———————. *Hollywood The Movie Factory*. New York: Popular Library, 1976.

Marx, Samuel. *Mayer and Thalberg: The Make-Believe Saints*. New York: Random House, 1975.

Minnelli, Vincente, and Hector Arce. *I Remember It Well*. Hollywood: Samuel French, 1990.

Newquist, Roy. *Conversations with Joan Crawford*. Berkeley: Berkeley Press, 1981.

Powell, Jane. *The Girl Next Door*. New York: William Morrow and Company, 1988.

Quirk, Lawrence W., James Stewart: *Behind the Scenes of a Wonderful Life*. Milwaukie: Applause Books, 2000.

Rapf, Maurice. *Backlot: Growing Up with the Movies*. Langham, MD: Scarecrow Press, 1999.

Reynolds, Debbie. *My Life*. New York: William Morrow and Company, 1988.

Robertson, Patrick. *Film Facts*. New York: Billboard Books, 2001.

Rooney, Mickey. *Life Is Too Short*. New York: Villard, 1991.

Schickel, Richard. *Clint Eastwood: A Biography*. New York: Alfred A. Knopf, 1996.

Schulberg, Bud. *What Makes Sammy Run?* New York: Random House, 1941.

———————. *Moving Pictures: Memories of a Hollywood Prince*. Chicago: Ivan R. Dee, 2003.

Selznick, Irene Mayer. *A Private View*. New York: Alfred A. Knopf, 1983.

Spada, James. *The Secret Life of a Princess: An Intimate Biography of Grace Kelly*. New York: Doubleday, 1987.

———————. *Peter Lawford: The Man Who Kept the Secrets*. New York: Bantam Books, 1991.

Troyan, Michael. *A Rose For Mrs. Miniver: The Life of Greer Garson*. Lexington, KY: The University Press of Kentucky, 1999.

Turner, Lana. *Lana: The Lady, the Legend, the Truth*. New York: Dutton, 1982.

West, Nathaniel. *The Day of the Locust*. New York: New Directions, 1939.

Williams, Esther. *Million Dollar Mermaid: An Autobiography*. New York: Harvest Books, 2000.

Zicree, Mark Scott. *The Twilight Zone Companion*. New York: Bantam Books, 1982.

PERIODICALS

Bannon, Anne Louise. "The Studio System, Then and Now." *Ross Reports TV/Film*, January 1999.

Beber, Lori. "Going to the Source: MGM/UA Research Library." *MGM/UA Exclusive Story* 1, no. 2 (April/May 1983).

Belhmer, Rudy. "To the Wilderness for Northwest Passage." *American Cinematographer*, November 1987.

———————. "Oral History with J. J. (Joe) Cohn." 1987.

Blake, Michael, F. "Talk Silent, But Tell It to the Marines." *Filmfax*, May/June 1995.

Byrne, Julie. "Visions of Prom Dresses Dance in Her Head." *Los Angeles Times*, May 5, 1966.

Champlin, Charles. "Bye Bye Backlots." *Los Angeles Times West Magazine*, October 18, 1970.

Corliss, Mary, and Carlos Clarens. "Designed for Film." *Film Comment*, May/June 1978.

"The Day the Dream Factory Woke Up." *Life*, February 27, 1970.

Delugah, Al. "Urbanetics Petitions for Bankruptcy Protection." *Los Angeles Times*, January 16, 1974.

Downing-Olson, Robert. "Act of Vandalism." *Los Angeles Times*, March 8, 1978.

Edwards, Bill. "Levitt and Sons Outlines Plan for $60 Mil. Housing Spread on MGM Backlot." *Variety*, August 11, 1971.

Eller, Claudia. "MGM Deal a Bold Miscalculation for Sony." *Los Angeles Times*, October 20, 2006.

Erengis, George P. "MGM's Backlot." *Films in Review*, January 1962.

———. "Cedric Gibbons." *Films in Review*, April 1965.

Eustis, Morton. "Designing for the Movies: Gibbons of MGM." *Theatre Arts Monthly*, October 1937.

"Famous Movie Props Donated for Playground." *Los Angeles Times*, August 29, 1971

Faris, Gerald. "Movie Biz Will Never Be the Same." *Los Angeles Times*, March 14, 1974.

"Fiery French Designer Off MGM Lot." *Variety*, November 11, 1925.

Fire Rages at Film Studio. *Los Angeles Times*, November 23, 1940..

Fontaninf, Steve (photo). "Fish Rescue." *Los Angeles Times*, August 21,1971.

Gibbons, Cedric. "Art Direction by Cedric Gibbons." *What's Happening in Hollywood: Weekly News of Current Pictures, Trends and Production*, February 1, 1947.

Grossman, Andrew. "The Smiling Cobra." *VLife*, June/July 2004.

Hagberg, Pete and Dave Larsen. "Fire Destroys Sets at MGM." *Los Angeles Times*, March 13, 1967.

Hamilton, Jack. "Would You Let Your Daughter do it?" *Look*, September 7, 1971

Harvey, Steve. "Gone with the Wind Home Goes with a Crash." *Los Angeles Times*, April 17, 1966.

Hebert, Ray. "Famed Lot 3 Enjoys Final Fling." *Los Angeles Times*, August 11, 1971.

Hernandez, Greg. "Executive to Depart MGM." *Los Angeles Daily News*, December 8, 2001.

Hubert, J. "Movie Soundstages Exclude Noise and Reduce Resonance." *Building News*, February 1939.

Hubler, Shawn. "Stolen Lamppost is More Than a Light" *Los Angeles Times*, September 30, 1990.

Kiesling, B. C. "Biography: Cedric Gibbons." *MGM Studios Biographies*, January 22, 1958.

Kleiner, Dick. "Ann Rutherford's Goodbye to Lot 2." *Waco Tribune-Herald*, October 15, 1972.

Lachenbruch, Jerome. "Art and Architectural Artifice" *American Architect*, November 3, 1920.

Loper, Mary Lou. "Gone with the Wind Blows Up Storm for Charity." *Los Angeles Times*, July 2, 1967.

Mandell, Paul. "'Walking Distance' from the Twilight Zone." *American Cinematographer*, June 1998.

McFaden, Strauss & Irwin Inc. Public Relations. "MGM's Lot #2: The End of an Era, the Beginning of the New." Press release. 1972.

"One Dies in Studio Crash." *Los Angeles Times*, January 11, 1925.

"Opening of Cary Grant Theatre." *MGM/UA Exclusive Story* 2, no. 5, October/November 1984.

Randisi, Steve. "Eye of the Storm." *Filmfax*, June/July 1994.

Reed, Rex. "A Star Bids Farewell to the MGM Backlot." *Southland*, December 10, 1972.

Reeder, Dan "Culver City's tall Tower Looms as Monument to Movie Days" *The Daily Breeze*, April 5, 1978

Ripton, Ray. "Unresolved Issue of MGM Lot 2 Use Again Goes Back to Drawing Board." *Los Angeles Times*, January 16, 1977.

Robinson, Robert. "The Insubstantial Pageant." *Sunday Times Colour Magazine*, December 15, 1963.

Rose, Frank. "The Dream Factories Reborn." *Fortune*, February 16, 1998.

Ryon, Ruth. "Pasadena Home Copies Mansion of Famous Film." *Los Angeles Times*, July 2, 1978.

"64 Greatest Things about LA, The" *Los Angeles Magazine*, March, 2008

Stingley, Jim. "A Profile of Another Hollywood." *Los Angeles Times*, July 6, 1975.

Torgerson, Dial. "Props Become Stars in MGM 'Spectacular.'" *Los Angeles Times*, May 4, 1970.

Wanamaker, Marc. "Historic Hollywood Movie Studios." Part 1. *American Cinematographer*, March 1976.

———. "Historic Hollywood Movie Studios." Part 2. *American Cinematographer*, April 1976.

———. "Historic Hollywood Movie Studios." Part 3. *American Cinematographer*, May 1976.

Webb, Michael. "Cedric Gibbons and the MGM Style." *Architectural Digest*, April 1990.

Williams, Whitney. "Fading Ghosts of Filmdom's Glory Days Soon to Be Housing Site." *Variety*, August 25, 1972.

DVD COMENTARIES AND DOCUMENTARIES.

Brooks, Mel. "Commentary" B000G6BLWE. *Young Frankenstein*. Brooks, Mel (dir). Los Angeles, CA: Fox Home Video, 1974.

Donan, Stanley. "Commentary" B0006DEF9. *Singin' in the Rain*. Kelly, Gene, Donen Stanley (dir). Los Angeles, CA: Warner Home Video, 1952.

Hollywood: The Dream Factory B00005JKGZ (located on *Meet Me in St. Louis* DVD) Rosten, Irwin (dir). Los Angeles, CA: Warner Home Video. *1972*

Keel, Howard. "Interview" B00020XVDW. *That's Entertainment! III: Behind the Screen.* (located on That's Entertainment! The Complete Collection) Engel, David. (dir). Los Angeles, CA: Warner Home Video, 1994

Lumet, Sydney. "Commentary" B000CNESU8. *Network.* Lumet, Sydney (dir). Los Angeles, CA: Warner Home Video. 1976.

MGM: When the Lion Roars B001I2EQUO Warner Home Video. Martin, Frank (dir). Los Angeles, CA: Warner Home Video, 1992

Rush, Richard. "Commentary" B00005OCK7. *The Stunt Man (Limited Edition).* Rush, Richard (dir). Troy, MI: Anchor Bay Home Video, 1980

York, Michael. "Commentary" B00004VVNB *Logan's Run.* Anderson, Michael (dir). Los Angeles, CA: Warner Home Video, 1976.

WEBSITES

http://faculty.oxy.edu/jerry/homestud.htm
    Much info on studios and backlots.

http://groups.yahoo.com/group/StudioBacklots/
    A lively, backlot related discussion site.

www.associatedcontent.com/article/1069674/the_five_most_memorable_houses_in_american.html?cat=40
    Timothy Sexton's "Five most Memorable Houses in American Film History" essay.

www.bisonarchives.com/index.html
    Invaluable Marc Wanamaker's Bison Archives site.

www.ci.culver-city.ca.us/
    Culver City homepage, with a historical section

www.decofilms.com/
    The story of Marion Davies much traveled bungalow

www.eiu.edu/%7Emodernity/dgerst.html
    David Gerstner's writings on Vincente Minnelli.

www.faculty.ucr.edu/~divola/MGM.html
    Photographer John Divola's website.

www.hollywoodheritage.org/
    Hollywood's premiere historical organization.

www.imdb.com/
    The industries main "go-to" site.

www.pauldmarks.com or www.pauldmarks.blogspot.com
    Writer/director Paul D. Marks' websites.

www.swoyersart.com/james_christensen/featured_artist.htm
    artist James C. Christensen's bio.

www.thejudyroom.com
    Scott Brogan's Judy Garland site.

No Help
WANTED

Made in Hollywood USA